THE FORWARD MALE

WORLD-CLASS DAY GAME FOR THE MALE IN HIS 20S

MIKE MEHLMAN

Coalesced thought streams

A compendium this book

Passing the Baton

お前はこの文章が読めたら凄い笑

この本を書いてた理由は

俺の現在の考え方について感謝を持ってるから

この本を書かれてる時、俺が約２年半大阪に住んできた

最終的にお前はこれらの文章が読めるようになると

俺はやっぱりお前に西成区の自販機の日本酒を買って差し上げる

特に天気が寒いなら俺は夜道で飲むのが好き

ワロス

TABLE OF CONTENTS

MY FIRST APPROACH EVER

I was 25 and a half and living in Australia. I was at one of the university libraries at night reading by myself at a large table in the middle of the room. I saw a cute girl with brown curly hair stand up from one of the secluded corner study spaces.

She started walking toward me. I noticed she had short-shorts on and very nice legs. She was walking past me to go the bathroom it seemed. As she passed, I looked at her from behind and noticed there was a circular impression in one of her back pockets. I could easily tell it was a condom.

Couldn't have been more obvious it was a condom.

Did she have a boyfriend she was going to see after? That thought didn't even cross my mind at the time. All I processed was that I was very attracted to her and that she had a condom in her back pocket.

I wanted to say hi but I hadn't made any real approaches before. That is, using a mindset of true deliberation and decisiveness, I had never just gone up to a girl and said hi, unless it had been by accident.

Now at the time, it hadn't occurred to me that I could wait for her to come back from the bathroom and perhaps say hi to her near her study space. I felt some sort of temporal pressure, a feeling that I needed to act now. But I was nervous.

There were two thoughts that notably went through my mind that got me up out of that seat and over to approach her:

1) Success is not determined by the actual outcome of the approach. The success is in fact *just merely making the approach itself.*

In other words, you could walk up and she could instantly ignore you or wave you off, but the fact that you merely make the approach, irrespective of her response, makes the interaction a success.

Absolutely the biggest reason for approach anxiety is the guy is too worried about getting rejected. He's worried about *the outcome*. He frames success in terms of *the outcome*. If she's not interested, it was somehow a failure. Somehow he failed. And somehow that reinforces all of these insecurities he has about himself.

Oh it must have been because I'm not good looking enough, or tall enough, or because my hair doesn't look the right way today, or I didn't say the right thing. Suddenly the process becomes a reinforcing cycle of rumination. And in turn that makes future approaches even harder to make.

When you frame success as merely making the approach itself, you always have a 100% success rate.

I've literally walked up to girls before saying to myself, "Alright, let me just get this rejection out of the way." But I view it as a success before even saying hi to them because, regardless as to what the outcome is, I don't care. I realize that I'm approaching a girl because it builds positive momentum to help me with the *next* girl. That's my true incentive, really.

It's rarely about the actual girl I'm approaching and more about building a mindset for the next girl.

This isn't the movies where you see your one true love from afar and you're finally going to talk to her. You see an attractive girl coming out of an elevator, or in a subway station, or on the street - it doesn't matter - *she's just the girl who happens to be there that moment.*

No one girl is special to me before I get to know her. If she refuses me, great. I forget her instantly.

All of the girls you approach are essentially interchangeable. As men, we like to romanticize. But never fixate over any one particular girl you're approaching.

And even if you do "hit it off" with her, don't ever think, as you're scrolling through the numbers in your phone, "Ok, *she's* the girl I'm most keen on." Don't associate too much thinking with one particular girl. Treat them all the same. And the way you treat them all the same is by literally accumulating many numbers. If you have twelve new numbers in your phone, each one means less to you.

You can't fake that thought process. Truly not caring comes from getting many numbers and handling rejection (which I talk about in detail later).

So now going back, I will establish that the single biggest factor determining whether or not a guy will approach is *how he defines success in terms of the approach itself vs the outcome.*

If you define success by whether she turns out to be interested or not, you'll never allow yourself to approach at full potential. You'll always be held back by fear. Rejections from girls are a natural part of the process. They will never not occur.

It is my belief that the pervasive tendency for men to view an approach's success *in terms of its outcome* is precisely why they never actualize on their potential efficacy.

If you define success by *the act/process of merely saying hi –* that's it – you're always 100% successful. That's really, really important.

And by the way, the reason I have conviction in that is not just because it eliminates my own approach anxiety, but because, without thinking about it, that is the advice I have spontaneously given to guys I've been out with who've been afraid to approach, when something has to be said quickly before their approach window closes.

In other words, over the years, without processing it, if I've been out with a friend who's afraid to say hi to a girl, I'll tell him, "Look, saying hi in and of itself is the success. She probably will reject you. Good. Let her. It's her issue. But you saying hi – that act alone – *is* the success." And that usually gets them moving.

So that was one of the two thoughts that went through my mind that got me up out of my chair in the library. The other was:

2) I have missed out on hundreds (even thousands) of opportunities in the past because I was held back by fear.

If I think about high school, college, etc., a lot of the memories that come to mind aren't positive. I think a lot about opportunities I missed. Some so absurdly obvious. Some not so obvious. And many I could have easily created but didn't.

Essentially what you start to realize is that much of what drives many girls to be with guys older than they are isn't just the biological aspects of support, maturity, etc.; it's actually that younger guys tend to blow opportunities, and guys a little older know how to capitalize.

The girl who's 22 might date the guy who's 27 because he knows better how not to fuck up. He's also probably developed a little more confidence now that he's getting older and cares less about what others think of him. It's likely he approached her. The 22-year-old guys she meets don't close her. Or there's lots of guys in her classes and around campus who simply won't approach her out of fear. The younger guys tend to care more about what others think. They're blowing the opportunities. That's why guys like me cash in instead.

One of the biggest differences between your early- and late-20s self is that the latter knows far better how not to fuck up.

As we get older, there's a general transition we go through that involves caring less and less about what others think of us. It's more about what we think of ourselves that matters. The only difference between people is how quickly this transition occurs. You'll have guys who go through life always fixating on what others think. Guys in their 50s who never approached a woman in their lives. Their wives probably approached them.

In the library, I'm not sure why specifically those two thoughts came into my mind at that exact instant, but they did. And they were vivid:

"I've missed hundreds/thousands of opportunities in the past."

"Just saying hi – that act alone – is in and of itself the success."

I got up out of my seat.

I walked over to where the bathrooms were in this little corridor. I waited for her to come out. When she did, she started walking past me. I didn't think about what I was going to say. It just happened all at once.

Using a low voice, I said, "Excuse me."

She turned around.

"I'm Michael. I thought you were beautiful and wanted to say hi."

My voice was trembling. My lips were quivering. My face was red. I could feel it. In retrospect, I realize she must have found it profoundly authentic – which it was. And that probably never happened to her before.

If you've ever read Malcolm Gladwell's 'Outliers', one of the major themes in the book is that positive events in life that we often want to take sole credit for are actually largely shaped by external factors – e.g., had Bill Gates been born two years earlier or later, he wouldn't have been the guy to pioneer the computer industry and become one of the richest men in the world. Same guy. Same genetics. Different circumstances. Different outcome.

75 of the 100 richest people out of the entire history of human civilization were men born between 1830-1840 in the United States. Success can be attributed to their gender, country of birth, and the timing of the Industrial Revolution. Had these same people been born at any other time in history (or even at the same time in a different country), it would have been others instead who achieved financial success.

We like to believe that even though we have active control and responsibility over our lives that the outcomes we experience aren't in any way arrived at passively. But that's just not the case.

The girl who rejects you at the bus stop on Tuesday is the same exact girl who would have been receptive at the grocery store on Monday. That's not in your control.

Maybe she wasn't in the mood that day. Maybe they ran out of pearls when she went to get bubble tea. Maybe she's premenstrual. There's no purpose in speculating because the possibilities are endless.

In the library, I was incredibly nervous when I introduced myself to this girl. As I said, I was trembling. She could have easily ignored me or told me no right away, and I would have been left in the little bathroom corridor, alone, probably ruminating about my past and everything I felt was not perfect about me, and that those reasons were why she must not have been interested.

But I was really fortunate. And that wasn't because I was amazing. She just happened to be, in this select circumstance, receptive. Maybe she had a productive study night and was now just procrastinating. Maybe one of her friends liked her recent comment on Facebook and now she felt validated and social. So for whatever reason, she talked to me.

She smiled and said, "Hi, I'm Sarah."

Slurring my words and with a red face, I inched toward her a little and started asking about what she was studying. After about 60 seconds, I calmed down and we entered into a more normal conversation. We chatted for about 10-15 minutes in that corridor before I was the one who suggested we go back to study.

Now what happened after this I believe is a big reason I'm at where I am today. In my own life, this was my Malcolm Gladwell moment.

I didn't get her number. It didn't even occur to me. I just leaned in to sort of give her a half-hug to say bye, and then suddenly we just kissed on the lips. As my first approach, I have no idea how that happened, but it did. I was somehow hit with the perfect combination of factors, in that moment, and it set the stage for me making all future approaches. Had she rejected me instantly, it truly is possible I may have shrunk back to my diffident self, afraid to say hi to girls forever. I don't think I'm inherently special. I acknowledge that I've had various low-probability circumstances align in my favor.

The emotions of that approach were intense, and to not have been rejected was just a matter of chance. She probably liked that I was really authentic, but I had been nervous and authentic on many subsequent approaches that resulted in rejections. So really it was just that this particular girl, in this particular moment, was receptive – that's it.

I left the library that night without saying bye to her. I still had my girlfriend of a year and a half at the time (see chapter: End of the beta male). That was probably why. I recall I didn't want to be in the relationship but was too afraid to leave because I lacked autonomy. It was the approaches I did toward the end of this relationship that gave me the courage and confidence to be okay with being single. I didn't need to rely on anyone as a buttress for my emotional support. It was knowing that I could meet people that gave me the courage to break up with my ex.

I saw the girl at the library several times after that. We studied together and kissed sometimes, but it fizzled. I was still in a "committed relationship" and wasn't yet at the stage where I knew how to be forward, so I didn't know how to handle the situation. Looking back, I could have easily slept with her. Easily. And I do regret not having done so. I just didn't have game. But the process takes time.

And I'll tell ya, it's the regret of missing out on previous opportunities that got me to approach in the first place. And going forward, when I think of these lost chances (e.g., not sleeping with library girl), that gives me even more incentive to create opportunities in the future. Even now, part of the reason I still approach is because I don't want to miss out on opportunity.

In the beginning, the initial focus is merely making an approach. Stage zero is learning how to approach. After that, the focus becomes how to handle the women you actually meet and how to maintain them in your repertoire. But before any of that becomes a salient focus, getting over approach anxiety and saying hi is the most important thing.

You cannot control whether a girl will be receptive or not. No matter how authentic you are – no matter what you say – no matter how much experience you have – rejections will never go away. That's why the approach itself is the success. It's not the outcome that matters. Let her reject you.

If you internalize that the *approach itself* is the success, you always have a 100% success rate.

ABSOLUTE BIGGEST MYTH IN HISTORY

When I was in my early-20s and still living in Boston, I had numerous sexual opportunities that I lost because I wasn't forward enough with girls. That is, I didn't want the girl to think "I was a player" or "just in it for the sex," so I thought I was doing the appropriate thing by taking it nice and slow. What a joke.

I have no idea where the fuck this myth originated from, but taking it "nice and slow" with a girl so that she thinks "you're not a player" is the number-one way to lose her. Who the fuck came up with that.

I can think of numerous times I had been in bed with a girl (sometimes the same girl more than once) and didn't make a move to sleep with her. Yeah, and they all stopped hanging out with me.

When I was 22, I had met a gorgeous half-white-half-Indian girl from Northwestern University doing a summer exchange program at the Boston Medical Center. We took the same shuttle bus in the morning and, because it was always jammed-crowded, ended up next to each other one time and started talking.

I then ran into her in a courtyard one afternoon and had lunch with her. She said we should hang out some time and asked for my number. She texted me a short time later inviting me over to her place. I didn't even think anything of it.

After the gym one night, I went over to see her. She poured us red wine, and we talked for probably six or seven hours about every topic you could imagine. We were discussing strengths and weaknesses, and she said her weakness was that she was addicted to sex.

I am not kidding. She really said that. So what did I do?

I continued talking with her.

By about 4 am, after *talking* all night, a weird energy came over us and my subconscious mind was able to process that I had ruined my chances. I *apologized* to her and left. She went back to Northwestern. We remained Facebook friends for a while, but I ultimately removed her because I couldn't handle looking at stunning photos of her while knowing I had blown such a golden opportunity.

"You invited me over to your place, poured us red wine, and told me you're addicted to sex. So before leaving, I just wanted to apologize for talking to you for 6-7 hours and not making a move the whole time."

The start of the next year I moved to Australia and started medical school at the University of Queensland. I met an Aussie nurse who was also 22. By that point in my life, she was probably the most attractive girl who had ever shown any interest in me. I put her on a pedestal. I remember feeling like she was way out of my league. She came over to my place twice. We cooked dinner together both times, and she lay down on my bed afterward, both times.

I thought to myself, "I really like this girl and would want her as a girlfriend, so I don't want her to think I'm a player by taking it too quickly." She stopped responding to my texts.

Fast-forward one year. She randomly texted me again out of the blue and invited me over. Even at 23, I was still equally clueless. She lived in a Queensland-style flat surrounded by palm trees. I arrived at night, and as I was walking up to the door, saw her through the silhouettes of the palm trees and thought she was a goddess. We cooked together again and had a "long talk" about life, etc.

I stayed the night at her place, in her bed. I never made a move on her. That was the last time we ever talked or hung out. That experience really sucks to think about.

"So nice to have you on my bed here and not have sex."

Those are just two mere examples that stick out in my mind. My early-mid-20s were littered with these types of blown opportunities. I was always trying to be the nice guy who took things slow. Once again, I look back at that as such a joke.

In reality, the vast, vast majority of women are not looking for you to take things slow. Even if they come across really conservative or shy, they're not looking for that. The way you need to think about it is: *never ever let yourself* be the rate-limiting step in the equation. *Never let yourself* be the reason why you didn't sleep with her.

If you try to fuck her and she ultimately says no, you of course respect her wishes, but at least you tried. *She* must always be the reason you didn't sleep with her, not you.

If I ever have a girl in my room, no matter how reserved she seems, I always try for sex. Always. You have to ask yourself why she's in your room in the first place. She wouldn't be there if she didn't have attraction for you. So for you not to try to fuck her is stupid.

Anything can and will happen behind closed doors.

If she says no, it ends there, but at least you let her be the reason you didn't fuck; you weren't the reason. If you don't at least try for sex, she'll lose attraction and respect for you.

How you act in the bedroom defines your dominance/submissiveness balance in the interaction/relationship with a woman. There's no 50/50. Most women secretly aren't looking for that. Relationships with a 50/50 dynamic are sort of just a natural consequence of most guys being lame. A lot of women are in relationships wishing that the guy they're with would just be more dominant. They might even try to tell their guy, "Be more dominant with me. Man-handle me." Not every guy is James Bond, but every woman wants James Bond.

Let her know you're in control. If you're relinquishing control to her in the bedroom, it says she has control in the relationship. You can give her the illusion/impression that she's in control sometimes (that's different), but when push comes to shove, you're still in control.

A good gauge of how beta you are is the degree to which you are accommodating to a girl in the bedroom. In the bedroom, it's my way or no way. If she's pleased as a natural result of me being so incredible, that's awesome, but I don't service girls. That's not my job. I have zero interest in a woman who is about herself in the bedroom, even 10%.

Anyone who tells you healthy relationships are about striking the right balance, etc., my input is: the way in which you act in your interactions determines the types of relationships you foster.

If you believe a healthy relationship is accommodating to your girl here and there so that you have this "respectful 50/50 thing" going, it means you'll naturally foster a relationship where you set a precedent for pleasing her and/or suppressing what you want to do sometimes for her. You can reason your way around it any way you want (e.g., "Oh but relationships are about sacrifice," etc.), but what you're ultimately doing is changing your behavior for her.

Never change your behavior for any woman.

I meet women who are not happy with this sometimes, but if they're not happy, they can leave. And why should you be willing to let them leave? Because there are tons of women out there whom you won't need to be accommodating for, and who will fully accommodate to you. The women I screen for are fully accommodating to me. That's my style. That's what I like. The ones who like me would probably think you're a lame bitch. The ones who like you would probably think I'm a self-focused jackass piece of shit. To each his own. There's no right or wrong in terms of the types of relationships that you want to create for yourself.

I meet women now and again who get angry at this notion that the relationship doesn't revolve around them, and it's extremely easy to let them walk away forever because I have no interest in a woman who's about herself.

Some women like the idea of playing with fire but can't actually handle the heat. In other words, some women like being with a really dominant, forward guy for the strength he exudes, but they'll either refuse to go to your place, or once they get to the bedroom they'll refuse to fuck.

If a girl won't come home with me by the second date, I start losing interest. It's like, why are we wasting time. If she won't sleep with me by the third date, I don't text her again. It doesn't mean it's guaranteed over, but she has to work for me now. She might start texting me wanting to meet up, but I won't go out of my way for her whatsoever in terms of scheduling because I already know she's a prude.

I don't view sex as some magical, emotional thing. I tie zero emotion to it whatsoever. I respect that most women think of sex as an emotional process, but if a woman is overly attached to the idea of that, that's not a woman I match well with anyway.

It's a bigger deal for me to hold a woman's hand than it is for me to sleep with her. What you do with your hands says a lot. If you ever want to know if a girl is interested in you, go for her hands. If she seems hesitant to hold/touch them, pulls away, or seems like she doesn't like it, she's not actually into you.

Likewise, imagine you've slept with a girl but aren't really interested in her beyond that; if you go out together and she tried holding your hand, you'd do your best to limit it.

When I'm first courting a girl, I have no qualms about going for her hands. I'm not talking about in a needy "I really want to hold your hand, baby" sort of way, but more in just a playful way, for a few seconds here and there. It allows me to gauge how interested she is. If she's not interested in my hands, I correspondingly lose a little interest in her. And if she seems fine touching my hands, I'll generally try to be the one who breaks it off first by going for my phone, or in order to make a gesture.

If you're slow and nice with women, the best you'll ever do is a committed relationship. You won't ever hook up with women in your life and will waste your sexual prime.

And when I say "committed," I mean involuntarily committed. In other words, the vast majority of guys will enter into a relationship and "commit" to the girl, but secretly they know that if they could be polygamous they would be. They'll stay in the "commitment" because they know that's their only way to get consistent sex.

Every "committed" relationship I had been in up until I was 25, I was never actually mentally committed. Had I had the opportunity to hook up with other girls, I easily would have. That is, if you had asked me, "Michael, would you rather stay committed to your girlfriend or sleep with five different girls in rotation?" It would have been an obvious no-brainer. And truthfully, for most guys, that's a fucking no-brainer. The issue here is that the latter is impossible for guys who don't approach to conceive of.

If you're a beta male, a committed relationship is your only sure-fire way to get consistent sex. This mentality results in you being dishonest in your relationships. It can result in you developing cowardly ways to conceal your intentions and interest in other girls, and then if rare opportunities come your way, giving in to cheating.

There's no reason to ever cheat in a relationship. The way you can avoid cheating is to never tell a woman you're committing to her. If you're not entering into an explicit commitment then it's not possible to cheat. Her assumptions don't equal reality. She can say "our relationship" and call you her boyfriend, but unless you've explicitly said you agree to those terms, there's no commitment. And if she's not content with your lack of explicitness, you're not holding her there.

If anyone ever tells you that your silence equals dishonesty when it comes to commitment, that person is either a female or a beta male. I'll state firmly that no woman is ever entitled to your thoughts. Nor are you entitled to hers. If either person in an interaction is not happy with the communication of the other, he or she is free to leave.

It's when you overtly and explicitly say that you're committing to a woman that you open yourself to dishonesty. If she nags you about being explicit, make jokes to get around the topic until she stops. If she's incessant, you either terminate the interaction because of her neediness, or you just tell her your terms; the latter will often (but not always) result in her distancing herself.

Some women will tacitly carry the awareness that you're seeing other people. As long as you don't overtly admit it to them, they will often tolerate it insofar as you maintain high non-neediness and confidence levels. Some women are OK with covert polygamy in high-status (i.e., high confidence) men.

A couple years ago when I was still living in Australia, I met a cute, quiet Chinese girl at a bus stop. She was 24 and extremely shy, the type who you're certain wouldn't have sex until she's married. I made small chat with her and was very forward, almost for entertainment purposes.

We exchanged WeChats (the Chinese messaging app). She was shocked because, unless you're Chinese, or have many Chinese friends, *or have hooked up with Chinese girls*, that's not an app you'd ever use.

We met up one night around where she lived for a small bite. My plan was to meet her for an hour or two and then go see someone else.

I walked her back to her place and tried to kiss her. She pulled back in astonishment. I wasn't surprised at all and was like, "Alright, bye." As I was walking away, I had zero intention of ever talking to or seeing her again. But then she started messaging me about how she was sorry she was so shy and that she liked how I was confident.

Over the next few weeks or so, I met up with her a couple times on campus during short study breaks, and I would kiss her and virtually only talk about sex with her. She told me she had never been with a guy before, but that she had an ex-boyfriend in China for two years whom she only hugged. I was like, "Wow, what the fuck."

I told her we should study at her place and that I would give her the honor and privilege of making me special Chinese tea. Even though I was partially joking, she agreed earnestly that that was a great idea. I ended up hooking up with her three or four times, and it was awesome. She was actually amazing in the bedroom.

I would say in terms of all of the approaches I've done, she was probably in the top three in terms of how forwardness was exactly what an extremely "shy" girl was looking for (I currently live in Japan and have met a lot). Had I been slow and nice with her, I would have been just like the last guy who had only hugged her. She had strong attraction for me, and respected me, because I was straight and fast with her.

I lost enough opportunities in my past due to lame non-forwardness that now I know how to effectively push for sex.

I would contend that it's probably true – similar to how real confidence only comes through tried and true repeated rejection – that effective forwardness only manifests after handling the pain of reflecting on lost opportunities from lack thereof.

The number-one way to lose a girl is to not be forward enough. *She, not you*, must always be the rate-limiting step in the equation/interaction. Even girls who on the surface seem "shy" are still looking for forwardness, confidence, and directness.

THE END OF THE BETA MALE

When I was 24, I was living in Australia with a lively and hilarious Aussie housemate who was dating a Thai girl. The two of them knew I studied all of the time but invited me out one night because they were bringing a "hot" coworker along, and it was just going to be the three of them. I declined.

I was at the university library and my housemate texted me saying, "You're a fucking idiot. This chick is 18 and stunning. I'm not letting you fuck this up, so we're coming to pick you up."

They came and picked me up *from the library* at about midnight.

The plan was to drive to this girl's place in some distant suburb. When we met up, my housemate said to me, "Look, you're going in her car with her. I'm going in my car with my girlfriend. So you have to make conversation for 30 minutes. Can you handle that? And please, don't do any of your psychoanalytical shit. Just keep it simple and have a normal chat with her for the love of god."

I made conversation with her in the car almost in disbelief that I was sitting next to this gorgeous girl out of nowhere. My friends talked me up heavily beforehand, which is why she was so receptive. I couldn't have been luckier.

When we got to her place, we all essentially just got ready for bed, and she invited me into her room. She stripped down to just her light-purple underwear and got into bed. I lay there, and I didn't make a move on her. I asked her if she wanted to put on a movie or something. She gave me a weird look. Finally, she said to me, "Look, we should just have sex." And we did, three times. I was nervous because of how blunt and forward she was. Had she not been direct like that, we wouldn't have hooked up.

She went on to become my girlfriend for a year and a half, but she was the guy in the relationship. She wore the suit pants, and they were very stiff ones. Everything was on her terms.

She bought me shoes and clothes; told me how to do my hair; told me which shirts to wear to parties; told me on a given day if I should do cardio or lifting at the gym. She even told me when I was allowed to come during sex. She was the fucking guy and I was the lame beta who felt lucky to be reaching for her.

I remember feeling unhappy in this relationship but was afraid to end it because:

1) I felt really lucky to be with someone I perceived as much more physically attractive than I, so I thought that might never happen again;

2) Guys were after her all of the time, so if I broke up with her, I risked swift irreversibility and her immediately dating another guy;

3) I lacked autonomy, meaning I didn't like the idea of being single and not having someone there for me; and

4) It would have meant an end to consistent sex with a gorgeous Aussie girl.

Even sexually the relationship was on her terms. When she was 17, she had dated a 25-year-old sports car-driving meathead who I'm certain alpha-ed the hell out of her. She had particular ways she wanted to get fucked, and essentially gave me instructions. I actually learned a lot sexually from that relationship. But really, here I was as this 24-year-old guy taking sexual instructions from my 18-year-old girlfriend?

One time she came over to my place after she finished work, and I was in a fairly energetic mood. When she came into my room, without making any conversation, I swung her around and started taking her clothes off for spontaneous sex. She got really angry with me and scolded me. She said something along the lines of, "I don't care how spontaneous you think you're being; I'm not just some sex object." I was taken aback. This was my girlfriend of probably eight months who was saying this to me. "What was wrong with spontaneous sex," I thought.

Now it goes without saying that sex must always be 100% consensual, so she wasn't in the wrong in any way, shape or form (just to be crystal clear).

But what that event did reflect on is the sexual dynamic of our relationship: she didn't view me as a dominant male, nor had she ever submitted to me. She acted as the gatekeeper and controlled when and how sex would be granted to me. If I didn't meet the exact terms of being the boyfriend she was looking to control, then there was no sex for me.

A year or so into us dating, I met an attractive Israeli girl at a dinner party who took a liking for me. We had mutual friends at the university, and she had offered to pick me up on a later night to go meet them. I went out with her probably three times in this fashion. I didn't tell her I had a girlfriend because I secretly liked her and was a coward. I thought if I told her then I'd risk losing her interest.

I viewed the situation as one in which I wanted to date this second girl but was too scared to cut things off with my girlfriend. There was no guarantee at this early stage that the Israeli girl would even commit to me, so if I broke up with my girlfriend, I might end up with no one. So I didn't know how to transition.

The fourth time or so that I saw the Israeli girl "as a friend," she suggested after dinner that we stop by my place to pick up study materials and then go to the library together.

When we walked into my place, my girlfriend was, out of nowhere, sitting on my bed reading. She had come over uninvited and was waiting for me. I was really annoyed by that. I walked out of my room to get some water and contemplate the situation while the two of them engaged in awkward talk for a few minutes.

*As the fucking piss-of-the-Earth, dastardly scumbag that I was, I decided to move forward with the Israeli girl then and there, and told my **girlfriend** that I was going to go study with another girl. And then I just left, without even explaining anything to her.*

So while my girlfriend was imploding/self-destructing alone in my room, I got into the car with the Israeli girl and we drove off. She said to me, "I didn't know you have a girlfriend."

Then I spent the next few minutes explaining that we used to date and that now we were just friends, but she still liked me. For whatever reason, she accepted my conniving and mendacious explanation and we studied together.

As the absolute scumbag I was, I left my girlfriend to self-destruct on her own in my room.

My now *ex*-girlfriend and I then went onto non-speaking terms for about a month. In the mean time, I was flying home soon to visit family, and the Israeli girl suggested that because I had a morning flight, I could just stay at her place and then she'd drive me to the airport after we woke up. Sounded reasonable to me.

At her place, she was making me a sandwich and I remember looking at her ass thinking to myself, "This is going to be my next girlfriend." We went into her bedroom and I gave her a short massage. We turned the lights out, got into bed, and started kissing. I got on top of her and could feel that she was wet.

At that moment, I thought to myself that because I was going to date this girl, I didn't want to screw things up by going too fast too soon, so I didn't try having sex with her.

I got off of her and lay beside her. In an upset voice, she said something along the lines of, "I don't understand. I just don't understand." Not really directed at me, but in general. She was probably in disbelief at how pathetically lame I was. And what's even worse is, at the time, I didn't even think anything of it.

She drove me to the airport in the morning. The plan was she was going to pick me up after I got back from my two weeks seeing family. I remember sending her a fairly substantive email while I was home. Her response wasn't necessarily short, but it lacked substance and I could tell that she didn't have much interest when she wrote it. She then sent me another email shortly before I was flying back to Australia saying that something had come up and that she couldn't get me from the airport. I bought the excuse. But looking back, it was an obvious lie.

She didn't have interest in hanging out with me after that. I soon found out that she was dating someone else. Similarly, I found out that my ex-girlfriend was now sleeping with some new guy. There were pictures of them together on Facebook, *and he was jacked*. The whole situation hit me pretty hard and I felt like a lame piece of shit.

I *was* a lame piece of shit.

This was the beginning of a huge wake-up call for me. In particular, I found it hypocritical that while I was dating my ex, she would tell me to do cardio at the gym, telling me specifically that she liked the thin, ripped style, but meanwhile the first chance she had, she slept with a big, muscular guy. And I mean *big*. I didn't overanalyze it at the time, but I made note of it.

At this stage, I had new housemates, and one in particular was an Italian guy. He saw how distraught I was, and during one of our talks I was actually crying about my ex-girlfriend. He started telling me stories of his past, and how he blew countless opportunities with lots of girls and used to be incredibly shy.

He had binders of reading material and would give me different things to look at. I also started reading countless articles online. Every day, he and I would talk, sometimes for hours. He became a mentor for me. I felt really lucky.

There were two back-to-back days I can recall when he brought five different girls, both days (so that's ten total), to our house for lunch. No jokes. He was basically playing ElimiDate with them. The level of "what the fuck" associated with that is not something I could even put into words. His level of success with girls was something I couldn't relate to. But he and I kept talking every day, and he kept giving me stuff to read.

He was very athletic, and I started going to the gym with him every single day and lifting. I was already a gym person, but compared to the cardio routine I had when I was with my ex, I became a lot stronger. My ex-girlfriend and I were now starting to text a little. She said she could stop by my house and talk, but that we weren't together. I wrote her a note before she came over telling her how I felt. When she arrived, she read it and was touched by it. She said, "You got bigger." I remember thinking I wanted her back really bad and was hoping she'd change her mind.

Slowly but surely, we started dating again, but something was starting to change in me. I was now going to the gym and lifting almost every day, and I was reading everything I could get my hands on about approaching and being confident with women. I became closer friends with my housemate, and we did practically nothing but talk about women.

Likewise, I began saying hi to girls myself. And what amazed me is that I had some really great interactions. I was still overall very shy, but it started to become more of a habit of mine approaching new girls every day. I would then come home and share stories with my new friend about my approaches that day. He would also share with me the stories of his approaches. Many of them were ridiculous. This became a routine of ours.

We'd talk about our rejections and laugh at them. The fact that there was somebody there to discuss these things with in humor made the initial process a lot more carefree and fun. Had it not been for having met him, I wouldn't be where I'm at today.

My housemate started hooking up with a modelesque acquaintance of my girlfriend. She was allergic to latex, and my housemate found some special Ebay deal on lamb skin condoms and got a box of 500.

It was beyond overkill, but nevertheless it's what he bought. He said they were surprisingly really good and gave me a stack of 20 or so just for kicks.

My girlfriend was on the pill, but one day she found the stack of condoms in my backpack and asked why I had them. I told her my housemate found a special deal and bought 500, and then made up an excuse saying that he recommended them for us if she ever missed a pill. She wasn't happy about it, and said, "I don't care. I don't like Corey anymore."

For a period of about two months, I started getting numbers and meeting up with girls on campus. I was still in a "relationship" and wasn't hooking up with anyone I approached, but I was slowly starting to become more and more confident.

I started to realize that despite any insecurities I may have had about myself, I no longer had crippling approach anxiety. I started to become aware that I could meet and date other people if I wanted to. My autonomy started to improve. I no longer felt like I was dependent on my girlfriend for keeping my self-esteem intact. This transition in my mentality during the latter part of our relationship finally gave me the courage to cut things off with her and become single.

In truth, despite our differences in personality, she was an extremely selfless and nice person. She had a very good heart and never actually did anything wrong in the relationship. If anything, I had been the scumbag and coward at various points.

So for about a month I didn't know how to let her down. She would say to me at various times, "Just break up with me already." But I still didn't have the full strength to do it. Finally, on the phone one day, when she said it again, I cried and said, "I'm sorry." She cried too. And that was it. I was now single.

I was approaching ten to twenty girls every single day and starting to date and sleep around. Probably within a couple months' time, I was dating several people and was a lot more muscular. I was benching 120kg without a spotter. My ex-girlfriend and I saw each other, and still slept together, maybe every other week for four or five months after our breakup. I knew she was hooking up with other guys, but it was essentially a don't ask, don't tell sort of thing. After all, I was doing the same.

She came over one night, and while we were talking in my lounge room, I told her to touch my chest to feel how big my pecks had gotten. She said no. So I told her to leave. She was like "What the fuck?" But I was firm on it, "Yeah, you can leave. I said touch my chest." We had a bit of a strained back-and-forth, and I told her that if she wanted to stay she had to touch my chest. *She acquiesced.* After she did it, she was like, "Fine, are you happy now?"

I was seeing several other girls at that moment, so if she left, I could easily text another. My level of care was non-existent. Let alone the next day I could approach any number of girls and get more dates/sexual partners.

We went into the bedroom and I did things my way. As I was over her, I could see that she was staring at my chest and had a different look in her eyes. I didn't think anything of it at the time, but I must have remembered it for a reason. I believe it was the first time I registered that she felt something deeper and more visceral for me.

She told me that a new guy she was seeing for the past 6-7 weeks she lost interest in because he was too obsessed with her. She said she was straightening her hair one evening and he was watching her in amazement, probably idealizing her. She wasn't interested in that type of guy. She wanted a guy who wasn't needy for her and who would hold her accountable.

The next time I hung out with her, she picked me up to go for sushi. The conversation we had while we were out didn't interest me, and I told her that. I said to her, "This conversation doesn't interest me in the slightest. I don't see utility in it." We both stopped talking to each other. You would have thought one of us would break and say something, but neither of us did.

I got the check and we walked to the car in silence. She then drove me home in silence. When we arrived, I wanted to fuck her, so I asked if she was coming in or not. She got really angry and started shouting at me about how I didn't care or whatever, but I wasn't really listening. As far as I was concerned, she was either coming in or she wasn't, because that determined whether I was going to text another girl or not.

That was the last time I ever hung out with her.

WHAT IS DAY GAME?

Day game is not just approaching a woman literally during the day. Day game is something you'll do frequently after sundown as well. On the most simplified level, it generally refers to approach scenarios/venues that don't involve alcohol, dancing, or a party of any kind.

In other words, if you approach a girl at Starbucks at 11pm, that's day game. If you approach a girl at a university cocktail party at 3pm, that's night game.

*Day game generally refers to approaching women in scenarios where their **expectation** of getting approached is minimal. The exact venue/scenario is not so critical; it's the degree to which she **expects** to get approached that matters.*

At a bar, club or party, she expects to get approached. There are hungry and seedy guys lurking around everywhere. An approach in and of itself isn't impressive to her in these scenarios. You can be extremely confident, but any points you earn specifically for that reason are blunted because she's already expecting it.

In other words, the degree to which she's expecting to get approached is inversely proportional to how impressed she'll be if you actually do so.

"Hi, I'm Michael. I thought you were attractive and wanted to say hi."

Walking up to a woman on the street and saying that to her is an antithetical experience for her versus at a bar. At a bar she couldn't care less. On the street, it's suddenly a situation where she runs off to tell all of her friends about this "crazy encounter" she just had.

Alcohol is frequently used by men during night game as a crutch to overcome approach anxiety. They walk into a bar/club, and the first thing they do is get a drink. The idea is, have a few drinks, ease the nerves, then start approaching.

You don't need any of that bullshit.

Drinking alcohol when approaching women generally takes away any validity being extremely confident and forward with them has. If I have a beer in my hand, it's basically signaling to her, "Yeah, so here I am with a buzz, which I'm using as a crutch to hit on you, because without this buzz, I probably wouldn't have the courage to say hi to you." If I ever approach in a night-game scenario, I do my best to never have a drink in my hand.

The most powerful tool you can possibly have as a man is your directness and confidence, together.

Using that tool and confronting her when she least expects it (e.g., on the street) is a very profound thing, not just for her, but also for you.

I have dated plenty of girls who I am certain would not have dated me had I met them out at bars, clubs, or parties because it was my confidence on the street, on the bus, in the library, etc., that attracted them in the first place. In night-game venues, it wouldn't have meant much to them. These environments are just entirely disparate.

Almost all guys start out with some form of night-game experience (i.e., you're young, and you go have some drinks at a party/bar and maybe talk to a girl if you can rack up the courage). As you become more confident, you'll transition into day game. Then eventually, you'll see night game as mostly inefficient and expensive and drop it altogether.

The reason day game is so important is because most of the women you encounter in life are not artificially superimposed in bars and clubs.

Day game is really just a colloquialism for your normal, everyday life.

If you see a woman who seems interesting on the street, on the bus, or in the library, etc., learning how to say hi to her is an extremely important facet of being a man.

Day game is harder than night game because it requires more confidence. If you can do day game, you can easily do night game. If you can do night game, you can't necessarily do day game. Once you become effective with day game, you'll transition out of night game altogether.

THE MOST FUNDAMENTAL RULE OF APPROACH

The most fundamental rule of approach is as follows:

The manner in which you go about approaching girls naturally filters/selects for those with whom you'll pair.

That's probably one of the most baseline, standard, important rules regarding your interactions with women. I'm not a seduction star fox who created and conceived of that rule. That's well-known and perpetuated.

But now I'll add my magical Michael touch:

If there are 100 women in a room and seven might go on a date with you, depending on how you act, that number doesn't go wildly up or down.

*It's merely the case that the subset of **which** seven who'd date you would shift.*

If you peacock the hell out of your appearance with a crazy hat, earrings, trench coat, etc., you'll naturally filter for women who find that appealing/interesting; others might view it as try-hard and lame (but by the way, you can dress and accessorize however the fuck you want.).

If you play disinterested, neg, and try to poke at women's insecurities, you'll naturally filter for those who will play disinterested themselves and be condescending toward you.

If you walk in there as your natural self and are very direct and upfront with what you think/feel, you'll naturally filter/select for those who value confidence in a guy. Others might find it imposing or arrogant, or they might not want to hear inconvenient truths.

For instance, I'm extremely blunt with women. When I'm thinking something, I say it. If they don't like my bluntness and honesty, they naturally filter themselves out.

Why date a girl who can't handle you being upfront?

"Wow, this ravioli she cooked really sucks, but I don't want to offend her by telling her bluntly."

"I don't like when she raises her voice to me, but I'll just wait till she settles down. I don't want to make her more angry by calling her out on it."

Women sometimes say they want an asshole. They don't actually want an asshole. They want a guy who will tell it to them like it is – a guy who isn't afraid to act as he pleases or say what he thinks. When you carry yourself as you please, it's impossible that some people won't think you're an asshole. Just by the nature of it, when you polarize, you repel some as much as you attract others. I'd rather attract the women who like that I'm my own man. As I've already said, if a girl is repulsed by me because I'm too honest and upfront, then we happily screen each other out.

People will naturally pair with those similar to themselves. So you can act however the fuck you want to act and the actual number who are interested in you doesn't change wildly; it's just the subset of *which* women who are into you that shifts.

People will ask how you even get to the point of having enough confidence to make the first approach. In other words, if you're so deeply entrenched in stage zero and have absolutely no confidence, what's the trigger point to get you out of it?

I would say for me it was knowing that I didn't have to be or act a certain way. Those thoughts of, "Should I be saying a certain thing?" or "Should I look a certain way?" None of that matters because regardless of what combinations of personality traits or flair you present to the world, you'll find women similar to you with whom you'll mesh. So there's no fear in just being yourself.

Whether you approach as your natural self or with some lame facade, the only thing that changes is the mere subset of women who will be keen. The actual number doesn't go up or down. So there's nothing to force.

That was probably one of the most important things for me. I didn't have confidence before I started out. I was really apprehensive. So knowing I could just relax and be myself helped me get over my initial approach anxiety.

*Likes select for likes. People filter for those similar to themselves. Approach as your natural self and you'll pair with **somebody.***

THE DIRECT APPROACH

When you cold approach (meaning you've never seen a particular girl before), there's two ways to go about it:

1) Either you're direct about why you're approaching, and you tell her that upfront; or

2) You're indirect by playing to the surroundings, trying to naturally develop a conversation by rolling with your scenery.

You need to be direct with women. None of this indirect bullshit.

In other words, the vast, vast majority of your cold approaches should be direct, where you declare your intentions immediately.

If they are indirect, truthfully, it's more a matter of coincidence than anything else. That is, you should never plan to be indirect.

Never purposely come up with a topic related to your surroundings as a pretext to start the convo.

If you're in the same aisle at the grocery store, don't make a stupid comment about the price of the peanut butter. It's just lame.

Or even worse, if you see she's reading a book, don't open her by asking what she's reading or if it's interesting.

Girls are all hardwired with the same sixth sense of whether a guy is hitting on them or not.

If you're hitting on her, say so. Tell her. It's really attractive to her. And don't go halfway saying anything like, "I was walking and was feeling social, so decided to say hi." That's a lie too. Really, you were feeling social? No you weren't. You were just scared of telling her directly that you found her attractive.

There's two main ways I'll open women:

I'll say, "Hi, I'm Michael. I thought you were attractive and wanted to say hi."

Or, "Hi, I'm Michael. I just wanted to say hi."

That's it.

And those aren't canned pick-up lines. That's just the truth. You see a girl, you think she's attractive, and hence you want to say hi. So that's the most honest and simple thing you can say. Why would you need to say anything else?

And I'm usually super calm, not smiling, and looking them in the eye when I say it.

Why would I fake smile? What am I supposed to be happy about? You hear all of this bullshit about how you're supposed to smile because it makes you seem more friendly, etc. When I go to say hi, do I care more about what I think or what she thinks? My level of care about what she thinks is non-existent. So to artificially smile because it might make her more comfortable is irrelevant to me. Don't do anything that isn't you. Don't try to be a certain way when saying hi. Just say hi. However, if you're the smiley type, good for you.

Opening a girl with a neutral statement like, "Hey, how's it going?" or "What are you up to?" is always inferior to a direct approach, but is always superior to an indirect one. I've found neutral approaches are OK if (and this is going to sound unusually specific and weird) the two of you are incidentally standing/sitting beside each other, OR if she comes into your territory and sits/stands beside you.

In other words, unless she basically just appears out of thin air in front of you, you need to introduce yourself and tell her you wanted to say hi. If the direction of movement is from you to her, you need to be direct.

If she's sitting or standing at a bus stop and you approach, be direct – i.e., "Hi, I'm Michael. I thought you were attractive and wanted to say hi." If she comes and sits or stands next to you, a neutral opener – e.g., "How's it going?" is okay.

If the bus is mostly crowded and you end up beside her, a "How's it going?" is alright. If the bus is mostly empty and you go sit beside her, a "Hi, I'm Michael." Or, "Hi, I'm Michael. I just wanted to say hi," is far superior.

If the two of you incidentally end up beside each other at an intersection, a neutral approach is acceptable if it just happens to pop out of your mouth. If you see her at the intersection and walk up to her, tell her you wanted to say hi.

Why this pattern is ideal I'm not entirely sure, but over the years that's just what I've experienced to be the case.

A man physically uses his penis to penetrate a woman, so conversation is no different.

Essentially, if she's coming into your territory or you're beside her, you've got an "excuse" to open her neutrally, although it's at the expense of the points you gain for making a confident approach. That's why this isn't much better than the indirect approach.

If she's walking down the street and you skate or walk over to her and say "Hey, how's it going?" She'll usually deflect this type of encounter. Probably because it's obvious you're hitting on her but the approach comes off as indirect/weak so she doesn't bother engaging you. Even though, yeah, you approached her, it's sort of a lack of follow-through.

In general, the female subconscious mind just doesn't like to be approached by the "How's it going?" guy.

I can think of various interactions I've had where a neutral approach has worked for me, but I'd say these were spontaneous, unplanned moments. That is, I might arrive at a crosswalk not having noticed the girl next to me until the last second, which at that point "what are you up to?" just pops out of my mouth.

But, for instance, if I were to see a woman from 20 feet away standing at an intersection or in a grocery store, I wouldn't plan on ever approaching her like that. I don't ever think about what I'm going to say as I'm approaching. A direct approach – "Hi, I'm Michael. I thought you were attractive and wanted to say hi" should be a fairly automated way to start a conversation because it's the truth.

When I think of most of the simple deflections I've received, they occur when I approach a girl with a neutral opener, especially if she's walking. If she's sitting still, a "Hey, how's it going?" or

"What are you up to?" approach will usually result in her just looking down again at her phone, or not looking up at all.

If a girl is walking/going somewhere, it's especially paramount that you are direct. Immediately tell her your name and that you think she's cute. This is the best way to stop her in her tracks. If you say, "How's it going?" she's going to keep walking.

My suspicion is that when a girl who's physically moving/going somewhere is approached in any neutral or indirect way, her subconscious mind interprets it as "This guy is chasing me." This feeling of hers is also heightened in crowded areas.

You're more likely to get a simple deflection when you approach in places such as busy shopping streets and bus/train stations, etc., where pedestrian flow is dense and fast. Why crowded areas are unfavorable I'm not really sure, but possibly because women are more likely to put up protective guards in these scenarios. But regardless, don't ever chase anyone. I don't chase women. I set the tone immediately by intercepting them in their path with directness.

Your most powerful weapon is your directness.

I can't reiterate that more. So even if you want to start debating when and where a neutral approach could work, you'd be missing the point: *neutral approaches shouldn't ever be something you strive to make.* I was more just opening up this topic briefly because they're probably the number one way guys say hi to girls. It's the rarity of the direct approach that makes it so effective and attractive.

If a girl asks me why I said hi (i.e., if I had approached her with "Hi, I'm Michael. I just wanted to say hi."), I'll be nothing but straight with her: "I thought you were cute." She'll usually blush when you say that. If she blushes, that's a positive sign that you're creating attraction. And often times it's the fact that you said that so directly that causes her to be attracted.

If she's not attracted because you said that, she wouldn't be attracted no matter what you say because nothing beats that. That's the best thing *you can* say.

I also want to raise another subtle point. When you are direct and honest about your approach, don't go overboard with supporting details. If you say something like, "Hi, I'm Michael. I was walking over there and saw you and wanted to say hi. I was just coming from lunch and thinking about where I'm going to go to study because I've got a test tomorrow, and I just looked up and saw you," it starts to come off weird. You have to learn when to shut the fuck up.

Too much detail, despite a solid and direct approach, communicates neediness and turns her off. It shows you can't handle the tension of your own approach and are defusing it by not shutting the fuck up. It comes off as though you're trying to justify to her somehow why you said hi. There's no other reason why a guy would go excessive on detail.

I've sometimes used variants of my opener, e.g., "Hi, I'm Michael. I thought you seemed interesting and wanted to say hi." I'll probably say that if the air she gives off is a bit alternative/skater-type and appealing to me. You say whatever is on your mind. But usually, I just tell them I think they're cute.

Either way, some form of short comment declaring you think she's attractive and/or seems interesting marks the superior approach.

If she asks why you thought she seemed interesting, tell her. Just say you liked her outfit, or her piercings, or her hair. Whatever is on your mind is the correct answer. Don't even think about your answer. Just say it.

Also, if the type of moment occurs, where she perhaps blushes and looks a little uncomfortable, do not try to defuse tension in any way by rapidly changing the subject. The existence of tension creates attraction.

If she gets uncomfortable and starts to leave, don't follow her. Let her leave. The one thing you never ever do is follow a girl if she's walking away.

If you go to say hi and she's moving away from you, terminate the conversation immediately. Only extremely rarely have I violated this rule and it's worked in my favor. But truthfully, I'm not proud of that because it's needy. I'll generally stand there, solid with my footing, and I don't react to her moving away. After she's moved outside of five feet of me, I don't even say bye and walk away.

In these situations, my mindset is that she is lucky that a confident guy like me approached her out of the blue to start a conversation. It's true. Every other guy she encounters in life is probably too scared to walk up and declare his intentions. The fact that you're confident to approach her is something she will rarely encounter in life, and perhaps never again, especially during the day. If she wants to leave, it's goodbye forever. She'll go off and brag to her friends about her "crazy" encounter today, but as far as you're concerned, you've forgotten it the second she disappears.

Regarding the outcome of any given approach, my level of care is non-existent. Women who accuse you of being too direct or forward are generally testing you to see if you'll waver. If she rejects you because you're forward, that's the best case scenario. The only type of girl you want is the type that appreciates and loves your confidence.

I once went out with a very attractive Vietnamese girl who, via text message, didn't want to go out with me a second time because I tried for sex on the first date. She felt I came across too sexual. I told her to go find an Asian beta who would cater to her. I was serious. She was outraged. I didn't get defensive. Instead, I told her I thought she was awesome and would love to go out with her again, but because I'm not some Asian beta, I'm not her type. I wished her luck. She told me to go find a trophy wife. And that was the end of it. I didn't chase her. I said what I thought. I wasn't interested in her if she actually felt that way.

A month and a half later, she texted me again. I told her we should meet up. After all, what other purpose did our text exchange serve? She asked if I would care if we didn't meet up. I responded, "I've never cared so little about anything in my entire life." She was once again outraged. She thought I was supposed to care. Anyway, she agreed to meet up, and when I suggested the city, she countered by suggesting my place instead. She came over and it was great sex. Looking back, it was clear to me she was ovulating and her instinctual side knew I was the guy to contact that day. I had passed her confidence test. We hooked up for probably three or four months. She ultimately wanted a committed relationship. But I stuck to my guns. I told her to go find an Asian beta.

When you're dealing with girls who obviously pick up on your confidence and lack of stability factor, if they ask you, "So is that your thing. Do you just skate around approaching women?" I don't tell them yes. That isn't being dishonest. That's just being smart. If she's confronting you about it, she obviously knows you do. I hold myself to never overtly lying to women just out of the sake of non-neediness. But what I will do is simply not answer their questions. If they don't like that, they're under no obligation to talk to me. I'm not holding them there.

It's usually in a girl's best interest to stop asking these types of questions (e.g., "How many girls have you been with?"; "Do you always approach?"; etc.) because even though at first I perceive this as a predictable byproduct of tension on her end, if she persists, I interpret it as neediness and my interest evanesces.

At various points I have told them "Yes, I do (approach women)," and have even had chats about how other women respond, etc., and generally the result is they distance themselves. That's not to say there aren't women out there who wouldn't appreciate having this type of chat and admire your honesty, but the problem is it immediately takes away any element of her feeling special. She wants to feel special, even if her primitive brain knows she's just one of many you're approaching. If you enter into this type of conversation, just know it won't go anywhere with her.

And this isn't caring about what she thinks either. It's not like you're withholding information because you're trying to make her feel special; she'll feel special as a natural result of you singularly approaching her. This is about calibrating your answers to stay honest while not being overt about absolutely everything.

Somewhere, somehow, there was this notion created that if you're not being completely overt 100% of the time then somehow that's equivocation. Somehow that's intentionally misleading. But that's simply not true. No one is entitled to your thoughts. I'm not there asking her about her past relationships or whom she's fucked. I don't care. She got banged by an unusually big and dark cock four months ago? That's the last thing I want to know. And if I were asking her for details and she didn't reveal all of them, is she lying to me? Absolutely not.

Truthfully, if a guy started asking those types of questions on the first approach, I'd consider that very needy. If she's discontent with the answers you're giving her in any way – if she doesn't feel you're transparent enough – she has the right to leave. You're not forcing her to talk to you.

When they ask you about whether you go around approaching other women, the best way to respond is with an exaggeration factor: "Yeah obviously, hundreds." And she'll say, "So you do?" And I'll reply, "Yeah, hundreds, thousands. I've lost count." – whatever random things I need to say to jump around her tests without actually giving her the satisfaction of having her suspicion confirmed.

If you say something outrageous like, "Yeah, (I've approached) thousands," she obviously won't believe it, but it's not a lie. It keeps you honest, but the exaggeration let's her believe that maybe there's a chance you really are joking. This type of response is often satisfactory.

A girl's primitive mind will often know she's just one of many you approach. But don't confirm that suspicion of hers overtly. Just joke around with her, exaggerate a bit, and ask her questions to change the subject. If she's not happy with your answers, she can leave.

I've had plenty of girls reject me for being *too confident*, and I'm okay with that. They can filter themselves out.

Women want a balance of forwardness and safety in a guy. They all want forwardness in the beginning. They need some sort of demonstration of confidence. After that phase is completed, they'll look to see that you're safe – i.e., that you have a relationship stability factor. And the threshold is different depending on the girl. If she's too needy for stability, you're better off not getting involved. As I said, let her filter herself out.

In terms of the trajectory of the approach, it should always be head-on if she's standing still, or if she's walking in an area where there aren't lots of people.

If the area is busy (e.g., a train station or crowded shopping street), I will most often pop up alongside her with the flow of traffic. In busy areas, my choice to intercept her head-on will always be improvisational and usually only if she is slow-moving.

My housemate several years ago flashed me a page of some random manual/book, showing some diagram (yeah, the author had actually drawn such a thing) about approaching girls from 45 degrees from behind while they're walking. At the time, I didn't think much of it. Now I see that as incredibly dumb and lame. Approaching a girl from that angle shows you think the same way: indirectly. It also shows you care about what she thinks. It shows you're worried about whether she'll find you too confronting. It shows you're thinking about how to make her less uncomfortable.

As I said, unless I'm approaching in very busy areas, I don't open women from any other direction apart from head-on. No matter what angle I see her from, I always come around to the front and place myself immediately in her path so as to cut her off. If I'm skateboarding, I'll pop off my board about ten to fifteen feet in front of her, then walk back to her and say, "Hi, I'm Michael. I thought you were attractive and wanted to say hi." My presence almost always gets a response from her, even if it's a flat-out no.

There is absolutely nothing superior to the direct approach. When you see a girl who sparks your interest, walking up to her, saying your name, and telling her you think she's attractive is the best thing you can do.

APPROACH STANDARDS

Only 1% of the time will a woman be over-the-top ecstatic when you say hi to her. The other 99% of the time you need to have some standards in place.

A lot of what prevents a guy from relaxing when he's approaching a girl is the thought that he needs to qualify to her somehow.

When you approach a girl, you're never qualifying to her. You say hi to her with the mindset that she is your equal.

This isn't to necessarily say she should have to qualify to you, but the act of approaching is already your ante on the poker table. Where's hers? She has to show you something.

There's this pervasive false notion that because you're approaching her, that for some reason you need to prove to her that you're good enough. Somehow you're supposed to qualify to her, as if she's interviewing you. My answer to that is fuck that.

The fact that you're approaching her directly is in and of itself all of the qualifying you'd ever need to do.

"Hi, I'm Michael. I thought you were attractive and wanted to say hi."

If she's not at least neutral or mildly receptive to me within ten seconds, I leave.

I don't flinch or react even in the slightest. I will just abruptly say, "Okay, goodbye," or, "Alright, see you later," and then I vanish into thin air. As soon as the interaction is over, I'm like a phantom into the night. I'm gone.

If we're moving/walking in the same direction, I don't change my pace because of her. I don't walk faster or slower to distance myself from her. Her issue, not mine. Let her slow down or run off if she wants.

If we're sitting beside each other on a bus or in a cafe, I just put up an electromagnetic shield and go back to whatever I was doing/reading. Literally, end of interaction.

If there's another girl to approach immediately after, I'll do it knowing the first girl can witness it plain as day.

If she's at least neutral toward me but is boring or strikes me the wrong way, I'll leave within 30 seconds to a minute.

And a minute is generous. I don't waste time. When I say something, I allot an additional second or two of silence to allow her to respond. If she is particularly silent, even if seemingly neutral, I'm out of there. I'm not there to impress or entertain her. I don't care. I'm giving her the extraordinary opportunity to have a conversation with me.

Extraordinary.

If I say, "Before I moved to Japan, I lived in Australia for six and a half years," and she has nothing to say back (e.g., "What were you doing there?"), peace.

I tend to make very open-ended statements so that the conversation can flow better. I might say, "I teach on Skype to support myself." If she is incapable of saying something like "Oh yeah? What do you teach?" Peace.

I can think of several instances when I've rejected girls on the spot because they weren't interesting enough or were too silent, even when they were at least neutral or receptive toward me. And sometimes they're taken aback by it. Their expression is essentially, "Wait really? You just made the approach and now you're rejecting *me*?"

Correct.

I'm not mandating that she get down on one knee in genuflection to me. I'm not entitled to every girl being interested in me. I'm just offering the opportunity for simple conversation. And if it's not going anywhere, why would I waste our time.

I once had a date at a bookstore cafe starting in fifteen minutes, and I saw a cute girl at a nearby table. She got up and was poking at some books on the shelves. My plan was to maybe get her number and then just sit down. Then subsequently, if this girl observed my date, she might get turned on by seeing me with another girl; however if she were put off by it, I couldn't care less and goodbye forever. But either way, I wanted her number.

So I walked up and opened her. "Hi, I'm Michael. I thought you were cute and wanted to say hi." She smiled, blushed, and made small-talk with me. But she was boring as fuck. Mainly she was just too silent for me, but not particularly in a shy way (if she's quiet *because* she's genuinely shy, that's different and OK). But in this case, I got the impression that she expected me to qualify to her. I wasn't there to entertain her. Within 45 seconds I just abruptly said, "Okay, well, see you later."

She flashed a quick look of surprise. I could gauge she was willing to continue talking with me, but I didn't care. As I said, I had a date starting soon. So I sat back down and my date arrived shortly. Meanwhile, for the next hour or so, this girl undoubtedly watched from a short distance away as I was chatting and flirting over coffee. My level of care couldn't have been lower.

The bottom line is: you should always be willing to walk away from the girl you approached if she is either unreceptive or, if neutral or receptive, is boring or strikes you the wrong way. Have some standards. Never feel the need to qualify to any girl you meet. Approach with the mindset that you are equals.

Never carry entitlement to a girl's interest in you, but bear in mind that your direct and confident approach is actually a big deal. Most guys don't approach this way. If she doesn't meet your standards for basic communication, just move on to the next girl. Women are an abundant resource.

SMALL VENUE APPROACHES

I want to make some important points about what to do if you're in the same small venue as the girl you're approaching.

In other words, if you approach a girl on the street and she's not interested, you leave immediately. You vanish. But let's say you're in a coffee shop and there's a girl ten feet away from you. If you go and say hi, and she rejects you, then what? Do you leave the cafe out of awkwardness or do you go back to your seat?

Firstly, it doesn't matter what she thinks, so you can do whatever you want immediately after. But let's say I plan on spending maybe another hour relaxing and studying at a cafe, and even though I don't care what she thinks, I'm not interested in being in the same physical space as she after the rejection. I like clearing my mind. I don't need to see her there in my periphery. One could argue that if you really don't give a fuck then why would it be awkward in the first place. I would say it's more just a feeling of wanting to move forward and away from that situation, end of story.

So I first ask myself how interested I am. If I'm decently attracted to her but not overly eager, I'll often times wait until I'm getting ready to leave and approach her then. If she rejects me, I just leave the cafe as I was going to anyway.

If I'm decently attracted to her and I'm not ready to leave the cafe yet, I might wait until it looks as though she is getting ready to leave. Then, if she rejects me, I go back to my seat and she leaves as she was going to anyway. No awkwardness. Also, because she's leaving, you don't have to worry about wasting time having some long conversation with her. You can literally spend a few minutes chatting with her and say, "Ok, well, I don't want to hold you." That's it.

If I'm really attracted to her, no matter what I'm doing, I don't waste any time and approach her as soon as possible. If I walk in and she's already been sitting there for an unknown amount of time, I approach in under 60 seconds. If I'm there first and she is just sitting down, I'll wait 1-2 minutes depending on the circumstances, because I've approached girls before only for the boyfriend to arrive with his soy latte 30 seconds later.

Even if she doesn't look like she's leaving any time soon, you never know. She might just take her coffee a few sips in and abscond. It's happened before, where the girl abruptly gets up and leaves with the full coffee, and I've kicked myself for it.

If the girl rejects you and neither one of you is ready to leave the cafe, you go back to your seat and handle it. And, no, you don't change locations either. You put up an electromagnetic shield. The approach never happened.

One time there was an attractive girl who sat down at a small table directly in front of mine so that we were basically face to face. She pulled out her phone and didn't notice me. I got up and sat down in front of her. Before I could even open my mouth, she immediately started shaking her head and waving her hand no as though it was some sort of traumatic experience for her. Essentially, "Oh my god, a guy is saying hi to me!"

Because of my level of experience, this wasn't an issue for me and I handled it very easily. But I could only imagine, for instance, if this had been my first approach ever, that probably would have been fucked.

Without flinching or saying anything, I just calmly stood up, walked backwards literally five feet, sat back down in my seat, still practically face to face with her, and continued with my study. And it was like, "Yeah, no kidding it's awkward now bitch." But I dialed that feeling back and just kept studying. Within five minutes she got up abruptly and left. And I was thinking, "Yeah, exactly, get the fuck out of here."

She couldn't handle the tension and broke, so she left. Not my issue. It was hers. She probably had nothing better going for her that day – wake up in the morning, spend time putting on expensive makeup and fitted clothing, go to a cafe alone, and then reject the confident guy who says hello so that we can retreat back home, once again alone, swipe around on Tinder, and be depressed – sounds like a great plan.

I half-joke, but sometimes you just have to own getting rejected harshly. We are never entitled to a girl's interest. In truth, this particular girl was just in her "state." She hadn't even looked at me. It could have been any guy saying hi to her whom she would have waved away.

Situations like that are the reason why I've analyzed my timing a little bit for small venue approaches. I can handle any awkwardness better than any girl I'll ever approach, and I don't care what she thinks, but it's more just not wanting to deal with distractions while I'm studying/relaxing. For that reason, I much prefer street/campus approaches. That's my forte. But naturally I'm not some ninja dude who only exists on the street, so learning how to manage small/closed venues is important too.

THE TIME TO HESITATE HAS CEASED

When I was 22 and still living in Boston, long before I ever had the confidence or ability to approach women in an integrated way, I was out for the first time with a friend of a friend. He was 27. We saw two attractive girls looking at us smiling. I didn't take any initiative whatsoever to get us to approach, nor was that something I would have done had it not been for him.

As we stood there not approaching, he looked at me for a moment, almost as though we were fools. Then what he said next still powerfully resonates with me today:

"The time to hesitate.....has ceased." And then we just walked up.

Sort of like you're standing at the side of a pool nervous about jumping in because you know it's cold, but on the count of three you just jump anyway, no questions asked.

Basically, if you don't act quickly enough, even if your approach target is stationary, you run the risk of blowing the approach window, because any additional time you spend thinking about or analyzing things ruins the spontaneity of the moment and the degree to which you act naturally.

Sometimes there might be cases where you make eye contact with a girl across a coffee shop or library. Then an hour later, before you leave, you go to say hi, etc. *But for the vast majority of your approaches, you're not going to have the luxury of copious time to play around with.*

Maybe you'll be on a sidewalk and a girl will briskly walk out of a store, pass in front of you, then cross the street. In that case, your approach window, before she crosses the street, is about 2-3 seconds, and if you don't act instinctually and immediately, there's no chance to open her, unless you chase her, which changes things entirely.

Even now, occasionally there will be times when I don't act as quickly as I could. If I ever catch myself in these moments (i.e., stalling and blowing an approach window), I have the tools to essentially blast open an emergency valve and just make the approach, no matter how much I've increased its awkwardness. Sometimes I'll *tell her that*.

Sometimes that's the only way to bring the interaction back to equilibrium – "Hey, I saw you crossing and thought you were beautiful, so I had to run over here. I'm Michael."

But mostly, what allows me to blast open that last-second valve is my awareness that if I blow an approach, it's negative momentum for my following approaches.

I will say to myself *"The time to hesitate.....has ceased."* And then I just approach, no questions asked. That's my one-second "count of three" at the pool, and it always works for me. None of this "Ahh shit, sorry, I just can't jump on three" bullshit. You have to be strong and own it. When you say that line to yourself, you approach. That's it. There's no thinking. You just do it.

I don't really care about making some last-second, slipshod approach that ends in rejection because as long as I say hi, no matter how creepy or weird I come across, *that is the success*, and my next approach only becomes better.

In fact, if you're on the verge of blowing an approach but save it, that's probably an even greater gain than if you had just done a normal one.

That doesn't mean purposely hesitate, but no matter how experienced you get, you will always blow approaches. That never ends. However what you do become better at is how to save some of them.

Whether it's to prevent an approach from being blown, or to just say hi to a girl in a situation you think she's likely to reject you, in order to have success with women, you've got to risk coming off creepy sometimes.

If you're aggressive and make high-risk approaches (e.g., cutting her off at the bottom of an escalator to tell her you wanted to say hi), it's impossible for some women to not think you're a fucking creeper.

If she likes you, you're sexy and confident. If she doesn't like you, you're all of a sudden a fucking creeper. Same guy. Same exact approach. But depending on the girl, not you, all of a sudden the perception is completely different. The first girl thinks you're a creeper; the second girl likes you. But really, this point emphasizes that polarization, by it's very nature, ensures that for the very reasons some girls are attracted to you, others are repulsed. For every girl who is put off by your confidence and boldness, another will be drawn to you for it.

So in short, if you see a girl and feel yourself hesitating, say: "*The time to hesitate.....has ceased.*" And then you just walk up. That's it.

FEMALE NON-RECEPTIVENESS IS THE MALE NON-APPROACH

"Hi, I'm Michael. I just…"

Most women are prone to be non-receptive even if you approach them in the most attractive way possible.

That's why you can't take it personally. It's almost always never about you and almost always about her. If she's non-receptive, she's in her "state," where she's not going to be receptive to anyone. The specific guy saying hi to her is essentially interchangeable and irrelevant, the same way the specific woman you're approaching is interchangeable and irrelevant.

Girls don't take it personally when a guy doesn't approach. So why should you take it personally when she does the female equivalent, i.e., not be receptive.

Her default setting is to be non-receptive, just as most guys will never approach.

There's no way to know who will be receptive and who won't be, which is why if you want to say hi to her, you should do it. The guys who try to make this assessment beforehand are the ones who aren't aggressive enough. They wait for when the moment "looks right" or "seems right."

I once approached a girl on the sidewalk of a busy road. Because we were going same direction, after I said hi, I walked and talked with her for 20 seconds. We made small chat, but she wasn't receptive, and she turned to go down another shopping street. I wasn't there to entertain her, so I just let her walk off without following her.

Probably about two hours later, I randomly bumped into her again, this time face-to-face in a corridor of an enclosed cafe-mall area.

As soon as she saw me, her face got red in an unusual way, almost as though she was relieved to see me. (Call that weird all you want, but that's just what I was able to gauge).

She stopped for me and we exchanged contacts instantly. Then I told her I had to go.

My impression of the situation was that her initial, biologic response to my street approach was to be non-receptive. For her, that was just her instincts acting. Then after I walked off, her more conscious thought-process probably kicked in and said, "Ya know, that was actually rare. Guys don't really approach during the day like that. I actually wonder what could have been." So when she saw me again, she was relieved. Because otherwise she would have always wondered.

Had I not bumped into her a second time shortly thereafter, I would have had no way of knowing that she had a change of mind.

I was at the University of Queensland biological sciences library one night and saw an exceptionally beautiful blonde Aussie girl studying by herself. I approached her and said, "Hi, I'm Michael. I thought you were cute and wanted to say hi." She said thank you. The very next thing out of my mouth was, "Let's take a 5-minute break," signaling that we could talk outside of the quiet study area. She politely declined. I then very calmly said, "Ok, see you later," and walked off.

I went up to the next floor and started studying by myself in an enclosed glass study room. The staircase I had walked up was across the floor, but I had an unobstructed view of it from where I was. Maybe about five minutes after I started studying, I randomly looked up and saw her near the staircase searching for something.

I could tell she was looking around for me.

She then went back down the staircase.

I packed up my shit, ran across the floor, and flew down the staircase. She was leaving the library. I caught her out in front and said, "Were you looking for me?" And in a relieved voice she said, "*Yes, I thought you deserved a chance.*" We walked around campus for probably ten minutes talking and getting to know each other.

"Yes, I thought you deserved a chance."

I could tell by our initial conversation unfortunately that our chemistry was fairly weak, but I was really attracted to her so opted to go out with her anyway. We met up and had dinner together. Once again the conversation was boring. I kissed her goodbye and that was the end of it.

But the point being: here was this beautiful girl who had rejected me as her initial response, but after spending a few minutes contemplating it, appreciated the confident approach and came looking for me. Had that been a street approach, for instance, I never would have known she had a change of mind.

Similarly, most guys won't approach, and then their approach window closes. And that opportunity is gone forever. So if you by chance encounter the same girl again and can re-open an approach window, you might feel *relieved*.

The female natural state is to experience hesitation receiving an approach the same way a male hesitates making one. That's another reason you should never take anything personally.

There was another time I approached a cute redhead in the University of Queensland Great Court. She was neutral, and I talked to her for about 60 seconds. Then I told her we should hang out and exchange numbers. She declined. So I left. As I was leaving the courtyard (maybe 15-20 seconds later), I saw something in my periphery.

*She came…**running**…after me.*

She gave me her number and said we should hang out. I remember telling my housemate about this because he liked redheads, and he was like, "What the fuck!"

So once again, never take female non-receptiveness personally because it's her default setting. That's her normal state. A fair number of the women who reject you on the spot will have "non-receptiveness remorse," and you'll never know because you won't see them again.

One of the most important calibrations with respect to saying hi to a girl is *to do it as soon as she becomes aware of your presence.* The coffee shop/library scenario is sometimes variable. I'm talking about, let's say, you're on the street and a girl sees/notices you, even in her peripheral vision. If that occurs, *do not linger* (i.e., walking in the same direction as she for 30 more seconds) before saying hi. As soon as she sees you, walk straight over to her so that there is zero discontinuity.

When a girl gets cold approached, no matter how you go about it, she's going to have to handle the situation as much as you are. When you confront her directly and quickly, **you don't give her time to decide whether she's going to close herself off.** If she's closed off, let it be more instinctual from her end. That's okay.

If you linger, you let her subconsciously process the idea of what it would mean to get approached in that situation, and that will only make her less, not more, receptive.

Have you ever thought too hard about whether to approach a girl? The longer you wait, the harder it is, right? You have to just not think and go do it. Well if you give her time to think, or if she senses you hovering or following, she'll close herself off.

A similar situation could be said for, let's say, a girl who sits down at the table next to you at a cafe. If at the instant she is sitting down you say, "Hey, how's it going?" It's very natural and there's no second thought about it. If she clearly sees you, sits down, and then you're both just sitting there in silence for however long, **the increasing hesitation on your end to open her is met with a corresponding hesitation on her end to be receptive.**

"I should have just said hi earlier."

In the beginning, your initial challenge as a male is making the mere approach. That's stage zero. Over time, your challenge will become more situational than anything else. Timing means a lot. Not just for you, but for her. As soon as the approach can be made, make it. Don't wait. You are most natural if you engage the spontaneity of that moment. Even if she doesn't see you, sometimes you'll blow your own approach window if you wait too long. You'll second guess yourself and the window will close. Never let that happen.

The majority of women will be non-receptive no matter what you say or do. Whether it's at the moment of the approach itself, or ultimately through flaked text messages/dates, most women will not follow through. That's expected.

Sometimes if, even for just one second, I notice myself becoming frustrated by a girl flaking, I catch myself immediately and discard the thought *because it's my expectation* that most women won't follow through.

Most guys won't approach. Similarly, most women won't be receptive.

That's important to remember because it keeps you reasonable.

Why get frustrated? *That's how it's supposed to be.*

Female non-receptiveness occurs not just at the time point of getting the number; it also is a standard part of the texting/follow-through process. Most of the numbers you get will lead nowhere. Most of the women you say hi to won't be interested. Just remember that.

THE MORE EXPERIENCED YOU ARE, THE LOWER YOUR PERCENTAGES

With regard to the women you approach, the more experienced you are, the lower your percentages.

At the outset, you're probably wondering right away what the fuck I'm talking about and/or are already in vehement disagreement. But I'll say it plainly again: the more experienced you are, the lower your percentages.

*That's because with experience comes the confidence to be more aggressive. And if you're being aggressive enough, you **should be** getting rejected a high percentage of the time.*

There's no such thing as an experienced guy with high percentages. Even if he's "fairly good with the ladies and so good looking," the implication of high percentages is he's actively avoiding approaches in situations he doesn't feel he'll get a good response. In other words, he's thought about approaching at times but lays off. That's not true calibration. That's actually approach anxiety.

Many guys secretly know they avoid approaching in situations that are likely to result in rejection. They wait for situations they think are likely to be less imposing on the girl. It doesn't matter how good your social calibration is; you never actually know which approaches will result in the outcomes you're looking for.

Most of your approaches *should be* resulting in rejection. If a quarter of your approaches turn into dates, that means you're doing something wrong, not right. That's a problem. *It means you're not being aggressive enough.*

For example, if we consider "safe" venues like coffee shops or bookstores, why are they even considered safe? It's because the environment can be used as a pretext, or excuse, for an "incidental" crossing of paths, essentially as a buffer against approach anxiety. In other words, these types of venues can sometimes carry a lesser degree of confrontation and intensity, essentially for men to avoid being as direct as they could be with women.

However if you approach a girl as her train is arriving at the platform, this situation would be considered "high-risk" because there's a much greater chance she'll reject you *regardless of your ability to calibrate*. But that's good. It keeps your percentages lower. It means you're being aggressive enough. And you know what, of those high-risk approaches you do, some will convert and become some of your most rewarding experiences in life.

In my experience, *on average*, the greatest chance of rejection is in crowded areas of transit (i.e., people are moving/walking in high density). That means these scenarios are considered highest risk and are good for practicing direct approaches and stomaching rejections.

I would probably guess that if a man is being maximally aggressive (i.e., not holding back because of any fear mechanism), his *sexual* conversion rate, with respect to the number of *raw approaches* he makes, should be around 1%. And I am **NOT** talking about kissing, "third base," or anything like that; I'm talking about actual, straight-up sexual intercourse. If you include non-actual-sex hooking up, then the % is higher.

Right away, a lot of guys reading this would probably shoot that down as though it's preposterous. Really, you sleep with a third of the girls you approach? Either you're sleeping with thousands of women (you're not) or barely any at all. See what happens to that percentage if you spend an afternoon only approaching in bustling subway stations.

*You should, in effect, essentially be "titrating"/adjusting your approach style **in order to reduce** your percentage down to around 1%.*

If you already consider yourself a seasoned approach veteran and think my 1% figure is off-the-chains absurd, as I said, go to a subway station or busy shopping area. Give yourself ten minutes to act like a pinball bouncing off of people as they walk by. Then, yes, now you'll understand the 1% I'm talking about.

Before I moved to Japan and was living in Australia, where a good portion of my approaches were on-campus, I'd guess my % was 2-5%. It's only now that my approaches are exclusively intra-city, fast-paced ones that my % has evolved to be around 1%.

*That is, the only way to hit the magical 1% figure is to be approaching in venues that are fast-paced and bustling. I consider **the choice** to approach in these venues to be a reflection of high audacity and experience; in addition, these venues will further spur confidence augmentation – essentially a positive reinforcement loop.*

Some guys will say that venues aren't in their control (e.g., you are still finishing university in a place that isn't a big city). My response is: don't dwell, and after you graduate, move to a big city.

*It's not a fucking accident that after spending 6.5 years living in Brisbane, Australia (a not-so-large city), I moved to Osaka, Japan (a big city). I made that happen. I wanted that. **Consistent intra-city approaches have allowed me to achieve high audacity levels incomparable to when I was living in Australia.***

If people want to pursue acting, they move to Hollywood. If they want to start a tech company, they move to Silicon Valley. If they want to be a stock broker, they go to Wall Street.

If you want to maximize your audacity and confidence levels, you need to move to a big city and approach in high-pedestrian-traffic areas.

Maybe Miami just isn't big enough of a city. Try New York. Or London. Or Seoul.

If you can't (or choose not to) move, then you have to accept responsibility for that. You have to own the consequences. You just won't reach your peak potential for confidence in life is all. And there's nothing wrong with that. Just don't ever preach that your 2-5%, rather than 1%, sexual conversion rate is a matter of experience and calibration. It's not.

So going back to the numbers, let's say in a couple-month span you make 20 approaches and sleep with two. That's not impressive. Firstly, you should be making 20-30 approaches *per day*; and secondly, 2/20 = 10%, which means the 20 approaches you did make weren't aggressive enough. It means you saw lots of women you could have approached out and about and simply didn't open them.

That means you should try being a little more courageous. Try talking to more women at the bus stop, on the train, at the gym, at restaurants, etc. That percentage needs to come down.

If you're approaching a lot of women and are aggressive, the percentage doesn't feel like it's 1% because you're conditioning yourself to immediately forget the interactions that don't go anywhere. As soon as a rejection occurs, the girl should be erased from your mind pretty much instantaneously. And you shouldn't even have to try to do it. It should be very integrated really.

Even the girls whose numbers you *do* get you shouldn't think too hard about. Sometimes there will be those whom you're more interested in, but it's actually a good thing to struggle a few days later and be like, "Wait, this Hannah in my phone was which girl again?" Sometimes putting them in your phone as "Hannah outside Starbucks," if that's where you met her, is a good way to set up your contacts. Or things like "Jess turquoise nails," etc., if there was anything that stuck out about her. I always put a little tagline like that next to names.

About 80% of girls you approach **will** reject giving you their number/app contact on the spot, irrespective of what you do. That means for every 100 girls you approach, roughly **EIGHTY** will either ignore you completely or make up some excuse as to why they can't give you their number.

But 20ish will give you their contact *if you attempt to get it*.

That's correct. If you're walking up to a girl, there's a 20% percent chance she'll give her number to you if you try to get it (and on a college campus, that's probably closer to 40%). *This is where some guys get the impression that their percentages are so high.*

So then why the absurdly low 1%?

It's a lot easier for a girl to give you her number and then flake than it is for her to say no to your face.

Out of every 20 numbers you get, one-quarter of those will be non-responders. Now you're left with 15 of the 100 you approached whom you're now texting in some capacity.

Of those 15, a third might return a hello or a few replies, but they're not interested and you can tell. There's nothing you can do. Don't worry about it and delete them.

So now we're left with ten of the original 100 whom you might now have a little text rally with. Of these ten, probably a third will initially sound excited to hear from you but will not respond when you try to arrange a meet-up; a third will say they're keen to go out (e.g., "Yeah, next week should be good!") but will flake, and about a third will go out on a date.

That means three out of 100 will go out on a date (3%). Of these three girls you go on a date with, you'll end up sleeping with one (1/100 = 1%).

This also assumes that you can calibrate to your date well and push for the bedroom and sex aggressively; most guys don't have that ability on dates, but I make this presumption because in order to get these dates in the first place, the implication is that you've got a minimal level of confidence and forwardness established.

This means if you approach 20 women every business day of the week, that's 100 women in one week, which means a new sexual partner every week.

And the thing is, the more women you start sleeping with, the easier it is to maintain them, because you become less needy. By a month or two, if you are genuinely doing 20 approaches a day, five days a week, you will pick up 4-8 new sexual partners. You think I'm lying? Try it. It's the fact that most guys don't/can't do this which is why guys like me capitalize. Just so you know.

If you are doing two approaches – that's it – every business day, that will probably net you one sexual partner every ten weeks or so, which means about five in a year.

However one important point to bear in mind is that the accumulation of sexual partners is **not** as simple as: approach 100 a week for eight weeks and pick up eight. Things tend to occur as waves of varying speeds. You need to be patient.

In other words, there might be one girl you meet, e.g., in January whom you start sleeping with somewhat quickly, whereas another you meet around the same time you won't start sleeping with until the summer. This could be for any number of reasons, but the long story short is, you'll find that some of the girls you enter into sexual patterns with you'll actually have met several months earlier. It merely takes time for the waves to hit the shore. That's why consistency matters.

I can think of one example where I had met a Thai girl at the university library in the spring, yet I didn't start hooking up with her until the following winter. There had probably been about a 9-month gap.

The result is: the first couple months you approach at a high level, you might carry the impression that you're doing "really poorly" because very few girls seem to be converting over into sexual partners. But then a few months later, "when the waves start to hit," you'll find you're all of a sudden seeing several people at once.

This statistical breakdown isn't something I've ever formally calculated or cared about. It's sort of just a retrospective impression I've garnered/ascertained by having made thousands of approaches. Some days you might approach 12 people and get zero contacts. Other days you might go three for four. It's really hit or miss.

Here in Japan, as of April 2019, I would guess I average 20-40 approaches per day, with a typical range of 4-11 contact acquisitions. I never count my approaches, so that range is subjective, but my # of contacts is objective since I can clearly look at them afterward. (Btw if you give a fuck and want actual "proof," go to my FB group and click through the photos I've uploaded. You'll be able to find some of my "field report screenshots" of contacts I've picked up. So if there's a percentage of you who imagine I'm bullshitting, the proof is there for you to see with your own eyes.)

There's an 80/20 rule of business/economics floating around out there somewhere. That is, 80% of your productivity occurs in 20% of your time; 80% of your revenue is from 20% of your clients/customers; etc.

Well I'd say there's truth to that with meeting women as well. 80% of the contacts you get will be in 20% of the time you spend approaching.

In other words, you might spend an entire afternoon skating around only getting one contact in total, and then have a random morning on campus between classes where you get four.

It also means if you're having a shitty day, you don't just say, "Alright, well this is one of those bad days so I'll just hold out for the next." You truthfully don't know the fate of any one day. You could go zero for fourteen, but your perseverance leads you to meet an awesome girl on the fifteenth attempt that day.

I've had days skateboarding around where I've literally picked up six contacts out of seven approaches – the kind of day where I'm like, "Yeah, I know, I'm so incredible." Then I'll go zero for twelve on the following day, or one for thirteen on the next. Or I'll forget that I went zero for ten the day earlier. It's just the nature of it. (I'm just making a point, but if you live in a big city you should be shooting for 20-30+ approaches per day).

I can recall, in particular, one summer, I had purposely spent four straight afternoons going to the city to spend an hour or two approaching, and I got zero numbers. It was ridiculous. Then, when I was going out on the fifth day, I skated past a beautiful 20-year-old redhead walking her dog in front of my house.

I passed her by about 50 meters, then flipped open my emergency approach valve (see chapter: The time to hesitate has ceased), and skated back to her. I talked to her for no more than 30 seconds and got her contact. She sat in my phone for about two months, as I had so many other numbers in there and people I was already seeing. Then I finally texted her and she came over. Within two minutes of being in my room, we had sex. I remember thinking afterwards that the total time I had known that girl, between literally first saying hi to her and sleeping with her, was two and half minutes.

So it's really important for me to reiterate that low percentages are **what you want.** I'm serious. If you are hanging around people bragging about their high percentages and how incredible they are, they're amateur. And if they've been at it for a while, then they still don't understand how to actually be forward with women.

My old housemate I had mentioned (see chapter: The end of the beta male) was once falling out of form, and he made a boasting comment that he was "doing really well lately" and was going on dates with about a quarter of the girls he was approaching. I said something along the lines of, "Shut the fuck up. You obviously aren't being aggressive then, and you know it." And he knew it was true. There was a girl on the bus that day he admitted to not saying hi to, and he was kicking himself for it.

*One of the best metrics that reflects how experienced a guy is is how **low** his percentages are. The more experienced you are, the lower your percentages. You're reading that correctly. You have the right to disagree, but that's one of the most important pieces of info anyone will ever tell you. Doesn't matter how "amazing" you think you are for whatever reasons; if you're bragging about high percentages, you're not aggressive enough.*

WHEN THERE'S A SURROUNDING AUDIENCE

People at the bus stop standing in silence? Good. Let them analyze things. Let them be the audience that observes and takes notes on how bold you are.

You have to genuinely override those thoughts and not care what others think. The same way a certain level of confidence is required to talk to your girl of interest and not care what she thinks, there's confidence required in not caring what the surrounding people think.

I've approached plenty of girls before on dead-silent buses, in silent library study areas, etc., where there have been close-proximity audiences of fifteen-plus people. And sometimes I've been rejected harshly. I swallow it. But I get mega "fire points" (i.e., big momentum) from these types of approaches. Sometimes people look on intently like, "Omg this guy is talking to a woman!" I know, holy shit, such a crazy thing. Fuck them.

The degree of tension associated with an approach is directly proportional to the amount of positive momentum and confidence you reap as a result. There are very few certainties in life (i.e., death, taxes), and this is one of them.

In other words, you will actually become more confident after having started up a conversation on a quiet, crowded bus, where the situation feels a bit tense, as compared to approaching a woman sitting by herself in the corner of an empty cafe. In both cases, your confidence increases, but the more difficult/tense the approach is, the more greatly you reap rewards from it.

Therefore, high-risk and tension-filled approaches are a blessing in terms of the number of confidence points they bestow to you, especially if you get harshly rejected. The outcome isn't important. It's the mere act of you saying hello that matters.

Tension undeniably is a real factor to consider, and in truth, the exact physical scenario surrounding the approach is irrelevant because the circumstances you're engaged in at any one moment are highly variable. What truly matters is the tension you feel in that moment and whether you act despite it being there.

Notice I don't say "nervousness"; I say "tension." Nervousness implies a negative feeling of apprehension about making the approach; the implication is your fear is holding you back as a result. In contrast, tension implies the identification of a slightly uncomfortable but positive emotion; you use it as an indication that following through on the approach is important.

No matter how many approaches you do, tension never fully goes away. Daily fluctuation is normal, and you will always encounter certain scenarios where you feel a little tense about opening someone. It's these times that matter the most and give you the most confidence after you follow through.

Ever have a day where you're feeling tired/like shit, but you go to the gym anyway? And what happens? You feel better afterward. It's those "off-days" that are most paramount. They're the ones that reflect your perseverance and determine how fit you stay/become. Well the same is true with approaching. It's the ones you hesitate on the most that are the most crucial to follow through on.

Despite the thousands of approaches I've done, I will still feel tension depending on the scenario. At my level, this never has anything to do anymore with the actual woman and is always related somehow to the surroundings.

Once again, the degree of tension associated with an approach is directly proportional to the amount of positive momentum and confidence you reap as a result.

I generally don't like audiences in quiet areas, but I do my best to ignore them. I practice what I preach. When I feel tension, I tell myself that the time to hesitate has ceased, then just mentally shut the fuck up and approach/open. It's being able to approach in these scenarios that breeds my confidence. I live it. And whether I get rejected or not doesn't matter. It's merely saying hi that counts. 99% of guys won't do that. And especially in high-tension scenarios? Probably >99.9% of guys won't go there.

I find when I'm with one or two guy friends, having them observe from afar as I approach alone in front of a surrounding audience relieves tension because a rejection for me is entertaining for all of us. I'll say, "Ok, watch this rejection. It will be entertaining." Then they watch. And if I do pull the contact, all it does is demonstrate the importance of being aggressive. If I get rejected, I'm even more fearless to make the next approach. It's a win-win. But in general, I'm almost always solo (i.e., not with friends) when approaching, because it's integrated in my daily life, rather than something I do periodically "as a sport."

If you're new to approach, you can start small and say hi to women sitting in coffee shops and walking in bookstores, etc., but ultimately you need to work up to introducing yourself to people on the street and public transportation.

If I'm approaching in a closed space and can't eject myself from the physical area immediately (e.g., on a bus), I'll put up an electromagnetic shield and make zero facial or bodily expression in response. I'll generally just continue reading the news on my phone, or whatever I was doing before.

Typically, if nearby people respond in any way, I've noticed it's with a smile. It's usually because they can admire your confidence, *not because they're laughing at you*. I say this because despite the fear one might have of opening a woman due to a surrounding audience, negative responses are actually exceedingly rare.

In fact, I've never had a surrounding person react negatively to any of my approaches, and I've approached thousands of women. Nearby people will never actually react negatively to any of your approaches. It's all in your head.

Some women will actually be *turned on* by having seen/heard you approaching other women.

I was once at a cafe sitting at a long table, with a girl on either side of me. I opened the girl to my right because she was actively swiping on Tinder, so I thought she'd definitely be receptive. She wasn't. Her responses were dismal, and even slightly hostile, so I stopped talking to her after about 10 seconds. It's like, go have fun with your Tinder swipes. Not my issue.

About a minute later I opened the girl to my left. She said, "I just heard you say hi to that girl there." My response was along the lines of, "Yeah, it's good to meet new people sometimes." I ended up going on a date with her. And that's just one example. I can think of many.

In contrast, might a girl become less receptive if she sees you approach another girl before her? Yeah, but it's not really her fault though. It's her biological safety mechanism because you've demonstrated yourself as highly confident. On the surface, she's probably saying, "I'm not interested in creepy guys who go around approaching women." But in reality, she's just projecting what her limbic system is telling her: "There's a greater chance he's non-committal and I should be more careful."

In general, I couldn't give a fuck if other women observe my approaches. And sometimes if I get rejected by one girl, especially if it's harsh, I'll approach another girl right in front of her to demonstrate my prowess and to show her she's not special. Not because I care what she thinks, but because it's entertaining to me. It feels good to reinforce your inner man sometimes.

I was once walking in a crowded shopping area and saw a cute girl. As I was approaching her from behind, at the last second, I saw about five feet behind her a stunning girl, so I approached this second girl instead. She rejected me instantly. Instead of disappearing, I proceeded to march up to the original girl, right in front of the one who just rejected me, and opened her. This one also rejected me instantly. But it felt good. It was a quick 0/2 on my way to 1/100 (1%). It only immunized me further for future approaches.

Nearby guys who see you approach will appreciate your confidence. They might be annoyed if they were thinking about approaching and you got to the girl first, either by timing or because they were chicken. But at heart, they admire the confidence and can learn from not having been more aggressive.

One time I was on a street and observed across the sidewalk four guys walking behind a very attractive girl. I crossed over, hopped off my skateboard, and opened her head-on. She rejected me instantly. The presence of the guys meant nothing to me, but I observed that they all smiled at the obvious bold pick-up I had attempted. I could have basically become their group leader after that had I wanted.

Approach anxiety never goes away. It just takes new forms. In the beginning, anxiety is mostly centered around the woman you're approaching. As time goes on, it becomes more circumstance-based and is often related to the presence of a surrounding audience (e.g., getting the number of a cashier while her coworkers are hovering around her in silence). This is ironic, however, because surrounding people won't respond negatively, so there's no reason to actually hesitate.

THE APPROACHES YOU MAKE EARN YOU THE NEXT GIRL, NOT THE ONE YOU'RE ACTUALLY APPROACHING

There is no stagnation when it comes to approaching women. It's sinusoidal. If you choose to not make an approach due to any fear-related mechanism, the result is negative momentum and you ruin your chances with the *next* woman. But if you do make the approach, irrespective of whether she rejects you, it's positive momentum and you build a bit of flame inside. Sounds weird but it's not a joke.

In other words, whether you realize it or not, you're always inadvertently increasing or decreasing your level of neediness with respect to the next approach. If you don't approach even though you secretly wanted to (e.g., you justify to yourself that you shouldn't say hi because she has her headphones in, even though the real reason you're not approaching is you don't want the people standing next to her to observe/analyze things), you're now more needy and are hurting your chances with the next woman. But if you just go and say hi, even if you don't hit it off, you're more likely to be on fire for the following interaction.

It is impossible that every woman will want to talk to you. Rejection is a natural and integral part of approaching. But by building enough positive momentum, what you're ensuring is that when you do genuinely meet a great woman who could go either way, you'll tip her in the right direction. **Therefore, the purpose of your approaches right now is to increase your chances with that great woman you're going to meet eleven approaches from now.**

For instance, I can recall one day in particular I was making approaches all afternoon on campus. I had probably made 15 or so, skating up to random girls saying hi, and they all rejected me. I got zero numbers. Maybe it was the weather that day. Maybe they had exams. I don't know. I don't care. But that evening, I saw a beautiful girl at the gym. I noticed she was leaving so I followed her out like a creeper. We ended up going on a date. That wouldn't have happened had I not built momentum from that afternoon. I was just in a zone.

There's an element of hardening that occurs as you get rejected over and over again – a form of resiliency.

This resiliency builds over time and becomes integrated, such that your confidence baseline a year from now is greater than at the present, but it also fluctuates on a day-to-day level.

That daily fluctuation is notably paramount, and when you combine that with your increasing confidence baseline, you can have rare bursts of super-high masculinity and attractiveness toward women that you never thought were possible for yourself.

Try making fifteen approaches in an afternoon and getting rejected harshly, or ignored, every time. The sixteenth girl you see, it will be like you're Rocky. You walk up. There's no bullshit. There's no smile. It's just purely metallic. Purely man. Now imagine a year or two of that. Try five years.

I say this from experience. Of innumerable examples, I was once in a park and saw an absolutely stunning woman. I'd say in the top 0.01%. I came face to face with her. She was 5' 10" and dressed in clothing that probably cost more than my whole wardrobe. I'm 5' 8" on a good day and carry a skateboard. It turns out she was a model (oh what a fucking surprise). And I'm not talking about the decently attractive woman who does a photoshoot in the woods, posts her photos on Instagram, and is now a "model." I'm talking about a real model who did runways in different countries and had photoshoots with well-known brands. The kind where I was that "average guy" with the tall, stunning woman, where guys would turn their heads wondering how the fuck that happened.

I wasn't thinking about it at the time, but the dynamic of my approach became the biggest and most enduring theme of our whole relationship.

I walked up and said, "Hi, I'm Michael. I thought you were attractive and wanted to say hi." Now that in and of itself wasn't special. That's a typical line I use saying hi to women. But in this particular case, based on my momentum, I had no smile. And I had locked eye contact with her and didn't unlock at any stage over the first two minutes or so. I didn't flinch. I don't even think I blinked. I was an actual fox. As I said, I wasn't thinking about it at the time nor was I trying to be intimidating. It just happened because I was so absurdly hardened and masculinized by my approach momentum, i.e., by getting rejected so many times in a row.

I took her on an "InstaDate" and she became *one of* my girlfriends for about 3.5 years. She had told me at various times that I was the only (not one of the only; I mean only, only) guy she had ever met who wasn't intimidated by her. And she continually referenced my unwavering eye contact when we met as nothing she had ever experienced before. I really wasn't intimidated by her going forward at all. Why would I have been? There's obviously an awareness that the person you're with is physically attractive, but when you approach enough, looks won't impress you anymore. And I'm serious about that. It's not a cliché I'm regurgitating. It's an important truth.

Just as the first ten approaches/rejections in a day will earn you the eleventh girl, looking back, she was that great woman I met as the **two-thousandth** approach or so. The first two-thousand approaches, and all of the nasty, embarrassing and painful rejections they entailed, ultimately "prepared" me for her. I wouldn't have been adequately conditioned otherwise.

That type of interaction at the 2000+ approach level you can't fake. This is not the same as going fishing and then 2000 later you just happen to finally catch a big one. This isn't that. The growth in confidence is literally the equivalent of going from fishing at a pond to a year or two later reeling ocean fish 12 miles offshore.

I just didn't have that same degree of confidence in the beginning. And even though I would have told you I was confident in my novice approach days, and objectively compared to most guys I was, the subtleties and nuances of behavior continue to evolve. That's one of the best parts of the process – the long-term changes in you, that is.

In addition, your **perception and interpretation** of what blowing an approach window even entails, or what a harsh rejection even means, will change as you gain experience. For example, at your 50-approach level (i.e., you're just starting out), blowing an approach window might mean simply not saying hi to a girl at a cafe and kicking yourself for it. But at your 7000-level, cafes you could do on salvia with your eyes closed. Blowing an approach window might mean not opening and closing a stunning girl in a 25-second span on a crowded train between stops, where she just got on and you're about to get off; this is a scenario, for instance, that even your 1500-approach self might not consider to be possible.

In short: on a daily level, the first ten approaches you do are to get you that great girl who happens to be the eleventh that day; the first ten rejections are irrelevant. On a more long-term scale, the grand summation of your approaches and rejections will induce lasting behavioral changes that allow you to hit confidence levels not possible early on. Confidence cannot be faked.

HOW TO GET ANY WOMAN YOU WANT

As you approach more and more and are direct with women, you start to identify your approach prowess and directness, together, as your most valuable asset – not your looks, not anything you own, not your job, etc.

You'll start to actually say to yourself, "You know what, this is a big deal. Not a lot of guys have the guts to do this." This asset cancels out any disparity in appearance level between yourself and a very physically attractive woman you're approaching.

Unless you are literally a pre-internet celebrity, your confidence will 100% triumph over any other asset you bring to the table.

Looks and material items (e.g., cars) are both essentially the same thing. They're both buttresses against approach anxiety, just the former happens to be built in. Doesn't matter how good-looking or rich you supposedly are. If you can't approach, it means nothing. It's the guy who is more average in appearance and income (like me) who has more "luck" with women.

If you're able to approach women during the day in a direct and honest manner (i.e., just straight up saying your name and telling her you find her attractive), that's a huge deal, because most guys won't/can't do that.

99% of guys will not approach attractive women directly. That's why if you do, it really is a huge deal.

A guy can compensate for "lack of looks" with confidence and directness; a woman cannot compensate to the same extent.

Now that doesn't mean confidence isn't important in a female. It is. But confidence and behavior are **more important** in a guy; they're a guy's core sexual asset; everything else is secondary. For a woman, her physical sexuality is more important; the rest is secondary. And you 110% have the right to disagree with me, but I'm firm on that.

A guy can, without a doubt, be impressed by and attracted to a woman who's confident. No questions asked. But he ultimately won't ever date her **because** of it. However a woman will date a guy **because** of it. It's the male's role to be forward. Pretty much universally across all cultures, it's the male's role to initiate.

*Sexually, the penis thrusts and the woman receives. So the same holds true for initiation: it's the guy's movement, thrust and forwardness that matter, and it's the woman's sexuality that is designed to attract this movement from the guy. It's not the woman's job to initiate with you. She **can** initiate, but it's not her job.*

In other words, when push comes to shove – when sexual partner selection ultimately occurs – a guy's attractiveness is determined mostly by his level of confidence, directness, and forwardness, whereas a woman must rely mostly on her physical sexuality to attract.

*Guys think that because they secretly fixate on looks that women must do the same. Yeah, women admire appearances, **but compared*** *to guys, they truly do not care nearly to the same extent, across all age groups.*

When actual sexual pairing occurs – all bullshit aside – that same woman who was just talking with her friends about some guy she thinks is cute, will actually hook up with and date the "average guy" who approached, is unwavering, and not intimidated by her.

A woman who's not physically attractive (even though beauty is in the eye of the beholder), irrespective of how confident she is, will experience difficulty attracting men no matter what. However, a guy's confidence can function as a substitute for "what he lacks." That means he can essentially attract any woman.

That's because a male's status is determined by his confidence level, and it's your status that wins you women.

Over time, you'll see that your "lack" of looks, money, etc., doesn't actually matter because your directness with women is what they're looking for anyway.

And when you see that your lack of something doesn't matter, you become more comfortable lacking it. As a result, you become more secure with yourself and happier.

Based on the numbers game, regardless as to how attractive the woman is, most approaches will end in rejection. We already know that.

So when an attractive woman rejects you, why would you automatically assume that looks were mostly to blame? That almost always is *not* the reason she rejected you. I've come to discover that women are often just in a "state." That is, they'll reject practically anyone at certain moments, and there's nothing you can do about it. Don't take it personally.

There are plenty of women who reject me instantly, *without even looking at me*. So in those particular cases, for example, how the fuck could my appearance even matter. When a woman rejects a guy on the spot, it almost never has anything to do with the actual guy or his appearance. The guy is completely interchangeable. As far as she's concerned, an approach is an approach, and she's not going to have it right now. You think I'm wrong? I'm not.

The vast majority of the time a woman says no, she would've said no regardless as to who had approached her.

The Italian housemate I had could have been a Gucci model had he applied. He was a tall, dark, handsome guy, who was very suave with women and had a great smile. He got rejected all of the time, both on the spot and through women flaking on him via text. That had actually helped prove to me, beyond a reasonable doubt, that looks really were not part of the equation most of the time. I'd say, "Wow, if *he's* getting rejected all of the time...that means even if I were as good looking as he, it wouldn't matter." He and I would actually laugh about it. I'd say, "Corey, you're not good enough for her! You're not her type!"

In other words, once an approach is made, good looks in a guy will not transform a woman who is unreceptive into being receptive. Looks function mainly to cancel out a little bit of male neediness **if the woman was receptive from the start.** That is, they slightly increase the threshold for which you lacking confidence will be overlooked. But if you're non-needy and confident, it doesn't matter what you look like.

The only difference that not being physically attractive as a male really makes is that if the woman is initially neutral or receptive, there's less wiggle room to come off needy in any way. You just have to be confident and not change your behavior because of her, because that's what will cancel out any looks discrepancy between you and her.

It's the act of you changing your behavior *because you think you're not as good-looking or as high status as she* that she will instinctually pick up on and get turned off by. It's your perception of yourself that she will read. It's not your "lack of looks" in isolation that she truly gives a shit about. What she is attracted to is the extent to which you're not intimidated by her. I've had lots of women intensely stare at me during an approach, some of them almost squinting; they're looking to see how strong I am mentally and if I'm holding it together.

If you approach a woman, that in and of itself is better than 99% of guys. But then let's say, inadvertently, you care more about what she thinks than what you think, and you're changing your behavior because of her; she can read that, and it's a turn-off to her. You have to stand your ground and not waver whatsoever. It means that if you want very attractive women, the only way to *match their attractiveness* is to be extra-confident. Don't waver. Don't flinch. Don't give a fuck about what she thinks. And you'll get her.

The only way to truly not give a fuck about what she thinks is to get rejected a lot, and to get used to it, because getting rejected a lot will make you unwavering as fuck. I promise. There's no way around that. You can't fake the confidence. You've got to earn it the real way. The hard way. Take pride in your rejections.

The face on a woman is largely interchangeable and unrelated to whether she'll actually accept your advances or not. Often times, less physically attractive women are *more difficult* to win over because they're less convinced your advances are genuine. A lot of the really hostile rejections you'll get are from very plain women.

Very physically attractive women are usually the ones most impressed by a confident guy approaching them during the day because they're probably used to most guys being intimidated, or just not approaching at all. So in this case, your confidence matches their looks and you pair accordingly.

When I am out and approaching, I'm the most attractive guy around because *I'm the one* who has the courage to say hi to any woman, in any circumstance. Any other guy out there doesn't come close. I'd probably say I comfortably clear the one in ten-million level for guys in terms of day game. I am 5-foot-8 and average in appearance. However in terms of confidence and approach ability, I am essentially the equivalent of a 6-foot-6 model. Now you can roll your eyes at how absolutely outrageous and ridiculous that sounds, but hear me out, because this is a big, big lesson here:

I truly know I can get any woman I want because I'll approach anyone I want, and I don't change my behavior because of anyone. If height, looks and wealth are supposed to get me that, I already live it. I'm aware that the vast, vast majority of guys are simply unwilling to say hi to a woman, let alone do it over and over again aggressively. Confidence is what a woman is really looking for, and I'm one of the rare guys who will just go for it. I am not in any way inherently special. I've just learned to own my rejections. Each and every one of them makes me stronger.

It's your ability to handle/stomach your rejections and continue approaching anyway that masculinizes your behavior and makes you high status. And that high status will get you women.

In other words, getting rejected gets you women.

The number of women you sleep with is somewhat unimportant and only an incidental outcome of your status; it is not the cause of your status.

If someone were to ask me, "Michael, you sound ridiculous and arrogant as fuck, but what would you say makes you high status?" I would probably reply, "That's a very good question. It's my ability to handle rejection. I've been rejected more than any guy in the world."

That means I view my status as nothing to do with the number of women I've slept with. Nothing to do with looks. Nothing to do with my job or anything I own.

My conviction in my status is knowing I can own and handle my rejections.

On an absolute scale, it's my fearlessness to go after what I want and not waver when things don't go my way. On a relative scale, it's my awareness that most guys in the population are too scared to approach; and if they do approach, they chicken out in tough surroundings. I own the tough surroundings.

HOW TO GET A WOMAN WHO'S IN THE TOP 1%

This section is not about putting women on a pedestal. Don't ever look at a woman and be like, "Omg crazies she's in the top 1%!"

This is more to address the common guy question of, "How do I get the absolute hottest woman out there? Michael, tell me what I need to do to get the hottest woman out there."

I'll tell you exactly what you need to do.

I'll break this down into two points:

1) The numbers game, with the incidental outcome being you date the hottest woman out there; and

2) How do you, literally, pick up a specific woman on the spot who you believe is the hottest woman out there.

To address the first point:

Based on rejection percentages, you'll sleep with 1 in 100 women you approach if you're aggressive enough, *regardless as to how attractive they are*. But of course, for every 100 women you approach, they represent a subset of women **who are already** somewhat attractive, otherwise you wouldn't have approached them in the first place. So let's say, arbitrarily, that your threshold for approach is the woman must be in the top 20%. I'm setting a very loose bar here to prove a point. That means, if she strikes you as cute/sexy at least in some way, you'll approach her.

I know some guys reading this are probably like, "Rah rah rah, I only approach women if they're *already* in the top 1%." My advice is to just hear me out, because this logic is less about how high your standards are and more about how to think in a different way about women you're going after.

Let's say you approach 20 women every business day (100 per week). That's 5,200 approaches a year. That means, in a year, if this is your frequency of approach, you will sleep with roughly 52 women (1% of your approaches) who are *all* in the top 20%.

Bear in mind the top 5% of the women you approach *must be in the top 1% of the population*, since those you're approaching are all in the top 20%, and assuming you're not actively avoiding any woman who is above your threshold.

In other words, 100% of your approaches = 20% of the population.

Therefore, 5% of your approaches must = 1% of the population (5% of 20 = 1).

So let's consider *your* top 5%.

5% of 52 women is 2.6 women. That means, in a year, if you are doing 20 approaches per business day, with all other probabilities and bullshit cancelled out, you will sleep with 2-3 women who are in the top 1% of the population.

On a smaller scale, two weeks would equal 200 approaches. Because they're all in the top 20%, 10 of the approaches must be in the top 1% of the population. If I get rejected by all of them, that 0/10 means I'm closer to hitting the 100 approaches I need to go 1/100 in terms of sex, and I'm okay with that. That means in 20 weeks (just five months), I've approached 100 and slept with a woman who's in "the top 1%."

One argument to counter my logic above could be, "Well of the 52 women you sleep with in a year who are in the top 20%, what if none of them is *actually* in the top 1%; in other words, what if the hottest 2-3 women you sleep with are actually in the top 3 or 4% of the population?" I would say that's probably reading into it a little too far because, **at the end of the day, the top 1% of women is only what you believe it to be.** Your friend's view of what the top 1% represents is not the same as your view. For instance, I am primarily into Asian women. Maybe you hate Asian women. So I can guarantee you already that our view of the top 1% is different.

Everyone's "top 1%" is different. A woman I find beautiful might not be someone you're interested in whatsoever, and vice-versa.

To address the second point:

Let's say you see a woman who you *already think* is in the top 1%. That is, you're walking on some random street and say, "Wow, she's unbelievably crazy gorgeous. Michael, how do I get her?"

I'll tell you what I would do.

I'd walk right up and say, "Hi, I'm Michael. I thought you were attractive and wanted to say hi." That's it.

The top 1% you're seeing on the street, on the bus, etc., as a subset in isolation, if you approach 100 women *in this grouping*, you'll get twenty of their numbers, go on dates with three, and sleep with one of them. That's pretty simple math. That means for every 100 times you approach a "drop-dead gorgeous" woman, you'll sleep with one of them. That might sound like a low number, but trust me it's not. If you're making active strides to approach women every day, this tally adds up very fast.

My old housemate and I used to occasionally mention when we'd get rejected by a "drop-dead gorgeous" girl on a given day, and the other would reply, "Well that's just one closer to the 100 you need, so yeah, that's good."

But in all seriousness, you approach these girls like you'd approach anyone else. No woman is different from any other woman. Seriously. Once you understand that, you won't treat her any differently, because she should never be treated differently. If you're treating her differently, it means you're changing your behavior because of her. Never change your behavior for any woman. If she doesn't like it, she can leave. And if you don't feel like you can be yourself around a particular woman, you should leave.

WHY DON'T YOU HAVE A BOYFRIEND

You're never going to see her again. So just say hi. Her headphones are not part of the equation.

There are two main types of encounters you'll have with girls:

Type A (you'll only see her once in a lifetime); and

Type B (you're likely to see her more than once).

Type A means you see a woman on the bus, or on the street, or shopping in a store, etc. You're likely never going to see her again (unless there's divine intervention).

Type B means maybe there's a certain girl in one of your classes, or at work; or maybe she's a barista at a cafe you frequent, whom you're fairly sure you'll run into again (there's no guarantees in life, but we'll run with it).

For type A encounters, for starters, the most important thing is not blowing your approach window and making sure you open her no matter what.

If you're not in a calm, clear headspace, you have to remind yourself that because you're already not talking to her / haven't even met her yet, you can't have less than that anyway.

You can only go up, not down. If you approach, and the interaction doesn't work in your favor, the net result is you're back to where you started – i.e., not talking to her – but now you have more momentum to make *additional* approaches. This is a win. The mere

103 MIKEMEHLMAN.NET

act of saying hi is in and of itself the success, not whether you get her contact or not.

If it's a street approach, I'll once again reiterate that I would approach her from the front and say, "Hi, I'm Michael. I thought you were attractive and wanted to say hi." Full stop.

That is the absolute best/strongest approach you can make, no matter who you are or what you look like.

When I say hi, I'm usually not smiling and act however I please. I have no reason to fake-smile and couldn't care less how friendly or unfriendly I come across. If you're the smiley type, great, but I'm just telling you what I would do.

If you don't feel like smiling, don't. Approach exactly as you are, in your own skin. Your mood will naturally be different depending on the day and circumstances. Don't change your behavior. And don't worry about what she thinks.

If she deflects your encounter/approach, the interaction ends instantaneously. That's it. That's the end of it. You move on to the next. You have to accept that rejection is inherently part of the approach process, and that no matter what the woman looks like, rejection will occur most of the time **for all guys.**

As I've talked about before, getting rejected on the cold approach is almost never about you and almost always about the "state" she's in. Do not ever attempt to push back against a girl's unreceptiveness. Attempting to fight through it isn't persistence; it's neediness. If you carry an abundance mentality, you leave immediately. Once again, **your rejections will almost always be because of her "state." Just let it be.**

If I were with you on the street and we were approaching together, and you were like, "Michael, show me how this is done." You would see me get rejected incessantly and laugh your head off. You'd probably be like, "Holy shit, this guy takes a fucking ton of rejections. This is nuts."

The aim is not to avoid rejection; the aim is to embrace it. Rejection is unavoidable, so don't try to side-step or circumvent it. Understand that it will never go away. I view any attempt to minimize or avoid rejection as a reflection of male neediness. Don't be so outcome-oriented. Understand that your confidence comes from the **process** of getting rejected incessantly. Embrace that. Own it.

If she starts talking to me after I've opened her, she'll usually say, "Oh, thank you." They usually don't say much more than that, so unless she counters by asking you a question back, you have to reply. If she doesn't tell me her name voluntarily, I don't blame her, and I probably ask for it only about 50% of the time at the beginning; the other 50% of the time I ask her name mid-convo or when I'm getting her number. It's not something I've ever thought about or hyper-analyzed, but when I reflect on it, it's what I do.

One could easily ask, "Why can't you just walk up and say 'Hi, I'm Michael. I thought you were attractive and wanted to say hi. What's your name?'"

You can do that, and by all means my conversations aren't scripted and you can say whatever the fuck you want to women, but, in my opinion, it subtly blunts the effect of your direct opener. Let your short, bold statement telling her you think she's attractive hit her like an arrow. Let her react to you saying that.

When you tell her your name and that you think she's attractive straight-up, there's nothing better you could possibly say.

The next thing I do is 100% wing my conversations. That is, I completely improvise and don't plan anything whatsoever. I'm an unequivocal advocate of **deregulation.** I have conviction that a male is his most natural if he's 100% deregulated and not thinking about what he's going to say. And if he's deregulated, he's not changing his behavior, and in turn, is his most attractive.

Any thought related to modifying one's convos, or even worse, any act related to the implementation of intellectualized "schemes" or "tactics," makes the male less attractive. This implies outcome-orientation and a *need* to not be rejected. That is, any form of regulation can be traced back to neediness because its aim is grounded in reducing rejection.

Deregulation is the natural result of being process-, rather than outcome-, oriented. It's not a purposeful implementation in and of itself. If you don't *need* a positive outcome and understand that rejection is normal, you should never do anything other than simply wing your conversations.

With respect to the following advice I preach regarding what to say during an approach, I want to make crystal clear that this is more or less just a general framework for how my conversations might progress. **In reality, I just wing everything.** It just happens to be the case, however, that you might ask certain things that are merely pertinent to any conversation (e.g., what she's studying, her hobbies, etc.); that's not synonymous with scripting or regulation.

So after approaching her directly, I'll typically say, "What are you up to right now." Notice I put a period there, not a question mark.

My enunciation would be similar to as if I'm *telling her* a direct statement, rather than asking her a question. "What are you up to right now." Period. I'm telling her that.

Then she might say something like, "I'm going to class," or "I'm shopping." Now this is where you have to calibrate based on how much time you think you have.

If you're not rushed (i.e., either one of you might be able to talk for 5 minutes), you can make a little small-talk with her, e.g., "Cool, what class?" Just have a normal conversation with her. Yes, you approached her because you thought she was attractive, and you told her that, but spend a little time demonstrating you want to connect with her person. If you're on a bus, find a way to ascertain when she might be getting off (e.g., at the university, or the next stop, etc.) so you know how much time you're dealing with.

If there's not much time (i.e., less than five minutes, or it's a crowded area such as a shopping street or train station), I pretty much engage her sharply, directly, and fast.

Whether you have a little time to play around with or not, I always ask her age in the first 30 seconds.

Asking the age quickly is important because if this isn't a university encounter and you're on the street, for example, and she looks like she's 19 but it turns out she's 17, you immediately just say, "Bye bye!" and walk away. So for one, it's a safeguard.

Secondly, if she's younger (e.g., early 20s) and probably not shy about her age, as soon as she says "24," I always reply with my age (32) even if she doesn't ask. Establishing the age difference is important right away because the last thing you need to deal with is for it to be some mystery that hangs over you guys, and then four days later you're texting about it, etc. Just get it out of the way.

If she's a little older (e.g., 30 and up), asking her age can make her feel a little pressure in the interaction, particularly if she's shy about it. Sometimes she'll say, "It's a secret." If that does happen, I don't even care and just immediately say, "I'm 32." End of story.

I used to preach back in late-2017 when I first started producing content about how I'd always ask in the first minute whether or not she has a boyfriend. And if she said yes, I'd leave instantly. I used to ask this 100% of the time as a matter of staying as non-needy as possible – i.e., why should a guy who has a pure abundance mentality waste one additional second on a girl who says she has a boyfriend – so just get the question out of the way. Pretty simple, right?

Over time, however, my mentality has evolved, and now I don't see it as mandatory to ask. The reason for this is because, especially through 2018, I had forgotten to ask the question on numerous occasions, only for the girl to hook up with me anyway, and then I'd find out she had a boyfriend after the fact. Additionally, I'd find she wouldn't even care. Therefore why should I? So I came to internalize: there are plenty of girls out there with partners who will be more than happy to hold a stable pattern with a beta male and then sleep with you on the side.

This is *not* the same as interfering in the relationship of a friend / guy you know (which I view as unforgivable). I'm talking about cold approaching a girl with a random, mystery boyfriend. In these types of cases, I don't view hooking up with her as a breach of one's integrity. That's just how the sexual game works. But once again, going behind a friend's back is unforgivable. There's a big difference.

If I do ask whether or not she has a boyfriend as a function of my deregulation, it's only if, as the convo gets underway, I find myself not super-attracted to her after all and I'm subconsciously looking for a way out. That is, instead of just abruptly leaving a convo sometimes, I might just randomly ask if she has a boyfriend. That way if she says yes, I have "a reason" to just leave immediately.

If she says she doesn't have a boyfriend, I'll always ask *why she doesn't have one.* This can sometimes jump-start tension in a positive way.

Once again, I enunciate as though I'm making a statement to her: "Why don't you have a boyfriend." Period. She'll usually get a little awkward and say, "I'm not sure.." If she gives you an exact reason (e.g., I don't meet a lot of guys), you can briefly talk about that. If she doesn't give a reason, I'll ask her if she meets guys often or if she goes out a lot vs stays in, etc.

"Why don't you have a boyfriend."

Asking her *why* she doesn't have a boyfriend is an extremely direct and confident question. Yeah, it's confrontational and weird. But it's a fucking awesome question. This is pretty much the best topic you can talk about when it comes to jump-starting a conversation you were about to leave out of boredom. It teaches you good information about her, conveys your intention, demonstrates your confidence, and kick-starts tension, all in one.

Now you want to know if she studies or works. That's the minimum extra information you want to know before any of your conversations end. You can make minimal small-talk around it, and that's not hard to do.

Some guys will ask about "InstaDates." That is, you hit it off and want to turn it into a coffee or ice cream date on the spot. If you think you can pull this off because the two of you have time on your hands and good chemistry, go for it, but be aware it can come off needy. Don't ever plan on turning a conversation into an InstaDate. If it happens, let it be because the circumstances of both of your days coincidentally dovetailed nicely, but don't ever make your focus pushing for an InstaDate.

If you do ever attempt an InstaDate, you do **not** need to ask if she has a boyfriend first. But bear in mind this can play out in two ways if she has one: 1) She'll withhold that information from you because she likes you; or 2) She will tell you late if she views you platonically. I've gone on InstaDates before only to have wasted time when she mentions her boyfriend 45 minutes later. However I've also gone on InstaDates with girls, whom I've hooked up with, when it later turned out they had boyfriends. So it's hit or miss and is your call.

In general, it's usually ideal to just get a girl's contact and then leave. Once again, don't make your focus going on InstaDates. This is generally how a good handful of my convos go (completely winging it, but a rough sense):

Me: Hi I'm Michael. I thought you were attractive and wanted to say hi.

Her: Oh [+/- wow] thanks.

Me: What are you up to right now.

[Possible trajectory #1]:

Her: Just going to work/class. (i.e., something that *is* a good convo starter)

Me: Yeah? What do you study? / Are you in university? / Yeah? What do you do for work? (Just wing it and see where the convo goes. That's literally it.)

[Possible trajectory #2]

Her: Just shopping. / Heading home. (i.e., something that *is not* a good convo starter)
Me: Oh okay. What are your hobbies? [super-childish / elementary-school-style question, but a fucking awesome one if it comes from a non-needy and genuine place. No, I'm not fucking with you. I tend to ask this question somewhat fast and abruptly in many of my convos. Once again, I'm always 100% winging it, but I ask this question **a lot.**]

Her: Hobbies?? Ummm (lols...) tennis, shopping, movies, etc.

Now you've got a conversational stem via which you can springboard things a bit easier.

I want to reiterate (because, for one reason or another, the hobbies-question takes a bit of criticism from guys) that asking, "What are your hobbies?" is an amazing, amazing question. People like to talk about themselves. And there's a certain ingenuousness that comes through with this question if you ask it from a non-needy place.

So after winging it for a few minutes, be forward and don't pussy out. Just tell her, "Ok, let's exchange contacts." Don't ask her. Tell her. If she says no, you just say, "Ok, bye," and walk off. Goodbye forever. If she agrees, awesome, you get the contact. Now she falls into the 20/100 approaches who gave you her number. Maybe she'll be that 1/20 you sleep with.

The more you get her talking, the better you're doing, since people generally like talking about themselves and will tend to leave a conversation feeling pretty good about it. But regardless, always be completely deregulated and just say/do whatever the fuck you want. Don't hyper-analyze the conversational dynamic. Don't worry about what she's thinking. Literally say anything that comes to mind. Anything. No matter how "stupid" you think it is, just say it. Even if it is, "What's your favorite animal?" Just say it. It's not what you actually say that matters; it's the act of you being genuine, non-needy, and deregulated that is in and of itself attractive.

Guys have asked me before if you should be making more statements vs asking questions in order to not come off as though you're qualifying to her. And my response is: statements have a purpose insofar as they drive an interaction forward – i.e., getting her contact, going on the date, etc. Apart from that, 100% wing your conversations. And if you're focused on asking questions vs making statements, that actually reflects neediness, which will permeate to the surface in any interaction. I ask lots of questions in my conversations. That's me deregulated. I can promise you she will not think you are "lower status or qualifying" simply because you're asking her things. If she's unreceptive, she's unreceptive, but that's not a function of you trying to get to know her.

Me: "Okay, well it was great talking to you. What's your name by the way."

Her: "Sarah."

Me: "Okay. Well again, I'm Michael, it was great randomly meeting you, but I have to get going now. Let's exchange contacts."

Her: "Okay…."

That's it. Shut the fuck up while she's getting her phone out.

Don't make some stupid statement to cut any tension or awkwardness that's there. Don't linger around after you get the contact making more small-chat. Just leave. Some people will suggest not leaving immediately so as to not give off the impression that your main objective was to merely get the contact, but my advice is to just leave. Getting the contact should be the close of the interaction; it's not some arbitrary midpoint.

The only additional calibration you can sometimes make after getting her contact is saying, "When are you free." This can be an effective way to set up a date on the spot (see chapter: "When are you free.").

Otherwise, that's basically how most of my conversations go. If she deflects you at the initial approach, you leave. Find another girl. If you asked if she had a boyfriend and she said yes, you leave. If she says no to the number exchange, you leave. I never linger.

My conversations are straight and to the point. They're not flowery. There's no screwing around. I'm not there to dance and ask her about what she's buying today. She's shopping? *Why would I fucking care about what she's buying.* Only talk about what you want to talk about. Asking basic questions like work/study, hobbies, family structure, and if she lives on her own, are probably the most pertinent if you're filling in time.

So in summary, my **deregulation** tends to unravel as:

1) Say hi. Tell her you think she's attractive straight-up.

2a) In the first 30 seconds: Establish your ages.

2b) Ask if she has a boyfriend if you're not super-interested after all and want "an excuse" to leave, as opposed to just abruptly walking away (even though the latter is perfectly fine). If she says she doesn't have one, ask why. InstaDating girls without asking if they have boyfriends is fine, as some of them will hide that info from you if they like you. Just bear in mind this runs the risk of wasting your time if she views you platonically and tells you late.

3) If rushed or in busy area: Find out her work/study. Tell her your work/study. Ask about hobbies. If not rushed: Beyond work/study and hobbies, 100% wing your convo. Seriously.

4) Tell her it was great randomly meeting her and that you have to get going. Tell her you're going to exchange contacts now. If you didn't get her name at the beginning, get it now. Improvise and ask her, "When are you free." Set up a date on the spot.

*I will be an annoying asshole and reiterate **again** that I have conviction in **conversational deregulation** as the number-one way to be your most natural and attractive. Having a sense of basic things to chat with her about is good, but apart from that, you should just be 100% winging your conversations.*

For type B encounters (i.e., you think you'll see her again, although no guarantees in life), a very important thing to consider is that "long game" never works. That is, don't try to "ease your way in" with random hellos and smiles here and there. There's no tension with this type of interaction and it generally goes nowhere. You need tension to create attraction. If your long game works somehow, it's truthfully lucky; it means she didn't encounter a guy like me somewhere else who's picked her up yet.

There's two main trajectories for type B encounters. The first is to take a fairly immediate and swift approach. The other option is to go into "hiding" and avoid most contact with her altogether until some later period (e.g., a month later when the class is ending), then pounce. The caveat is that the hibernation tactic is risky because she might get picked up before then – i.e., you have a greater chance of blowing the approach window. Hibernation might sometimes be, however, your only real resort if your aim is to sleep with teachers/professors, or anyone above you professionally. But whatever you do, don't long-game it.

Long game kills attraction.

Most of the time, I'm the guy who just goes for it right away, then stomachs the rejection if that's what occurs.

If the interaction with her is not something you can avoid (e.g., she is in a small class-based discussion group with you, or is literally your coworker at Starbucks or in an office), I recommend pouncing right away. Then if it's awkward, you handle it. You both will move on, trust me. It's 1000% better to have had the courage to just go for it than to have blown the approach window.

Overall, type B encounters are a little more complex, so I'll make light of a few examples.

If she's your classmate in a big lecture hall (a girl you see walking/eating on campus is a type A, not B, encounter), I'd wait till after class one day and then open her with a type A form of conversation – i.e., introduce yourself; tell her immediately you think she's attractive; ask her work/study + hobbies; then 100% wing it. Exchange contacts with her as you would a type A encounter.

If she's not receptive, I would just leave. Because she's your classmate in a large lecture hall, you don't necessarily have to cross paths with her again if you don't want to.

If she's in a smaller classroom with you or is a coworker, during the first one to two weeks of your interaction, tell her you think she's attractive and want to get to know her more. If you've already known her for some time and haven't overtly told her that yet, just do it now. Better late than never. If she rejects you, handle it, because the outcome is fairly simple: either you make your intentions clear and stomach the rejection, or remain a little boy forever and keep your thoughts hidden. That's my advice.

If she rejects you, you handle it, but this is infinitely better than any form of long game.

I once was in a small class of about 12 students. There were two girls who caught my attention. One was on exchange from Italy. The other was from China. I wasn't overly eager but was going to make my intentions clear regardless.

On the second day of class, I told the Chinese girl we should study together. She was receptive and we exchanged contacts. We met up for coffee and chatted a bit. She told me she was *married* (what the fuck? She wasn't wearing a ring) and that she and her husband were planning x, y and z about their future. From that point forward, I basically just didn't talk to her again. In class, I essentially ignored her. I really didn't care. I'm not interested in making female friends.

But the point being: the first week the class started, I had already determined a definitive outcome for one of the girls.

During the second week, I told the Italian girl we should study together and got her contact instantly. Taking into consideration my interaction with the Chinese girl, I asked her afterward if she had a boyfriend. She said no. I told her something along the lines of, "Well the reason I ask is because I don't actually have interest in studying with you. I think you're attractive." She replied saying she wasn't looking for any guys right now and that she just came out of a 5-year relationship.

From that point forward, because she was supposedly single, I asked her out twice more at fairly wide intervals of time, to lend space to the situation, but she declined both times. My level of care was non-existent. It was truthfully her issue, not mine. At the end of the day, there were two fairly attractive girls in my class whom I had driven some sort of conclusion with early. I didn't try to long-game them with the hopes that maybe three months later something would magically occur.

There is absolutely zero reason to expend any more mental energy than you have to. It requires less mental energy to get an early conclusion – rejection or not – than to have uncertainty hovering around you all of the time. For both type A and B encounters, quick and swift escalation is ideal.

And most importantly, if she says she doesn't have a boyfriend, the next thing out of your mouth should be, "Why don't you have a boyfriend." Period. Let it hit her like an arrow. It's the best thing you can say. That's it.

"WHEN ARE YOU FREE."

I'm beginning to find that saying, "When are you free" **in-person** *plays out the same exact way as it does via text.*

As of early-2019, one notable calibration I've started to spontaneously make is, after cold approaching and closing her (i.e., getting her contact), just very calmly and casually saying, "When are you free." It's not something I say in all of my interactions, as you sort of have to feel out each individual circumstance and just wing it, but I've found I'm saying it more and more often.

Don't worry about this potentially coming off needy. It's not. If she doesn't know when she's free, you either just leave, or you can open up your schedule and suggest a time. If she agrees, then you set up a date on the spot. If she's not free then, just leave and then text her randomly later on.

$$\text{Probability (P) of date} =$$

$$P_{\text{receptiveness on approach}} \times P_{\text{receptiveness via text}}$$

Think of it this way: when you eventually text her and she responds, you're going to say "When are you free" anyway. So I find that attempting to set up a date on the spot is highly effective for cutting out this texting step and can therefore actually reduce flakes. And not to mention, it can literally create at least one date per day for you.

Even if a girl "likes you" right away, she can still go on to be unreceptive through text. This is why sometimes you can have such an "amazing initial encounter, only for her to not respond and then you're so surprised by it. The more inclined you are to cut out the texting step, the greater your chance of actually getting the date.

Getting the date, period, is the most important step. Because insofar as you have her out and are forward and direct, there's ~1/3 chance she'll come back with you.

This is also why there's ~1/3 chance InstaDates will come home with you. Because as long as you are on the actual date, your "history" isn't actually as relevant as you think. Don't romanticize your prior texting, the amount of time you've known her, or the number of dates you've been on as important determinants of whether she'll come back with you. A girl coming home with you is often just a function of her "state," the same exact way her initial receptiveness is.

Once again, I don't say "When are you free" during the contact exchange for many of my approaches, but I'm doing it more and more frequently (I'd say at least a quarter of them [as of April 2019], but I never count or analyze). I view this as a significant fraction, considering up until recently I *practically never* arranged for a future date on the spot.

Not to sound like this is such a radically over-the-top or monumental revelation, but it really is the case that lately I've been saying to myself, "I can't believe I'm realizing this so late. This is such an effective and easy way to establish dates."

I think I used to arbitrarily imagine that attempting to InstaDate girls - and therefore probably to a lesser degree, attempting to set up a date then and there - must originate from a place of neediness. That is, your day shouldn't just start and stop the moment you meet her, so if you're trying to InstaDate her, doesn't that somehow reflect lack of other plans/options?

However my increasingly nascent sentiment is that if a male genuinely carries non-neediness, he can by all means attempt to

InstaDate and/or set up a future rendezvous on the spot **while simultaneously not having that fundamentally change the female perception of him in any way.**

You and I could essentially, to a T, carry out identical interactions at the same exact time and place with the same exact girl, but if I'm far more non-needy than you, she'll interpret my behavior as more attractive regardless as to how I close her.

In other words, if she for whatever reason were to view my forwardness regarding an attempt for an InstaDate or future rendezvous as needy in any way, *that's not a function of me actually having made the attempt; it would be because I would have been needy as my individual person, independent of how I closed her.*

My present awareness for that is derived from understanding that, based on my approach level and consistency, I'm always hyper-non-needy regardless. So that fact that *I* (of all people) sometimes push for InstaDates and future meet-ups *must mean* that the act of doing so cannot necessitate the conclusion of male neediness.

So my closures will sometimes go like this:

Me: Let's exchange contacts.

Her: Sure.

(Then 5-10 seconds go by as we do the exchange.)

Me: When are you free.

[Trajectory #1]:

Her: Umm let me think. Next week is okay.

Me: (While looking at my schedule) Which day is good for you.

Her: (She looks at her schedule too.) Wednesday is good.

Me: Ok. How's 4pm.

Her: That should work.

Me: Cool. We'll meet at the north exit of the station by X place.

Her: Ok see you then.

[Trajectory #2]:

Her: I'm not sure. I have work and school.

Me: (While looking at my schedule) How's next week.

Her: (Looks at her schedule) Thursday is ok.

Me: Ok. How's 4pm.

Her: That works.

Me: Meet at X place.

Her: Ok see you then.

[Trajectory #3]:

Her: I'm not sure. I have work and school.

Me: (While looking at my schedule) How's next week.

Her: (Looks at her schedule) Next week...I'm busy then.

Me: No worries. I'll just shoot you a text some later time then.

Her: K see you later.

[Trajectory #4]:

Her: I'm not sure. We can just message and sort it out.

Me: Cool. See you later.

That's it.

If you are arranging a future rendezvous during your closure and are contemplating when is ideal, I should point out that the amount of elapsed time between now and then is interestingly **not** strongly correlated with the probability that she'll flake vs meet up with you. I think I used to believe that a shorter gap is more ideal, but I've set up dates on the spot anywhere from the next day until weeks later, and I've had random flakes / conversions across the spectrum. So don't over-analyze that aspect either.

(In addition, the same is true for when you actually text her. I've messaged girls for the first time *months* after meeting them, and we've still gone on to hook up. So don't worry that she'll "forget you." The only real situation in which a shorter timespan is certainly paramount is when you're on the actual date. In this case, yes, your chance of sleeping with her is far higher the shorter the date is.)

Once again, don't worry about whether trying to set up a date on the spot is needy in any way. **It isn't.** True neediness vs non-neediness permeates to the surface no matter what. I can't emphasize enough that it's not about what you say during your interactions that matters; it's merely you being deregulated (i.e., not changing your behavior for her) secondary to your non-neediness that makes you your most attractive.

So yeah, next time you meet a few girls and exchange contacts, wing it with a simple "When are you free." Just see what happens. You might walk out of an interaction saying, "I can't believe I just set up a date tomorrow with this smokin' chick I just met."

And if you don't believe me or think I'm embellishing, it's because you haven't tried it. Exactly. So try it.

IF SHE SAYS "BOYFRIEND," YOU FUCKING LEAVE

If a woman mentions her boyfriend – early or late, it doesn't matter – you leave instantaneously.

Once that word "boyfriend" comes out of her mouth, you do not stick around. You do not be the nice guy. You do not continue to make small-talk as though she didn't mention it.

"Really, you have a boyfriend? Alright, well that's the end of our conversation."

If she mentions the boyfriend, that's her loss. It's not your issue. You just abruptly say, "Ok, well it was nice to meet you." And that's it. You leave.

Occasionally I'm even more abrupt than that and don't even say anything. I just walk or skate away. I vanish into thin air.

Sometimes this stuns them. Let it. Let her regret it. Let her cry about it. Let her be annoyed that she has a boyfriend. Let her live forever in dreamland with her boyfriend. Let her know that her boyfriend is the reason why you won't be talking to her anymore. Once you're informed of her boyfriend, the conversation between you serves no purpose. Leave.

Let her contemplate after the fact the rarity of your encounter and that it ended specifically when she said "boyfriend."

I encounter plenty of attractive girls where I feel as though (even within 30 seconds) I'm hitting it off with them. Then if they say they have a boyfriend, I don't even give myself time to get annoyed by it. I don't dwell on whether or not she *actually* has a boyfriend. In other words, is she just making it up? It's not relevant. The message she's conveying is that she's not interested or is closed off, period. A percentage of the time the woman is probably lying. Not every unreceptive woman will be cold or hostile. Sometimes the conversation is seemingly a really good one.

So if you hear the word boyfriend, you leave immediately. Let her regret it. Let her grieve. Her fucking issue.

"I regret so much having a boyfriend!"

99% of guys do not have the courage to approach a woman head-on during the day, stop her in her tracks, and say upfront, "Hi, I'm Michael. I thought you were attractive and wanted to say hi." And you know what the probability of that happening to her again is? Practically nil. In a bar, maybe. But during the day on the street? That is really rare for a woman to experience. And if she tells you it happens to her frequently, she's lying. No woman gets hit on frequently like that. Lots of guys will attempt indirect, dumb openers, but the direct and confident approach is rare. So if she's going to forfeit her opportunity with you by saying she has a boyfriend, not your issue. Peace!

When you say hi to a woman and declare your intentions openly, that's a really big deal for her. She'll go off and tell all of her friends about how this guy stopped her on the street and told her she was so beautiful. If you have the confidence to introduce yourself and declare your intentions with transparency, and she proceeds to tell you she has a boyfriend, you leave instantaneously. But more importantly:

If for any reason you forgot to find out during the initial encounter whether or not a girl has a partner, do **not** ask her through text about it. Sometimes she'll hook up with you anyway and then go back to him. No need to shut doors for yourself. If, however, you do ask via text message whether she has one, and she says yes, you end all communication with her.

I once met a girl at the gym and had a "great chat" walking out with her to a bus stop. I got her contact but realized after the fact that I didn't ask if she had a boyfriend, so I asked her through text. She said, yes, she did in fact have one. I replied literally to the effect of, "Well if you have a boyfriend we should just terminate all communication between us." She maybe gave a "hah ok," but that was the end of it. I saw her occasionally at the gym after that but completely ignored her, nor did I ever make eye contact with her again. As far as I was concerned, she ceased to exist. I let her know through my behavior that I was strictly a "sex guy" and wasn't there to be her friend.

I can recall one time I had approached a girl running in a park near where I lived. I introduced myself and told her I thought she was attractive. She looked at me with a half-smile, almost amused, and the first words out of her mouth were, "I have a boyfriend." I didn't even say anything to end the conversation with her. I literally just dropped my skateboard back on the ground and left.

So once again, if a girl says she has a boyfriend, you leave instantly. There's no being the nice guy. There's no "Hey, let's have small-talk anyway." Let her regret it. Let her grieve. Her fucking issue.

HOW TO AVOID THE FRIEND-ZONE

"We're not friends. We can either go on a date or just be nothing."

There's three main ways to avoid the friend-zone:

1) Never associate with a girl who has a boyfriend. Unless she is *literally* a coworker, colleague, or old friend from high school whom you've established a genuine, platonic interaction with, don't be "friends" with girls just for the sake of it. You should have very, very fucking few actual, legitimate female friends.

2) Declare your intentions immediately with a girl you're attracted to. If she rejects you, stop talking to her. Don't ingratiate your way slowly into some kind of safe interaction with her so that she's "comfortable first." Don't be her friend. Guys who end up tethered to women as "entertainers" are those who never racked up the courage to just declare their intentions. You need to force a conclusion early. Never allow for uncertainty as to whether she's into you or not.

I was once dating a half-Emirati-half-Irish belly dancer who used to go out hip-hop dancing at least once or twice a week. She was professional level. Every time she went out dancing, it was always with the same guy. He was also Middle Eastern. I could tell he was trying so hard to court her and secretly had a huge crush on her, but she didn't like him. I had absolutely zero care whatsoever that they used to go out dancing together because I had met the guy several times and knew he was harmless.

She would ask if I were jealous and I'd tell her absolutely not. I mean, here you had this guy, who was completely obsessed with my girlfriend and wasted so much time going out with her, all because he couldn't just be straight with her about how he felt, nor was he ever forward with her. This was years ago, but I imagine now if he's changed, he looks back at that interaction with her as one of those in life in which he should have just been more forward and direct. We've all been there.

If you declare your intentions and she suggests being friends, tell her, "We can't be friends. We can either go on a date or just be nothing."

I once gave a girl my contact and we had a text transcript that went like this (and this is an exact transcript because I had written about this a few years back when this happened):

Her: "Hey Michael, do you think we can be friends?"

Me: "No we can't be friends."

Her: "Oh ok, well all the best with everything then."

Me: "I think we should go on a date."

Her: "Is this some sick joke, oh god am I being Punk'd."

Me: "I'm saying we're not friends. We can either go on a date or just be nothing."

Her: "A date it is then."

Me: "Good move on your end."

Her: "I think so too."

End of transcript. (Yeah, yeah, I know. Maybe that doesn't seem to carry much buzz when you read it here, but at the time it was a huge score.)

The third way you avoid the friend-zone is to stop dating a girl who won't sleep with you quickly enough (i.e., after a few dates), or who sleeps with you early but withholds on the subsequent one or two dates in an effort to shape the interaction into some form of "stable" relationship.

I can think of several interactions off the top of my head where I've slept with a girl on the first or second date, and then she goes on to purposely withhold sex on the subsequent date, sometimes even communicating that she expects some sort of stable relationship pattern on her terms. If I ever experience this type of situation, I lose all interest.

Most women want a mix of aggressiveness and stability traits. The way some women go about it is they'll appreciate your confidence and sleep with you early. Then once you've passed that test/phase, they'll try to bring out your stability/beta factor in order to see that you'll form a relationship with them beyond just sex. This is actually an effort on the woman's end to bring the interaction into her frame, and if you submit, just be aware that you're relinquishing control in the relationship.

The way I see it is, if a girl withholds sex from you, especially after you've already slept with her, it shows her innate sexual desire for you is incomplete and is predicated on *transaction* - i.e., you provide for me and I'll sleep with you. One could argue this is a just a simple relationship shit-test and is based on where she is in the menstrual cycle (i.e., around ovulation she just wants to bang, but around menses she's looking to see that you have provisional characteristics), however I believe this is an overgeneralization. It is my sentiment that if a girl is truly into you, she'll want to have sex with you anytime and would never purposely withhold. I've interacted with plenty of girls who have been more than willing to fuck during inconvenient times in their cycle.

Bottom line is: Don't pursue women who have partners. Always declare your intentions immediately. Move on quickly if she's not willing to be physical with you early. And if she is physical with you and then withholds, she lacks desire for you and views the sexual dynamic as transactional.

HOW TO KEEP THE WOMEN YOU ATTRACT

After starting to approach, if you find yourself gradually beginning to get dates with women, the way to keep them around is to genuinely be able to walk at all times.

And the way you're able to walk is to know that you could simply go approach 20-30 more women tomorrow and easily find another to go out with. If you've got other women in your repertoire whom you could easily go hang out with the next (or same) night, that makes it even easier to walk.

So in other words, knowing you have approach prowess and can easily meet more women, as well as having other women you're simultaneously seeing, are the two determinants that factor into whether a guy is genuinely willing to walk or not.

These factors determine non-neediness. And you can't fake either of them. The good news: you don't need to be currently dating anyone and can still be non-needy enough to walk; all you have to do is **merely know that you are able to** meet more people the next day.

If you're just starting out approaching and obviously aren't seeing other women yet (i.e., you're still basically at stage zero), the mere approaching you do will go a long way toward making you less needy for any one particular woman you're out with. But then if you add on top of that four or five women you're simultaneously seeing, suddenly that one you're out with is super-easy to walk away from because you can easily get laid that same (or next) night by another woman.

When you are genuinely able to walk, the woman will know. She'll feel it because you don't change your behavior for her and speak what's on your mind. When I'm out with women, I don't censor what I say to them. I just say whatever is on my mind. If we don't jive for whatever reason secondary to how I naturally conduct myself, my level of care is zero.

Never change your behavior for women. If you're just being yourself and not hitting it off for whatever reason, feel free to walk. The way I go about this is by trying to get them home anyway, and then if they decline, I just walk them to the station and never talk to them again. If they do come back though, then all the better.

In my experience, the perception of good vs bad chemistry out on a date is often unrelated to whether she'll actually come back or not. Some really good hookups I've had have actually be with girls whom I've had ostensibly shitty dates with yet had entertained getting them home anyway. This is why I generally always push to get them home anyway, no matter how boring the date seems.

You being willing to walk signifies you have a core. You're leading the way and she has the choice to either enter your frame or leave. If you're changing your behavior because of her, you're entering her frame. Never enter a woman's frame. Let her be a part of yours. You act and say as you please. And if your frame doesn't work for her, it's not your fucking issue. She should be honored to be around you for the confident guy you are.

If she's not entering your frame (i.e., you're acting and saying as you please but the chemistry isn't good), you should always be willing to walk.

Why go on another date with her? Yeah, she's hot and you want to fuck her, but you can easily date other women. And if you're already dating her for whatever reason, don't be afraid to end things, otherwise you have no choice but to enter her frame.

Most guys live in women's frames. I observe it everywhere.

The typical male has an inner flame – an inner guy – somewhere, but it's suppressed by the woman he's with. She keeps him at bay. He's got to make sure she's happy in that moment, that her wants and needs are catered to.

Honestly, fuck that.

You get plenty of people who will say, "Yeah Michael? Well good luck forming lasting partnerships then, because relationships take two people and you have to make sacrifices." My response to that is:

Just like the manner in which you approach women determines those with whom you'll pair, the behavioral pattern you establish when you actually start dating women determines those with whom you'll form longer-term relationships.

There's someone out there for everyone. There are plenty of women who'd date me who would not date you in a million years, and vice-versa. I've had girlfriends who tell me *they like* that I'm not emotional with them and that I do and say as I please. They cater to and serve me. I like that. That's the type of relationship I foster. Maybe it's not the type of relationship you would foster, but we're not the same person. I'm not telling you to be anyone you aren't. My advice is to be the most confident person you can be within the scope of who you are, and to use that confidence as a tool to bring out the real you that you want to share with the women in this world.

My old Italian housemate would **prepare picnic baskets and bake apple strudel while wearing an apron** as some of his dates with women. I would smirk when I'd see it, then later on be like, "You are such a fucking tool," and we'd laugh about it. He and I were literally polar opposites, and yet we each fostered relationships with different types of women. What we had in common is the women were always in our frame. The women I dated thought that although he was physically gorgeous, his feminine demeanor was unattractive. They wanted a GUY, not a dude who fucking bakes. And I'm sure the women he dated thought my macho-man attitude and air of dismissiveness were cocky, arrogant, and a turn-off; they probably saw me and thought, "Fuck that guy."

I once went out with a stunning half-Thai-half-Chinese girl who initially wouldn't sleep with me because she was convinced I was just wanting to hook up with her. She was 100% correct. So one night I planned to meet her at 7pm in the city, but because I was seeing other people and wasn't needy, I purposely arranged to see a different woman, whom I was also very attracted to and already sleeping with, at 8pm. So when I met up with the Thai girl, after about 45 minutes I said, "Alright, well it was great to see you," kissed her on the lips, and walked. The next time I hung out with the her, we hooked up, and we ended up dating after that (until I moved to Japan). And it was awesome sex. Looking back at that interaction, had I not been willing to walk that one night, I wouldn't have ever slept with her.

Another interesting example is with an absolutely drop-dead gorgeous girl I had met from Colombia. She was probably one of the hottest girls I've ever dated. She agreed to meet up, and my improvised plan was for her to come meet me at the library computer lab I was studying in. But I noticed her texting behavior was a bit odd.

She came off very aloof, almost insincere about "not being able" to find the library I was at. Finally, she said she found the library, but when I told her to come inside the computer lab to meet me, now she said she didn't know where the computer lab was and that she was leaving. My thought was, "Ok, well the lab is as clear as day right next to the fucking entrance to the library, and even if you couldn't find it, you could easily just ask someone."

Out of curiosity, I walked out of the lab to the library entrance and saw her from about 40 feet away walking in the opposite direction. I didn't chase her. I just let her walk. It was obvious to me she could have easily come to the lab but expected me to chase her, as if it were a game.

From that point onward, I viewed her as an incredibly lame princess and lost interest outright. I stopped texting her after that. Two weeks later, she texted me again and wanted to meet up. She became one of the girls I was dating for about three years, and from my end it was exclusively sexual. She had an off-the-charts amazing face and an amazing Colombian ass. Despite her beauty, her lameness never really went away in my mind, which was mainly just due to her pattern of needy behavior across the entire time I knew her.

My confidence and non-neediness ultimately surpassed her beauty, and I was the one who was never fully interested. I always cared less than she did.

I was always willing to walk because I literally didn't give a fuck. She once said to me, after I had known her for probably eight months, "If I just dropped you home right now and didn't talk to you again, what then?" My response was, "I'd be like, alright." And I meant it. And she knew I meant it.

After two years, she was really annoying me one day, and I told her, "You already know I feel nothing for you." *But she stood by me,* because out of any guy she encountered (and trust me, this is a girl who went salsa dancing and met *plenty* of modelesque guys), it was my confidence that had her glued. She *liked* knowing that I was always willing to walk.

Then there was this gorgeous girl from Canada I was seeing. She wins the award for biggest eyes and lips of anyone I've dated. I told her that her estrogen levels were off the charts. As it turned out, she was an absolute daddy's princess and expected everything to be done for her. Apart from the sex, I had zero interest in her. I had once finished a long day, picked up a 6-pack of hard cider from a bottle shop near where she lived, and stopped by. She lived perched in a massive tower in the city that was both condominiums and hotel rooms.

I was relaxing in a chair in the front lobby. When she came down, I told her, "Take the cider up for us," and handed her the drinks. She paused for a moment, almost as though she was testing my authority, and said no. Then I said, "Please take the cider up." She again said no. A third time, more slowly, I said, "Please take the cider up." She said no. So I walked. As I was leaving, I texted and met up with another woman I was sleeping with who lived a half-kilometer away. I said, "I know it's a surprise, but I thought I would stop over with some drinks." She was ecstatic and thought I was so sweet.

I had probably been sleeping with Canada girl for well over 7 or 8 months at that point, and although we had texted a little subsequently, I never met up with her again after that. I was just straight with her and told her I felt nothing for her. And like the Colombian, *she still wanted to date me*. Why? Because I stood my ground. It was the confidence she was after. I was always willing to walk.

Women will be able to sense if you're willing to walk, and you can't fake it. Having conviction that you can easily approach/meet new people, as well accumulating simultaneous sexual partners, are the two determinants that factor in to this ability on the male's end.

THE INITIAL INTERACTION MEANS ABSOLUTELY JACK SHIT

"So magical meeting you today. You are the most amazing, handsome guy ever."

Literally. The initial interaction *actually* means nothing. It doesn't matter how certain you are that she's interested or not. The mercurial nature of women is a very unwavering thing.

The initial interaction has zero correlation with whether she will actually follow through or not.

That is an unequivocal truth. It's fucked up, I know, but it shows we really don't know what goes on in women's minds most of the time. I have met women who I swore would have been future girlfriends who have flaked. Similarly, I've met women who have explicitly told me they were interested in me, who were very affectionate, and who paid me numerous compliments, who have flaked.

However I've also met women who I was certain were 100% uninterested in/annoyed by me who have followed through to be sexual partners.

No matter how awful or great you think the initial interaction goes – no matter how much you think she seems consternated or ecstatic by your approach – *it means nothing.*

I was at a university bus stop one night and saw a very attractive woman in her mid-30s sitting and waiting. My thought was, "Wow, who is that extremely attractive older woman." I walked over to her, carrying my skateboard, and opened her with something like "Hi, I'm Michael. I just wanted to say hi." She looked up at me and was very neutral, willing to make perfunctory small-talk. She wasn't wearing a wedding ring. I surmised she probably worked for the university because she was dressed very well.

The bus came probably 30 seconds later. It was nearly empty. She stood up and was taller than I. I let her go first so I could sit next to her once we boarded. Had I gone first, she wouldn't have sat with me. On the bus, she told me she was teaching law at the university. She wasn't interested in me and was looking out the window while we spoke. She was just jumping through the hoops of making small-talk with a random student.

"I'm teaching law here at the university."

She said she was not seeing anyone. My bus stop was one of the first, so I had about five minutes to play around with. I was sure she wouldn't give me her number, but about 20 seconds before I got off, I went for it anyway. She looked annoyed and rolled her eyes. I mean actually annoyed. She didn't want to give it to me but started saying the numbers anyway.

The doors to the bus opened and she was still saying the numbers. I literally was walking out the door still typing. I vividly remember thinking, "Well, that's a rejection out of the way."

It's always easier for a woman to give you her number then ignore you than it is for her to say no to your face.

I might as well have deleted her number instantly, and I thought about doing just that, but decided to text her anyway. She replied, and for some reason, agreed to meet up with me. Not for a coffee. Not for a date. Just literally to meet up on campus one evening after she finished work. I believe the reason she agreed is because I was a mature-age student (27) and our university was massive (meaning I'd probably never run into her again), let alone I had no ties whatsoever to the law school. She probably thought, "There's no harm having *just a plain conversation with a student on campus.*"

It was an interesting talk I had with her. We were very different people, with very different views. I told her I wouldn't have liked her had I met her in a classroom setting. Likewise, she told me she wouldn't have liked me. And we both meant it. She felt I came off too imposing on others and defiant of authority; I felt she came off too uptight and sensitive to the idea of that. I told her nevertheless we were going to get a small bite before heading home. There was no harm in that. We walked to a quiet area off campus that had a pizza place. Afterward, I walked her to a non-university bus stop and tried to kiss her. She didn't kiss me back.

Maybe about a week later, I was studying at night in an empty classroom on campus in a remote part of the university. She would often be in her office late because she liked doing work there. I decided to text her. She agreed to having another conversation and came to meet me. I tried kissing her again, this time in the classroom. She gave in and kissed me back.

I told her we were going to go to my place. She gave me a look as though that were impossible. I told her there was nothing to think about. Let's just go. I took her back to my place, and without even telling her to do so, she immediately took off all of her clothes. It was awesome sex. Over the next month or so, I hooked up with her probably three or four times in her office. One of the times I threw the condom out her third-floor office window and she was like, "Omg you're crazy!" I brought out her youth a little bit. It was fun.

The bottom line is: of all of the thousands of approaches I've done, even to this day, that is probably one of the most salient examples in my mind of when I had met someone who I swore wasn't interested at all during the initial interaction, but went on to become a sexual partner anyway.

Text every number you get, even if you couldn't care less after the fact or are convinced it's just a waste of time. Don't analyze how well or shitty an interaction supposedly goes.

Just entertain yourself by saying a simple, "Hey it's Michael." If she doesn't respond, it's over. Delete the number within 24 hours. But seriously, no matter how interested or uninterested you think she might be when you first meet, it doesn't mean anything.

The reason that's important is because you can literally talk to a woman for 30 seconds in a train station, engage in some extremely mechanical and player-esque convo, basically just saying hi and extracting out her number, and she could go on to sleep with you. Whereas you could share life stories for three hours in a park with a woman who ultimately flakes. I've experienced the full spectrum, and continue to do so. It also keeps me reasonable and prevents me from ever getting over-excited.

I once essentially scared a girl at an intersection by abruptly cutting her off with my skateboard. I was with a guy friend who was watching from afar; he found it hilarious. We talked for no more than 60 seconds and I extracted out her number like a robot. I was having a "good day" and probably picked up six numbers in the three hours I was with my friend. Out of anyone, I would have been convinced she was the least interested. As it turns out, *she ended up texting me* a few days later *asking me out*. I told my friend, and he was basically like, "Send the screenshot. No way did that chick ask you out."

So as I said, you never fucking know.

I met a girl once on a nearly empty shuttle bus. She got on and sat across from me. I was getting off at the next stop, which was literally coming up in 30 seconds. I got up out of my seat, walked over, and swung myself into the seat next to her.

If you want to get anywhere with women, you sometimes have to risk coming off like a creeper. If she likes you, it's confident and attractive; if she doesn't like you, you're all of a sudden a creeper. Same scenario. Same approach. Different woman. Different interpretation.

I said, "Hi I'm Michael. I thought you're attractive and wanted to say hi."

She was just like, "Oh, hi." She was my age and didn't have a boyfriend. Next I told her what I was studying and asked if she worked or studied. Then I just said, "Alright well yeah, it's random as fuck I know, but I have to get off at this next stop, so let me just take your number. We should catch up or something." She gave it to me. The interaction from start to finish was under 30 seconds. I ended up hooking up with her for a few months. She was a really chill girl with a thick Aussie accent. Her ass was massive too.

Another example is with a half-Aussie-half-Chinese girl I met once at the University of Queensland biological sciences library. As I was walking up the stairs to the fourth floor, I saw her sitting at a table by herself on the third floor. She had her headphones in, with notes sprawled out everywhere. She was studying pharmacy. I walked over and half-sat/leaned on the table she was at. She took out her headphones.

I said, "Hi, I'm Michael. I thought you were cute and wanted to say hi."

Her pupils dilated as though we were in the jungle.

She looked uncomfortable and didn't say anything. I said, "Are you half-Asian?" She was like, "Um yeah......" Then I obnoxiously and firmly said, like an arrow straight between her eyes, "Yehh, cuz you look Asian." She was like, "Oooooook...."

"Yehh, cuz you look Asian."

She wasn't receptive. *Because she wasn't receptive, I did what I normally do in these situations: I left.* I told her, "Anyway, it was nice meeting you." And just abruptly, but slowly, walked away, up the stairs to the fourth floor. That was it. Had I attempted a number exchange, there's a very low chance it would have happened.

Now this is where a little experience with situational calibration worked in my favor. I demonstrated I wasn't needy because I was immediately willing to walk away from her unreceptiveness. But in reality, she hadn't *actually* rejected me yet, so I had the inclination she might transition into a neutral state if I gave her 20 minutes to process the interaction and its rarity.

I will reiterate that it's in a female's biology to be non-receptive to the majority of male approaches. But occasionally, if they have time to process/reflect on your approach, particularly if it was bold, they'll appreciate the confidence and question themselves as to why they weren't receptive.

After 20 minutes of haphazard study and scanning for girls on the fourth floor, I walked back downstairs and straight over to close her, rejection or not.

As soon as she saw me, she was half-startled and knocked over her almost-empty thermos of room-temperature coffee. I didn't even say a word and walked to the bathroom, got her some paper towels, and helped her clean it up. I made small-chat with her for another 60 seconds or so, then told her I was leaving. I went to exchange numbers with her but she "couldn't remember it" and didn't have her phone on her. It was obviously a fucking lie. I wrote down my number on her notebook and left. As I walked down the stairs, I explicitly remember thinking, "Ok, well I 100% will not be hearing from her."

She texted me the next day. She asked if we could go on a date. I was like, "what.........the.........fuck."

I met up with her and learned that guys throw themselves at her and she was sick and tired of it. She said she was 24 but still hadn't ever slept with a guy. She said she only had guy friends. Usually she'd hang out with groups of five or six guys. She was a very clued-in and smart girl. I'd say one of the smartest I've dated.

She told me she was aware I approach women all of the time and that I sleep with a lot of people. She said she knew I had been with someone the previous night and that I probably had a minimum of three women in rotation (in truth it was probably six or more).

I would joke back without answering her questions but she was straight/serious with me. She knew my type and communicated that she respected my right to engage in the dating patterns of my choosing, but told me she wanted me to try and connect with her.

That impressed me. I never overtly admitted I was seeing other people, but I opened up to her a bit, acknowledging that her thought process was good.

She told me she wouldn't sleep with me unless I committed to her. Under ordinary circumstances, I would have just dropped out of the interaction immediately because I wasn't looking to commit to anyone. But I felt I genuinely had a strong conversational connection with her, so I told her I would think about it, and that, correct, I wasn't looking to commit to anyone just yet.

I told her that I would be willing to hang out with her a little more to figure things out in my head. And truthfully, after a couple weeks of kissing and second-base, I thought for a change that I could genuinely attempt "the relationship thing." After all, she was really smart and really hot.

Note, by the way, that my natural non-neediness was reflected by hesitation to commit to her. All of the other guys she encountered would have immediately committed.

So without formally cutting ties with any of the girls I was seeing, I decided to essentially put them on "standby." I would just be "busy" for an unspecified length of time and try going at it alone with this one girl. I slept with her for about 7-10 days committed, before deciding that I genuinely thought she was boring after all.

In no way, shape or form was I obligated to be in any committed pattern with someone I thought was boring. But of course, she knew my behavior and could read the truth in me, and it was either commitment or zero, so I told her it had to be zero. She protested, but that was the end of it. That was an honest decision I made on behalf of respecting her. I saw her at a grocery store about a year later and she was with some other guy, so she had no issues moving on. That's how real life works.

I had told myself I was 100% sure that this girl from the library would not contact me, and she did. It could have been a serious relationship. You really have no way of knowing how an interaction will play out based merely on the initial encounter.

As I've said, I've had interactions at the opposite end of the spectrum as well. I once met a girl on campus, and we walked and talked for over six hours, holding hands and kissing down by a lake, watching a sunset as her head was on my shoulder [insert corny movie title that you wish]. I'm not exaggerating. She flaked.

Then there was this other girl I thought I had awesome chemistry with. I told her I was going to a BBQ so she came with me. We were holding hands and kissing all night. She was very affectionate. Everything in my instincts and experience told me it was mutual. She told me how much of an awesome time she had and couldn't wait to see me again. She wanted to plan then and there when we were going to meet up again. I was excited to see her going forward. She flaked.

So there's no way to know who will follow through to become a sexual/relationship partner and who won't.

Many of your interactions will come down to pure chance and timing. No matter how spectacular or shitty you think an initial interaction goes, there is zero correlation with the actual outcome. Some of the best interactions you'll have with women will stem from seemingly "terrible" initial interactions. Follow through on everything.

SOUP TEXTING

The number-one important thing to remember about texting is that the manner in which you do it can never make a girl more interested in you, but it can make her less interested.

One could argue that the analysis of sending texts in and of itself is needy, because after all, if you're always being yourself and don't care what she thinks, then why should it matter how you text. That's a very good point, and by all means, be whoever the fuck you want to be, but there is a certain level of strategy and calibration that goes into getting a first date and maintaining her interest before you sleep together.

*Texting should, the overwhelming majority of the time, strictly be an expedient/means for you to make plans to see each other in person. **That's it.** Don't use texting to talk about much else apart from when you're going to meet up.*

Do not try to be fancy. Do not start talking about your day. Do not ask about her day. Never say "How was your day?" or "How's your day going?" If you don't have something important to say, don't say it.

A model I was dating once told me, "The number-one thing I hate is when a guy texts me and says, 'How's your day going?'" Never fucking text that.

Have you ever seen Finding Forrester, with Sean Connery? There's a concept in that movie called a "soup question." A soup question is one that strictly seeks to obtain information that is important to you (e.g., "what are you doing later?"). If the information is unnecessary, superfluous, or just for the sake of your curiosity (e.g., "how did your exam go?"), it's not a soup question.

Your texts need to be 100% soup. Check yourself on that next time you send a girl a text. If it's not a soup text, don't send it. Don't worry, she won't be offended. She'll be glad you're not being needy.

Don't use big vocab or grammar/punctuation that's too purist (e.g., semicolons). You shouldn't be putting in any effort whatsoever. Your mindset when you're sending a text should be as though you're trying to launch something off quickly while waiting at an intersection before the light turns green. If you're putting in too much effort, she'll sense it, and it will turn her off.

If I, for whatever reason, find myself with a text window open thinking about what to say, I erase whatever I'm writing and don't send anything. I'll return to it however many hours later, or even the next day.

It is always better to text something from a spontaneous mindset, even if it's a delayed reply, than to over-think whatever you're sending.

It really is absurd that texting can have so much of an impact on the dating dynamic, but the truth is that you can actually ascertain a lot about someone's level of neediness by how he or she texts. It's one of the modern tools for screening potential partners in or out.

Because most of the women whose numbers you get will end up flaking anyway, the main purpose of effective text strategy is therefore to prevent unnecessary flaking by women who would have otherwise gone out with you.

If a woman doesn't respond to your first text, that's the end of it.

She didn't lose her phone. She didn't accidentally pass over your message. If she has interest, she will most certainly respond *the first time*. Sending her a second text after she doesn't respond to the first one is needy. Have some dignity. She isn't better than you are. You don't need her nor do you need to qualify to her. She is fortunate to have the opportunity to get to know you. She really is.

I had heard years ago somewhere about how persistence is supposedly one of the cornerstones of good game. I completely disagree. If you're *already on a date* with a girl and are persistently pushing for sex, that's a completely different story and, yes, I strongly advocate that. But if you're *trying to get a date* (or a second date), you shouldn't ever have to pursue/be persistent.

If a girl isn't responsive through text messages, it's over. Don't keep texting her. And especially don't keep her on standby hoping that three months later she'll become receptive somehow. If you have to "be persistent," it says you're chasing. It says you're needy. It says you don't have enough confidence to just go out there and find other women who'd actually want to date you. You can easily date a lot of women and never have to chase anyone.

If I text a girl and don't hear back within 24 hours, I delete the number. Her issue, not mine. And I don't even consciously think about it. Sometimes I delete it within a few hours. It really depends on the vibe I got from her initially. A percentage of the time she'll text back after you've deleted the number and you can re-add her as a contact if you wish, but the point I'm making is that under general circumstances, get in the habit of moving on immediately if she doesn't respond fast enough. You need to *send and forget*. Don't keep checking your phone to see if she got back to you. Try really hard to stop yourself from doing that.

I tend to erase my phone's entire message history every two weeks or so. I do that to stay non-needy and maintain the mentality of always moving forward. What purpose do old messages/numbers have in my phone from girls who didn't initially reciprocate? If I ever get a text from a number I don't know, I either don't respond or tell her, "I don't know who this is. I deleted your number because you didn't respond fast enough." Only once has the latter worked to get things jumpstarted again, but the interaction turned out to be volatile. In short, don't bother.

I'm not interested in girls who are tepid/lukewarm about me. I've had girls text me back five days, or even weeks, after I've messaged them. It's like, go fuck yourself. And by the way, if you're thinking right now, "Yeah, but couldn't one of those girls who texted you a couple weeks later now have different circumstances; in other words, maybe two weeks ago she wasn't open to your advances but now she is." My response is: if you're approaching girls at a high rate and accumulating many contacts, you should have absolutely zero reason to devote energy to a flaky or poorly responsive girl. If you're a manager and receive 100 job applications, and one of them arrives late, why would you even bother looking at it. You'd toss it immediately.

The way you need to see things is: there is no reason you would have deleted her number unless she had screwed things up by not reciprocating fast enough. You originally got her number because you had some form of interest in her. Therefore, if you get a message from a number you don't know, it means you're receiving it from a woman who didn't meet your standards for a decent interaction. She can get lost.

The frequency and length of your texts should always be slightly less than hers.

Don't overanalyze anything here. The gist is that you shouldn't ever be sending essays when you message. This is an easy trap to fall into if you believe you're hitting it off with someone. But trust me, *do not* fall victim to it regardless as to how well you think the initial interaction went. Women test us instinctually. They're subconsciously trying to evaluate how needy you are and whether you have alternative options. If you are too enthusiastic in your messaging, you lose. This is not intentional on their end or part of some grand scheme. It's biology.

I have lost very receptive girls before through having been overly eager and enthusiastic in my texting, and I've learned my lessons as a result. It sounds fucking dumb, and it is, but no matter what a girl actually says to you – no matter how excited she seems – keep your texts short and relaxed as fuck.

If a girl is excited while texting you, she'll go out with you no matter how stiff/boring your texts are. But if you're too excited, she might change her mind. Females are fickle.

Once again, you could argue that if you're genuinely eager and enthusiastic about meeting up with a girl, and she doesn't reciprocate, that's her problem, because you were being honest. Trust me, I agree. But my point is that *you can be very eager and enthusiastic about meeting up with a girl* **while simultaneously** *chilling the fuck out with how you actually text her.*

If she sends you a long, enthusiastic paragraph, don't send her a long, enthusiastic paragraph back. Now I am *not* telling you to be dishonest or pretend you're disinterested. That is not what I'm saying. You can most certainly convey interest in her while still keeping your texts short, simple, and direct.

Remember that the purpose of your texts is to strictly negotiate when and where you are meeting up with her. That's it. If you are texting her about anything else, you're being superfluous from a texting standpoint. Save your questions about her life, hobbies, work, study, etc., for when you see her in person.

Your texts should be fairly stiff/boring. Pretend you're texting one of your guy friends about when you're meeting up to go to the gym. Your texts should almost always be one or two lines at the most.

And avoid text-tennis. In other words, if you find yourself unable to resist talking to her, don't engage in too many ongoing text volleys back and forth, especially if they're non-soup and not direct answers to her questions. You can have great chemistry with her, but once you sort out when and where you're next meeting up, leave it at that. Let any tension/feeling you think you have for each other simmer.

It's a good thing if you've been able to solidify plans with her to meet up *and* she is the last one to respond (i.e., she says "sounds good," or "ok, see you then"). There is a subconscious positivity when she sends the last text and you don't need to respond to it. If she sends you non-soup questions, respond if you wish, but just keep your answers short.

I'd say I only have "extended" text conversations with under 1% of the women I ever message. One I can think of in particular resulted in her flaking on me because I was too eager. Another I can think of resulted in a date that didn't go anywhere anyway (i.e., our "text chemistry" didn't translate over into real life whatsoever).

The bottom line is: how you text will never make a girl more interested in you, but it can make her less interested. Do your best to stay within the fucking soup bowl.

WHEN TO TEXT HER / ARRANGE A DATE

The perfect time to send her (or respond to) the first text is: whenever the fuck you feel like it.

You need to do what you feel is best for you.

If I get a number around lunch time and get the urge to send her a text that evening, then I do it. If I don't have any urge and she isn't on the top of my mind, I may send the first text in 3 days' time instead. I've sent first-time texts anywhere between seconds to *months* after getting the number. It just depends on when you want to do it.

In your case, should you wait 24 hours before sending her the first text? How about 3 days? Don't over-think it. The answer to when you should send her the first text is: whenever the fuck you feel like it.

If she doesn't respond, good. I can guarantee it has nothing to do with the timing of your text. If she's interested based on your initial conversation, she *will* respond, regardless as to when you send it.

When I do get around to sending the first text, I just say, "Hey it's michael." That's it. I don't even use a comma after the "Hey" or capitalize my name. If she doesn't respond within 24 hours, I delete her. If she responds, it will usually be a standard, "Oh hey! [smiley]".

Based on how long it took for her to get back to me, I'll take that into consideration. And I say that not in a condescending way; it's more just a situation where my thought process regarding the girl (if I had one to begin with) evolves. If she is unable to respond to you quickly enough, there's a certain ingenuousness, or purity of reciprocity, that evanesces in my opinion. Call it dumb all you want, but that's just how I view things.

If she gets back to me quickly, I'll respond the same day. If she takes several hours, or most of the day, to get back to me, I'll usually respond around 24 hours later. I won't respond faster than she does. This isn't something I ever overanalyze; it's really just engrained in me at this point from having established habits over time.

*I'd say most of the girls I text – and this is a rough guestimate at best – I will typically send **only one text to in a 24-hour period if I haven't slept with them yet**. When I'm in a straight soup convo, I'm usually not more frequent than that. After I've slept with them, things tend to loosen up a bit on both ends, but the texting should still remain, overall, pretty fucking soup.*

If I'm using a texting app such as LINE, KakaoTalk, or What'sApp, where she can see if I've read the message or not, *I will not read the message* until I'm going to respond to it. Once again, texting games are fucking stupid, but how quickly you read her message she'll use to determine how needy you are. This is what you call natural selection in the 21st century. We don't have to agree with it, but we have to get over it.

If I'm not planning on responding at a particular moment, reading her text doesn't serve an immediate utility. I don't need to process and gestate what she said to me for the next six hours before coming up with my ribboned response.

This also keeps you more spontaneous with your replies. If you're using iMessage, adjust your settings so that the people you text don't receive a "read" indicator. The texts they send you will always just stay as "delivered" from their end; they won't see when you've read them.

The next thing I'll typically say is, "When are you free." Notice I don't use a terminal question-mark (you can either leave it off altogether or use a period). And also make note that it's soup because the purpose of it is to strictly arrange to meet up. As I said before (depending on how attracted I was to her), she's got about 24 hours before I delete the number. If she responds three days later and I still know who she is, I'll have an awareness that I could be getting into drama, but either way, she's lost "ingenuousness points" for not reciprocating fast enough. Her issue, not yours.

The reason I say "when are you free" instead of immediately suggesting a day and time is because her schedule might genuinely be busy, and it's never a subconsciously positive thing for the woman to reject any plan or suggestion of yours, even if she legitimately has something else she needs to attend to. You want her brain to be in the subconscious state of agreement-mode. Let her tell you when she's free, and then you can make a suggestion within that time frame.

When it comes down to arranging a time and place, step up and make the decision.

If you agree to Thursday evening and she asks "Ok, what were you thinking?" Give her a time and place (e.g., "Meet me at the Three Monkeys at 7."). Keep it simple. You don't need to ask if that's okay with her. And definitely don't end your plan with "if that works for you." If your suggestion doesn't work, she'll let you know and will make a counter-offer.

Don't ever say "I'm pretty flexible. Did you have any thoughts?" Women want a guy who can make decisions. You also don't want to reveal to her that your schedule is too open.

So in summary, my typical texting conversation with girls is direct and to the point. I'm short and boring. I text essentially as though I'm meeting a guy friend to go to the gym. Assuming she responds and is interested, it will go something like this:

Me: "Hey it's michael"

Her: "Oh hey! [Smiley]"

Me: "When are you free"

Her: "This week is busy, but next Tuesday afternoon is good."

Me: (Three days later, on Sunday) "Ok. Tuesday at 3pm by the great court fountain on campus."

Her: "Okeii [insert random, dumb emoticon]"

Never jump on the time she's suggested. If the time works for you, wait an ever so slightly longer moment to respond to her before telling her that works. Do not wait too long though. Just don't respond instantaneously is what I'm saying.

If she suggests that evening and I'm interested, I'll respond probably within the hour. If she suggests tomorrow, I'll respond in a few hours. If she suggests two days from now, I'll respond that evening or tomorrow.

The only time I will take more than 24 hours to respond is if the time she's suggested is more than two days later. For instance, if next Tuesday is five days later, I might respond three days later. And if my response at that point is "too late" for her (e.g., she says, "I didn't hear from you so I already made other plans [crying/sad face])," I don't even respond and delete her number instantaneously. For one, she clearly wasn't interested enough to double-check with you before making other plans, and two, she's communicating that she's not willing to roll back her plan B for you. The message coming from her is: "You're less important than my Plan B. If I had to choose whom to delay seeing, my Plan B or you, it will have to be you." She can get lost.

ARRIVING FOR THE FIRST DATE

In terms of confirming with her beforehand (e.g., the morning of, texting her, "Just confirming 7pm today."), that's up to you and really doesn't matter. There's nothing needy about this. Nothing to over-analyze.

If she doesn't show up for whatever reason, I'll text her, then wait up to 15 minutes depending on the circumstances. If she flakes, I delete her number. It's one and done in my books.

If she's going to be late for whatever reason, it's her communication about it that matters the most. If she's actively telling me she's sorry because she's still on the bus and will be there in fifteen minutes, I'll probably overlook it, but she loses points. In other words, if you had somewhere important to be, such as a job interview, you wouldn't be late, so it shows disrespect.

I've had women tell me, "I'll be there in 5 minutes," only for them fifteen minutes later to say it will be another ten minutes. If this happens, I leave without even replying to them.

A woman is actively disrespecting you by making you wait if she is not effectively communicating with you about it.

I once met a really hot black girl at a mall food court and was waiting in the city for her for our 7 o'clock first date. I texted her at 7:03pm asking if she was still coming. She said she would be ten minutes late. *Note that she didn't text me beforehand letting me know.* She didn't show up by 7:15, so I asked her again. She said she'd be another ten minutes.

I was really interested in her during the first interaction, which is why I was waiting it out.

But at 7:30, I left without even telling her. There were no ifs, ands, or buts. She texted me 45 minutes past the hour saying she had arrived. I was probably a 5-minute walk from that area of the city and could have easily turned around, but replied, "I left. You were 45 minutes late." She said sorry, but it was over, and I was already approaching other women instead.

Had she perhaps just been straight with me from the start with something along the lines of, "Listen, I'm really, really sorry, but I think I might be 30 minutes to an hour late. We can reschedule if you want, otherwise I'll be there because I'm looking forward to seeing you." I might not have dropped her. I probably would have just told her to meet me an hour later (while I was approaching other women in the mean time).

Now I never waste time anymore. If she's not physically there by 15 minutes after our meeting time, I'm gone. If I happen to be off to a cafe, or somewhere else that has a definite address, I might subsequently text her letting her know my location, but my level of care as to whether she proceeds to meet me or not is non-existent.

In general, I don't really see a flake as a negative because I'll use the time I would have spent on that date as "bonus time" to approach other girls instead. Maybe I'll hit the lottery with someone else. You seriously never know.

That is, maybe I'll encounter an awesome girl I never would have otherwise. I've had girls flake on me before where I've gone on to pick up others immediately after.

Rather than dwelling about flakes, it's important to identify that they're a natural part of the dating process. Yes, they're annoying, but as guys we have to be in the habit of moving on instantaneously and being productive. If you're meeting a lot of girls because you actively approach, it's impossible to avoid flaking. So as I said, internalize it as normal.

The bottom line: It's one and done in my books. If she flakes on the first date, she's gone. If she's going to be late, pay attention to how she communicates with you. If she keeps you waiting without effectively letting you know, that is active disrespect toward you and she can fuck off. Understand that flakes are a normal part of the dating process. Don't dwell over them. Just use that "bonus time" to meet others instead.

GETTING HER HOME / ONCE SHE'S AT YOUR PLACE

If there's ever a situation when a girl suggests dinner or drinks over a simple coffee, I'll often counter by saying we should just get tea (trendy here in Japan, but essentially akin to coffee).

Now why the fuck would I do that you might ask. Because doesn't dinner or drinks handedly insinuate a more night-time mood, and hence a greater chance of getting her back? Yeah, but there's a big reason I still don't prefer the "dinner or drinks" type of date:

I've come to realize with unequivocal conviction that the shorter the date is, the more likely you are to get her back. What you do / where you go on the date is actually irrelevant and not part of the equation. A simple tea or coffee outing is by far and away the fastest type of date. I view dinner and alcohol excursions as absolutely inferior because they're always longer and more expensive.

All of my dates are the same: hyper-short, -fast, and -direct.

I'm not exaggerating for the sake of projecting a player-esque and cool facade. The average duration for all of my dates is no greater than 45 minutes. I'd say 30 minutes is one standard deviation fast; an hour is a standard deviation slow. That means I'm guesstimating that ~70% of my dates are 45 minutes +/- 15.

When I arrange a date ahead of time, it's always at either 4pm or 7pm. This enables me to create first and second slots so that I can stack dates on any given day. I can therefore try to get Girl #1 home, sleep with her, and then still have enough time to meet my second date. I'm not saying I do this all of the time, but let's just say it's often enough (at least once or twice a week that I stack).

What I'll do is arrange to meet a girl at a main train/subway station in the general vicinity of my place. (I live a 2-minute train-ride, 7-minute skateboard-ride, and ~20-minute walk from the nearest major hub here in Osaka.)

I'll then walk with her to a tea place that is literally across the street from the station. I would say >90% of my first dates entail going to the same tea place. If we meet up and she pleads that she's hungry and really wants to eat something, I'll get takoyaki with her, which is only a slightly prolonged outing.

Takoyaki is a famous Kansai region street food.

The people who work at the tea place have seen me walk in with innumerable girls, and it has essentially become a comedy, but no one would dare say anything, as this is Japan and the baseline propriety is polite and reserved.

I'll order first and then give her ~7 seconds to decide what she wants. If she's still unsure, I'll say, "I can order for you if you want." You don't have to try to be manly by automatically ordering for her. It's nothing I've over-analyzed, but I believe an ability to show forwardness and make quick decisions is good. Some girls prefer guys make simple decisions for them, e.g., "We'll take two matcha lattes. Hot. Medium-sized."

I'll sit in the same exact seat I normally do - as will she the same seat as my other dates - and I'll essentially interview her for 20-30 minutes, completely winging the conversation.

My conversations are 100% deregulated and improvised. I never know what I'm going to talk about.

What you talk about on your dates isn't important. It's the act of being comfortable in your own skin and not changing your behavior for her that makes you your most attractive. And the way you don't change your behavior for her is by genuinely being OK with losing her in the interaction.

I'm always OK if the girl I'm out with doesn't want to come back with me. I tie zero expectation or care to it whatsoever. This is for two reasons: 1) I'm always creating tons of options for myself because I'm constantly approaching in high numbers on a near-daily basis; and 2) If she chooses to not come home with me, I allocate that time I would have "donated" to otherwise having her at my place to approaching other girls instead.

Whenever a girl doesn't come back with me, I just use my time productively and approach. If I get contacts, great. If I don't, the rejections add to my confidence. So whether she comes back with me or not, I view both situations as a win. I never need the girl I'm out with.

So after 20-30 minutes of 100% deregulated / improvised conversation, I'll transition by asking if she likes movies. She'll almost always say yes. If she says no for whatever reason, I just pivot to TV shows or something else similar.

I'll then ask her what kind of movies, e.g., action, comedy, etc. She'll give me her response. Then I'll ask if she wants to watch one. And I always ask it openly.

They almost always say yes in this situation. And if they say no, I still proceed with the movie idea anyway (e.g., if she says she doesn't have a ton of time, you can tell her you guys don't have to watch a whole movie; just some is fine.).

I'll then tell her I have a bunch of movies on my laptop at my place, followed by saying that I live two minutes away by train. I then tell her the sequence of stations from where we are to where I live. You might think that's weird, but I do this in order to communicate beyond a reasonable doubt that I'm about to suggest a movie at my place, not a theater. It also paints a clearer picture for her as to how close my place really is (i.e., I'm not suggesting we take a 20-minute train out of town).

I then just say, "Let's go." And we go.

Following my 20-30 minutes of 100% deregulated conversation, my movie transition almost always goes like this (in Japanese, but same meaning):

Me: So do you like movies?

Her: Yes.

Me: What kind of movies do you like / what's your favorite movie?

Her: I like comedies, yeah.

Me: Do you wanna watch a movie?

Her: Sure. / Right now? (Even though you haven't yet specified where/when, I find she usually says yes.)

Me: I have a bunch of random movies on my laptop at my place. I bought them on YouTube. From here (Station X), it goes Station Y, Station Z, Station W, and takes two minutes. (I'll gently tap four dots in a straight line on the table as I say the station names.)

[Then there's usually an incidental 2-second pause.]

Me: Yes. Let's go.

Her: Ok.

And I find about one-third of the time she'll agree and come back with me.

This has worked for me on InstaDates as well. That is, I've taken girls back to my place, middle of the afternoon, just after meeting them on the street / in the station.

If she declines, I'll still make the suggestion once more. What will generally happen is I'll chat with her for another minute or so, and then say, "So let's go watch a movie." (This time a bit more forcefully). And if she again declines, I just say, "Ok, I'll walk you to the station." Then I walk her back across the street and say bye to her. I'll always go for the kiss in this circumstance.

End of interaction.

Then I'll just approach other girls after she leaves. It's a win-win.

The last thing you want to do is turn your date into an escapade of walking around the city going to cake places and looking at bridges over the sparkly water. Any time I have entertained that type of trajectory, it has been in the setting of a girl who wasn't willing to come back with me after my initial forwardness at the tea place. These types of dates *always* get drawn out and never lead anywhere.

A girl will often be in her "state" as to whether she'll be looking to come back with you or not, the same exact way she'll be in her "state" during the initial approach when she's receptive vs unreceptive. If she's not going to come back with you after the 30-minute tea date, extending the date an extra hour won't change anything. I'm serious.

If she does come back with me, I'm very short and fast at my place as well.

The number-one thing you should never do once she's at your place is *service her* in any way.

In other words, don't enter your place and say, "Can I get you some water, or maybe some wine?" Don't do that. Just go directly to getting your movie setup underway.

The longer a process takes, the less likely it is to lead anywhere. As with the actual outing you were just on, once you've got her back, don't stall. The more you dither or cater to her at your place, the less likely you are to sleep with her.

Catering behavior also signifies beta tendencies, which runs the risk of turning her off subconsciously. Your goal is to not be in comfort-mode; it is strictly to escalate as quickly as possible.

The lucky thing for me living in a super-tiny apartment here in Japan is that my entire place is essentially just my bedroom. The silver-lining of not having some souped-up pad with a nice lounge room, etc., is that there's nowhere "to go" after walking through the door except to sit on my bed. There isn't even room for her to stand around aimlessly.

She'll generally look at the kanji poster I have on my wall as I'm opening my laptop and getting the movie ready.

Then I sit on my bed and tell her she can sit next to me. I then make a move to kiss her within 30-60 seconds of the movie being on. And then the rest is history.

If she is resistant to your advances, calibrate as you need to, but **always be forward, and always let *her, not you,* be the reason**

you didn't hook up. If you don't have sex, she must always be the rate-limiting step in the equation. Always be forward and persistent in the bedroom. A no is a no, but always try for sex. Always. There are plenty of girls you bring back who will be seemingly shy or reserved but who will ultimately sleep with you. This is sometimes normal female demureness.

If she doesn't allow for my escalation after 15-20 minutes of calibrated advances, I'll generally start to be direct with her conversationally (e.g., "When's the last time you were with a guy?" Or, "Are you shy?" Etc.). During the first 15-20 minutes, however, I make practically zero conversation and am strictly engaging in physical escalation.

Bedroom escalation will play out as a bell curve-like spectrum of outcomes, where some girls will instantly take their clothes off, even without you saying anything, whereas others won't even let you put your arm around them. I'd say in most instances, the time from when we enter my place to sex is, on average, under 20 minutes. I don't waste any time.

If the girl I have over is ultimately unreceptive in the bedroom despite my most nuanced and experienced calibrations, I will tell her I'm just going to walk her to the station. I'm not afraid to be abrupt about it either. I can even think of one example where I walked the girl to the station after just 10 minutes. In this particular case, she was hostile about me simply trying to put my arm around her. My thought was, "Well why the fuck did you come back to my place then?"

So in summary: Keep your dates hyper-short and forward. Going for coffee or tea next to a station (or your place) is ideal. Dinner and alcohol dates are longer and more expensive and don't improve outcome despite their night-time mood. 45 minutes is a reasonable date length. Consider over 60 minutes too long. 20-30 minutes into your 100% deregulated conversation, tell her you guys are going back to your place to watch a movie. Act cool and calm and don't be weird about. Once you get to your place, don't service her. Just get the movie ready. Be very forward and persistent for the first 15-20 minutes. If she's not budging, you can attempt more direct conversation about sex. If she's still a no-go, tell her you're walking her to the station. That's it.

"MAYBE NEXT WEEK"

When arranging to meet up for a date, if the time and place you suggested don't work for her, *pay attention to whether she offers an alternative.*

If she responds by saying "I'm actually not out of work by then [sad face]" and nothing else, probably 90% of the time I will delete the number instantaneously. I'm not interested in games, and I'm especially not interested in girls who decline any plan I make *without offering an alternative.* It's not fucking hard for her to say, "I'm actually not out of work by then. Is 8pm better? Or is Saturday doable?"

Imagine if the tables were turned. If a girl you're interested in were arranging with you to meet up, you wouldn't say "I'm not out of work by then." You would either stretch your schedule to accommodate her somehow, or you would 100% give her an alternative.

If a girl responds to me that way, and I was *really* attracted to her, I might just calmly say, "What is better for you." Notice that I don't use a question-mark. This isn't a question. It's a statement and I'm serious.

That in my books is actually a really big deal. That's the closest I'll ever come to "chasing" a girl or fishing a response out of her.

If she gives an alternative, she's in the clear, but she very rarely will, which is why I don't even bother and delete her instantly.

One could argue that my abruptness deleting the number after a girl doesn't initially offer an alternative sometimes results in me losing an actual date. My response to that would be that I lose interest very quickly if a girl comes across lukewarm to me. So to me that's not a loss. *I really no longer want to* go out with a girl who responds that way to me. And what I can tell you is that of numbers I delete, it's really, really fucking rare that any of them text me again anyway, which proves my instincts are correct in these situations. In other words, it's not like those girls were ever planning on offering an alternative anyway.

Essentially, if you ever text a girl a time/place and she says anything other than "sure," or "sounds great," or "sounds good," she's not interested.

Imagine if a girl you're genuinely interested in texted you a time/place to meet up. You would do everything you can to meet that arrangement. And if you couldn't, once again, you would definitely offer an alternative.

One of the absolute easiest ways to determine that a girl is not interested is if she says "maybe," "maybe next week," or "I'll let you know."

In addition, if she replies with a vague/ambiguous emoticon (e.g., a person thinking), she's also not interested.

"Maybe next week" is by far the most famous line a girl can use when she is not interested but responds anyway. If you say, "When are you free," and she says, "Maybe next week," or "I'll let you know," she's not interested. Believe it. It's the truth. I've even had women go so far as to say, "The rest of this month is really busy. Maybe next month?" It's like, go fuck yourself.

Firstly, the use of "maybe" shows she's equivocal/lukewarm about getting together with you in the first place, and secondly, the word "week" or "month" implies a deferral. It's non-specific and not necessarily any time soon. It also means you're not a priority in her mind.

If you met a great girl and she asked when you're free, you would fucking tell her when you're free. You wouldn't say "maybe next week."

*However, if a girl is **specific** about when she can meet up next week, e.g., "This week is busy. How is next Tuesday?" That is OK. It's the "maybe next week" that is a fuck-off statement.*

Pretty much any time I've entertained the idea by texting her a week or two later, she either doesn't respond or comes up with some lame excuse as to why she can't meet up.

"I'll let you know" is even more of a fuck-off statement coming from her. It's basically saying, "I don't want you to text me anymore until 'I let you know.'" And she'll never "let you know." Even with the time I've spent in Japan, the girls use a similar fuck-off statement (連絡しますよ; renrakushimasuyo), which is basically saying "I'll contact you." It's like, "No, you won't fucking contact me."

If a girl defers my intent to meet up without specifics, or tells me she'll let me know, I delete her number instantaneously.

The funny thing is, I learned that "maybe next week" is a rejection 99% of the time *after I started* rejecting girls with the line unintentionally. Although you are the one getting numbers and tasked with arranging rendezvous, as you approach more and more, *you* will actually be doing the rejecting a good chunk of the time. You might sleep with a girl here and there, and then start losing interest; then when she wants to meet up again, you might say "maybe next week" without really thinking about it. The best way to gain insight into how girls reject you is to actually do a lot of genuine rejecting yourself.

If a girl tells you she can't meet up because she's "busy" with school or work, delete her number instantaneously.

I've had times when I've been really busy/hectic, and when I want to make time for a girl, I make it, even if it's for just a half-hour to chat over a coffee. I once had a girl meet up with me for dinner, and she told me she had a final exam *the next day but wanted to see me anyway.* If a girl actually wants to see you, she'll fucking make the time. If she's "busy" for whatever reason, goodbye forever.

I once told a girl that we should meet up before next Wednesday because I was traveling home then. Her reply was (and I remember this vividly), "Sorry I'm really busy with work until next Wednesday." I told one of my guy friends about it and he was like, "Yeah ok, 'I'm busy with work up until the exact date you leave, sorry.' As though she doesn't have any time after work. She can go fuck herself."

Lame excuses on her end might also be her way of saying no if she's within one of your social circles or areas of school/employment, where she might run into you again, so she is trying to deflect your attempt amicably. Bottom line is: If she defers your attempt (i.e., "maybe next week"), is "busy," or is ambiguous in any way, delete her number. Her issue not yours.

LOLZ

Ready for some really dumbass, elementary school-level texting rules? Coolz, so am I.

drummmming

Eliminate terminal question-marks.

Now I know that might sound a little ridiculous. And that's because it is. This is one of the (incredibly) dumb "secrets" to coming off less needy through texting. One could argue that the mere consideration of this point in and of itself is absurdly needy, but it's not if you don't think about it and just integrate it into your routine texting style. Also, when I'm asking a girl questions in real life, I'm often fairly monotone and they sound like statements anyway, so for me, the lack of question marks actually makes sense.

"What are you doing later?" becomes "What are you doing later." Nothing dramatic.

It gives off the impression you're putting less time into your texts/thought process and that you're *not waiting* on her response. Likewise, the period makes your sentence a bit sharper and directed (which it is).

Eliminate capitals if they're not the first word of the sentence, and eliminate commas if your sentences are short (which they should be anyway).

If you write, "What are you doing later." Your texting app will automatically capitalize the first word, so if it's not capitalized for whatever reason, it appears as though you edited your initial writing. So first words should stay capitalized.

For subsequent words that normally take capitals, leave them out. Also drop the commas. So for instance:

"Hey, it's Michael." becomes "Hey it's michael"

You can use a period or no punctuation at all. I don't think about it, but I'd say 50% of the time I don't even use a period. That includes my "What are you doing later" statements as well.

*Absolutely never, ever, use smileys or emoticons in your texts with girls **who are not Asian.***

You don't have to "like" this rule, but it doesn't change the fact that women will view you as some lame guy who's smiling and nodding at their responses. I rarely smile in real life as it is, so especially for me, not using them reflects me not changing my behavior.

In the past, I used to use occasional "hi" or "sup" emoticons, which would show up as a face of some kind, and almost always the girl would counter with a dumbass emoticon in response (e.g., a hand waving). It's like, "Okay, that was pointless." Now I've eliminated them altogether and am literally just soup.

Now for Michael's extra-unique touch (warning: welcome back to second-grade):

The furthest I will go in terms of "text levity" with girls I'm *already dating* (and this is going to sound absolutely, off-the-charts ridiculous) is the occasional usage of "lolz," "lols," or "lulz" (correct, not "lol"), but never because I actually think what she is saying is funny. It's more an obnoxious gesture to avoid replying to what she's written about a topic I couldn't care less about. Or if I just don't know what to say otherwise.

It's basically my tacit way of expressing humor while also conveying that I don't care, without actually ignoring her. You need to avoid getting involved in her petty dramas. She might tell me something her friend told her, or mention something that's going on at work, and she wants some sort of reply from me, and I'll just say "lols." That's it. You might be thinking, "what…the…fuck?" Yeah, I know, to each his own.

Across the thousands of girls I've approached and all of the texting experience I've acquired as a result, I have no fucking clue why, but the rare usage of solitary "lolz," "lols," or "lulz" **in conjunction with otherwise short, boring texts**, *is the optimal style I've converged on. I have had plenty of girls tell me I'm the weirdest texter they've ever met. Weird in female terms means appealing.*

Keeping your texts short, focusing on meeting up, and not using smileys/emoticons or non-critical punctuation shouldn't be difficult to turn into habit. Remember, you're not trying to be dishonest in any way by playing indifferent or disinterested, but making these changes will reduce any extra impression that you're qualifying to her, which is always a good thing.

Lolzzzz

USING FACEBOOK AND INSTAGRAM

Whenever I meet a girl and go to exchange contacts, if she asks for my Facebook or Instagram instead (or in addition to the contact exchange), I'll tell her I rarely use it, or I'll say I don't use it. I always decline the Facebook/Instagram exchange.

If it's a Facebook/Instagram exchange or bust, I bust. If our interaction rides exclusively on whether you have the privilege to see my Social accounts, get the fuck out of here.

For one, a Social exchange is a step *below* getting an actual contact. It's less personal. Everyone uses Facebook and Instagram (at least in 2019) and a "friendship" means jack shit. To that effect, you might as well just accept her friend-zone invitation. Don't fall for that trap.

In fact, sometimes a girl asking for your Facebook or Instagram, *after you've attempted a standard contact exchange*, is her way of rejecting you on the spot. It's easier for her to ignore you that way. You know how that goes: your Social friendship gets buried in the mix.

The other really important thing is: a Facebook/Instagram friendship, nine times out of ten, will only work against, not for, you.

Yeah, you're some dude she hasn't met before, and maybe it's a trust thing. But she's going to meet dudes for the rest of her life whom she (obviously) hasn't met before. That's sort of just how life works. Sure, I'm a stranger who told you you're cute. Handle it. That doesn't automatically entitle you to analyze photos of my sister's wedding or the wording of a post I made two years earlier on a road trip.

*You need to avoid people who request access to your Social **too** **early**, even if it's seemingly benign. If I encounter a Social seeker, I lose all interest.*

I don't think I can recall a single situation, either for me or for any of my guy friends, in which a Facebook/Instagram connection has worked to help us fuck, let alone get a date, with anyone.

The Facebook/Instagram connection primarily does two things:

1) It immediately cleaves all tension, curiosity, and uncertainty she may have had about you. At first you were that slightly mysterious guy who was bold with her. She has that memory singed in her mind. But once she sees your Facebook, she starts analyzing and filling in gaps here and there, aligned against her own insecurities, and then it's over; that is, her curiosity has been slaked and she has no reason to ever meet up with you again.

2) It turns your bold, real-life encounter into an online dating experience for her. In other words, it undeniably enhances the superficiality of the interaction. Online dating is a completely different story. The woman will apply for her 6-foot-5, green-eyed German who drives an Audi A8. Real life doesn't work that way. Be aware that unless you have your photos and posts really fucking tightly wound up (almost heterochromatically) in terms of privacy settings, they will get hyper-analyzed/-scrutinized, *almost always* not in your favor.

As I said, if the initial interaction somehow rides on whether I give my Facebook/Instagram or not, I'm not interested. I'll just say, "Nah I'm good," and leave.

My old housemate was once friends with a very attractive, tall Spanish guy who was soon going to meet up with a girl for a date. The three of us were hanging out and he said, "She just texted me. She said she's with friends and they want to see my Facebook first before she goes out with me."

It was a little bit of an awkward situation to be in. Had it been me, I would have written back something like, "Maybe after our date we can consider a FB exchange." And if that didn't suit her, goodbye forever and I couldn't give a fuck.

But in his case, he gave her his FB and made a little joke with it too, "Ok now you can do your analysis/evaluation." Several minutes later, she wrote back to him saying that regarding their date and whether or not she could still make it out tonight, she'd "let him know." That became the phrase of the week: "I'll let you know." No, she didn't ever fucking let him know. She flaked. It was a complete joke. And truthfully, from an objective, completely heterosexual "guy perspective," there was nothing wrong with his FB at all; he had pictures playing soccer, etc. I mean, what was the issue?

Never fucking give your Facebook or Instagram to a woman you haven't slept with.

No one has the right to your privacy. If you're some UFC fighter, or a runway model, or a political candidate, with photos of you on stage in front of thousands of people, and you think your Facebook account will help you get women, by all means, rock on. Likewise, if you're a new-age, true, non-hacked influencer with 4.9 million followers, and you think girls will fall into your lap because of your numbers, go for it.

I'm talking about most people here. As I've already said, I'm of very average appearance, and on paper I'm not what most women on dating sites "apply for." My edge comes from the confidence and directness I exert when I approach women in real life. As soon as social media gets involved, it ruins everything.

Social media almost never wins you women. It is light-years more likely to kill any zing factor a woman has in her imagination about you.

If you insist on connecting via Facebook or Instagram with women you meet, your best case scenario is to recognize that less is more. Yes, I know, you might be willing to have her see all of your profile information/photos, etc., but just be prepared for her not to respond after her curiosity is quenched, is all I'm saying.

You don't have to adjust your settings specifically for *her alone.* I'd recommend adjusting them in general for everyone who sees your FB. Mine is set so that you can't see most of my photos and posts.

And don't allow people to see all of your FB friends. You can adjust your settings so that only your **mutual** friends can be seen. If people can see all of your FB friends, even if they're not mutual, what fucking purpose does that serve apart from giving others the ability to dive into your private life, or to see how many or few people you choose to link accounts with. Instagram is a bit different, as followers don't necessarily equal people you have any form of relationship with.

I've had women search through my FB friends before looking for the thumbnail photos of other attractive women, and then analyze their profiles to see what their relation is to me.

By the way, this isn't just about the initial interaction either. Once you start sleeping with multiple people and you're beyond the point that Facebook or Instagram even matter, if you choose to connect, be aware that if one girl posts something, another will see it.

I used to accept Facebook requests from girls I was *already* dating. This resulted in them occasionally "liking" my photos and posts, or writing "cute, xo" on my photos/wall. Essentially women want to mark their territory. Sometimes I would even delete their comments. This used to set off bombshells. This caused some women I was seeing to make fake accounts in order to message other women to learn if I was dating them also.

Facebook is a bit weird, where if you're not friends with somebody and he or she sends you a message, it gets filtered into an "other"/"message requests" folder. And if you're not vigilant or fully aware of how to use the messaging platform, you might never see the messages until many months (or years) later. I had one woman I was seeing tell me, "I received a message from a deleted account asking if I'm dating you. The message was from a year ago. I wasn't able to message them back. What's that about?" And I was thinking, "Yeah, what the fuck is that about. Who sent her that message?" It's that sort of thing that really put me off social media.

To this day, no one can write on my FB wall. If people genuinely want to contact me, they can DM me. That's just my style/the way I use Social. But obviously you're free to do as you please.

So, in short, my advice is:

- Decline girls who seek your Social too early;

- Don't give your FB or IG to a girl you haven't slept with;

- Keep your FB privacy settings tight – less is more;

- If you start rostering women and your FB privacy isn't tight, expect bombshells.

Is all I'm sayin'.

WHY ARE YOU FUCKING STARING AT ME

When I'm out with girls, I will look at others if I want to. This is not to prove a point in any way, but your freedom to look wherever you want can serve as a slight reminder to her that she doesn't have you wrapped around her finger, or anything.

If I'm mid-conversation with a girl I'm out with, looking her in the eye, and there's something attractive that walks by, I'll pay her respect by not glancing away. But if we're in a lull or walking somewhere, etc., if there's an interesting shape that draws my attention, I'll look at it.

If you knowingly want to look at another girl but don't because you're afraid of how your date/girlfriend will respond to you, or you consider the abnegation of your freedom to look at something as synonymous with paying her baseline respect, you're changing your behavior for her. Just be aware: that's the type of relationship you're fostering, one where you change your behavior, and that's your call.

I used to go out with one girl in particular who was so insecure, that anytime a hot girl would appear, she would glare at me to see where I was looking. One time she did this while she was driving. I said bluntly to her, "Did you just seriously take your eyes off the road to see if I was looking at that girl?" Sometimes I would stare right back at her, implicitly communicating, "Why are you fucking staring at me." The only reason I dated her is because her face and ass were amazing. It depends on what kind of trade-offs you can tolerate I suppose.

My view is that if you are changing your behavior for a girl for a long enough period of time, you will start to feel restricted/trapped and will ultimately begin developing resentment. You should never *date a girl where you feel your natural behavior **when you're around her** is restricted in any way.*

I also like to make small-chat with clerks/waitresses at cafes, convenience stores, etc. I do that whether I'm out with a girl or not. The only difference is I might try to pick up the clerk if I'm on my own; I'll leave that part out on dates. But really, if I like a clerk's hat, want to ask her age, or if any other thing pops into my mind, I'll just say/ask it.

For one, I'm not changing my behavior for the girl I'm out with. And two, in the subconscious female mind, it can serve as a reminder to her that you're a confident guy who doesn't need her there.

When I'm on a date, I don't go out of my way to interact *more* with clerks/waitresses, nor do I go out of my way to look *more* at surrounding hot women. I just don't change my behavior at all.

When I was dating the Vietnamese chick I mentioned earlier (see chapter: The direct approach), I was once at a phone store and one of the floor staff was super cute. She looked Vietnamese and late-20s. As she was addressing my questions about phones, I abruptly said to her, "How old are you." She said 28. I said, "Are you Vietnamese." She said, "yeah…" I said, "Yeah, cuz you look Vietnamese." She was like, "Alright.." Then I said, "Is your last name Nguyen (a super-common Vietnamese name; asking her this was a little obnoxious, but my way of exerting humor)." She said no. And that was the end of it.

The Vietnamese girl I was dating said to me later on, "You know when you talk to people like that it sounds like you're flirting, right? She probably thought you were flirting with her." *And she had said it in such a way that I could tell she was actually attracted to me for it.* It's like, well yeah, no fucking shit I was with her. I just didn't change my behavior at all (apart from not asking her out on the spot).

If I'm out with a girl and some guy who looks like a bodybuilder randomly appears out of thin air wearing a Golds Gym singlet, she has the right to look at him. I'm not going to get offended. It's like, "Yeah, he's massive. That's impressive." I'm not going to get jealous over it. I'm not asking her to *not look at something* because of me. That's just needy. So I expect the same in return.

The bottom line is:

Look at whatever the fuck you want to look at;

Don't censor what you want to say just because she's there;

Don't worry about what she thinks.

Done and dusted.

WHO PAYS?

"Shit, I thought we were just going to split."

In terms of who pays for what, if on the first date the tab is relatively cheap (i.e., under $20), I'll cover it. If it's still cheap-ish but getting a little higher (i.e., $20-30), I don't have extraordinary qualms about covering it, but I'll generally look to see if she at least offers to pay half. If she offers, I always split.

If the bill comes out a lot more expensive than you were planning (e.g., you were just ordering more and more sushi, or you didn't check the price of the beers and had a few each), I will *usually* just stomach it if it's upward of 50-ish dollars. If it's above that, I'll either tell her we're splitting or will ask her for a small contribution (e.g., if the bill is $79, I might say, "Do you have a 20-dollar note.").

Why do I split? Two reasons:

1) Because about 2/3 of those women you go out with on the first date you'll never end up sleeping with or seeing again, and I'm not there to pay $$$ for women I'm not going to sleep with. A coffee or sandwich is different. But a proper dinner, for instance, I'm not going to enthusiastically cover for a woman who might not sleep with me. As I've already talked about (see chapter: Getting her home on the first date / Once she's at your place), a simple tea or coffee is ideal for first dates (cheap and fast). For second dates, I *usually still* go for tea, or maybe a light meal. "Fancier" dates for me are actually rare.

2) Because of the Benjamin-Franklin effect, where if she invests a little in the interaction then she's more likely to care about it.

*No woman is not going to sleep with you specifically because you didn't cover the full bill out on a date. If a woman ever didn't sleep with you because you split a bill with her, she's declaring herself a prostitute. If there's some woman **who feels entitled and expects** you to cover the bill, regardless as to how much it is, she doesn't respect you and can go fuck herself.*

Plenty of women will voluntarily split the tab out on dates. Plenty. And it's not some covert test to see "if you're a cheapskate and will accept her offer"-type of thing. I've even had women, despite my gentle protest, *insist* on paying the full tab on a date; if this occurs, I will genuinely say thank you and tell her next time it's on me.

I tend to be more forgiving of a girl in terms of not splitting if she is a lot younger than I or I know she doesn't have/make a lot of money. If she's 18 (I'm 32), I would almost actually feel weird if she paid anything. There's no set rule on my end, but if she's 18-20 I will 100% of the time cover all tabs. Just a subjective thing based on relative age.

At the end of the day, there's no right or wrong regarding how you want to split bills, but my general piece of advice is to be mindful of whether a girl *merely offers* to at least split with you. Especially if she's around your age or older, if she's not capable of at least volunteering an offer, she's a crown princess and loses points.

Some of the dates I go on here in Japan are essentially a veiled form of prostitution: pay for the tea; waste my time chatting to her in boring English if that's what she's after; and then maybe sleep with her if she's in a sufficient "state." It's a value-exchange essentially.

DRESS CODE

A point I want to bring up is dress code, which is an interesting element of dating actually.

If you're ever wondering how casual or dressed-up you should be when you go on a date, the correct answer is: ***wear whatever the fuck you want to wear.***

If your plans are ever unspecified (e.g., meeting up in the city on Friday at 7pm, but you haven't decided yet where you're going), don't ever text her asking how dressed-up or casual things should be. Nor should you ever need to text her saying anything like "casual is good" if you're concerned she might accidentally out-dress you. Just rock up as you please.

If you're on campus till late, or are in the city approaching, etc., and you're meeting up with her in a couple hours, *if you feel like it's a hassle to go out of your way to go home and get changed, etc., don't bother*. Just show up as you are.

I once met up with a woman in the city on a Saturday night for a first date. I had been approaching in the city and felt it was too much out of my way to go home, get prepped, etc., so I just rocked up with my skateboard and wearing plaid shorts and a T-shirt. When I saw her, she was literally "dressed to the nines." She was wearing designer boots (and was already around 5'10") and decked out in full designer clothing.

I told her that because she literally lived a 5-minute walk away, I should just leave my skateboard at her place, then we could go eat. We didn't leave her place. I slept with her within 10-15 minutes of being there. I dated her for a while and she joked with me at various points that I had "good strategy" doing that, but in truth, I really hadn't thought anything of it. My point being: that was the most under-dressed I could have been relative to my date and it went well for me.

*I would say it's actually **worse** to be over-dressed.*

I was once wearing a suit because I had important obligations to attend to that day, and I met my 20-year-old date straight afterward in the city. She was wearing ripped jeans and a sweatshirt. It felt really awkward, especially since I rarely dress up as it is.

First dates should be fairly chill. It can come off like you're qualifying to her if you appear too fancy or spend too much money the first time you go out. Unless you normally wear nice attire to work and are going from there straight to your date, don't feel you need to go out of your way to dress-up. The idea that you have to dress-up, as though it's some sort of important occasion or interview you're going to, signifies you feel you're qualifying to your date. You should be very relaxed about it and wear whatever you want.

So yeah, the correct answer as far as what you wear out on a date is:

Whatever the fuck you feel like it. Don't go out of your way if it inconveniences you.

HAVING YOUR AUTHORITY QUESTIONED

One of the most important things to realize is that as you venture out of beta male territory and into a hardened routine of approaching, you'll naturally get your authority questioned with greater frequency.

Essentially, you need to be prepared to have an occasional person call into question the way you approach women and be able to stand your ground. The convenient element, however, is that as you approach increasingly more and begin seeing results, you'll develop greater conviction in your ways and start to see the periodic negative responses you get as merely reactive to the strength you exude.

Anyone demonstrating dominant behavior will get tested. And a lot of that testing is aimed at seeing if you'll buckle when antagonism is thrown your way. There's a natural tendency for people to be antagonistic of what they don't understand.

I used to live near a ferry stop, and when I was disembarking one day, saw a very attractive girl with an alternative style. She was covered in tattoos and piercings, had purple streaks in her hair, wore thick black shoes with spikes, and a short, red plaid skirt. I said hi, and we walked and talked for a few minutes, as we lived in nearby neighborhoods. We exchanged numbers and I texted her some time later. She never responded. I just deleted her number after that.

Maybe about six months later, I was on a bus close to midnight and saw a very attractive girl with an alternative style. At first I didn't realize it was the same girl, but as we got off and started talking, realized it was. We walked to a quiet intersection between our neighborhoods where we were parting ways. We both knew we recognized each other, but neither of us said anything. Right then and there, I made a move and we started making out. I took her number again (not giving a fuck or saying anything about having deleted it six months earlier). I texted her a week or two later. She didn't respond. I deleted the number again. And that was the end of it.

Now this will sound a little weird, but during the time I was living in Australia, I had met quite a few lesbians here and there who, for whatever reason, all had similarly gaudy alternative style. That is, it's as though there was some cultural Renaissance ensuing in the form of an alternative fad within the LGBT community. I didn't think anything of it, nor did I care, but it was an observation I had probably noted on the back of my mind over a several-year span.

Based on the way she enthusiastically and energetically made out with me, I had the impression it was more of an "event" for her that marked momentary excitement, rather than actual attraction. It's hard to explain, but it's something I could just sense, almost as though she didn't do that with guys often and decided to just experiment with me, given how forward I was. Then on top of that, she had a significantly alternative appearance and didn't respond to my texts both times. *In no way was I entitled to her interest*, but I nevertheless just had the impression after that that she was a lesbian.

Now fast-forward a solid year and a half since that second encounter. I was walking in the city (Brisbane), and from behind I saw a very attractive girl with an alternative style. I didn't recognize her at first, but as I was approaching, in the final five feet or so walking up to her, realized it was her. I said hi. She looked at me. The next words out of my mouth were, "Can I ask you something? She said sure. I said, "Are you a lesbian?"

She got a little red, pulled back an inch or two, then said no. Then I said, "Are you bi?" She said yeah. Then I was like, "Ok, that makes sense then."

She became irate. This was in the middle of probably one of the busiest pedestrian crossing areas in the entire city. She said something along the lines of how dare I approach her like that asking if she were a lesbian. I didn't mention her dress, but I told her based on how she didn't respond to my texts, in conjunction with how she acted when we made out, suggested to me she was. Her preferences were her prerogative, but the clarification elucidated things for me. I suspected she was probably in "transition," where she hadn't fully come out of the closet yet.

"Are you bi?" "Yeah." "Ok, that makes sense then."

She said angrily, "You think it's okay to just say hi to women the way you do?" And I was firm with a resounding yes. I told her no woman is forced to talk to me if she doesn't want to. Then we had a bit of a contentious parley where I essentially inculcated that people pair with those similar to themselves, and I screen for those receptive to my approaches. She had the full right to not be interested, as does any woman, but likewise, I hold the right as a man to confidently and directly approach women.

I told her there's a lot of guys out there but very few men.
She rolled her eyes at my aphorism. There was no concrete end to the conversation, and after a couple minutes of exchange, we walked in different directions. I don't know what she took away from that conversation, and I don't care, but I held my ground and it felt emboldening. Had I not been very experienced by that point, I wonder if I would have been able to handle her tempestuousness as well as I had.

That was probably the strongest confrontation I've ever had with a female about the way I approach women. Apart from that, maybe once a year or so I'll have a woman say to me somewhat hostilely, "So is that your thing? Do you just go around approaching women?" In these situations, make sure you don't change your facial expression whatsoever, and just calmly say, "It's good to meet new people sometimes." If she's unreceptive, she's unreceptive, but **never, ever** get defensive if someone – guy or girl – tries to shoot down your confidence.

Likewise, I have also had women now and again say to me, "I have a partner, but by the way, I really admire your confidence and I think more guys should be like you. Keep doing what you're doing." I'd say probably once a year a girl I approach says that to me.

In terms of guys questioning my approach prowess, this has only ever happened to me once, and it was probably about 15 months after I moved to Japan. I was at a skateboard shop chatting with the 35-year-old African-American owner, who had been married for the past seven years, and he was saying that if I wanted to meet women, I should just go to parties, and that approaching women on the street wasn't okay. He said, "You just don't wanna do that sort of thing. It's not okay."

I told him it's not for everyone and that most guys are too scared to say hi to women on the street. He seemed a little aggressive and said he didn't think it was okay. I told him some guys prefer alcohol and parties, but that wasn't my thing. Guys like me prefer the street, stations, cafes, parks, etc. To each his own.

I told him that introducing oneself on the street is absolutely a good and important way to meet women.

I didn't care if he didn't see eye to eye with me. I don't waste energy trying to change people's views. You can't get angry over others holding different perspectives. Let them live out their existence in their own heads. People will have any number of reasons for the viewpoints they hold. Maybe he resented being a subjugated beta in his marriage for the past seven years. Maybe he resented not ever having explored his own approach potential before getting married. I didn't think about it at the time, but in retrospect, I can see that conversation was a heavy power play, and I'm glad I held my ground.

I should also point out that, irrespective of any specific encounters in isolation, it is the general male propensity to shoot down the notion of approaching women. That is, it's actually very common to have guy friends or housemates, etc., who tell you it's "creepy" or weird to introduce yourself to new girls. I bring this up because most guys are *not* positive influences when it comes to confidence and putting yourself out there.

My advice is to cut negative "bros" out of your life and add those who support you in your quest to actually fucking meet girls. Remember, people will always have their views and judgments. Not your issue. And don't try to convince anyone of anything either. Just keep approaching. Keep doing your thing.

The bottom line is: As you approach more people and become less beta, expect your dominant behavior to get questioned/tested. Hold your fucking ground and never, ever let anyone talk down what you do. Understand that most guy "friends" are actually negative influences when it comes to approaching and meeting girls. Don't be hesitant to edit certain people out of your life. Add confident friends instead. And if you can't find them, there's always the fucking internet.

TWO THINGS YOU SHOULD NEVER DO

"Why should I be sorry for dating twelve other people and not telling you?"

1) If a girl finds out you're dating other people, don't apologize for it.

Let's say you were dating a girl whom you were absolutely obsessed with and had strong emotions for, and she never overtly told you that she was committed to you. Then let's say you became aware that she was seeing other guys, and you got all upset about it. *That's not her fault, nor is it her manipulating you.* Your fantasy of being committed to a girl you were obsessed with didn't equal reality.

If a guy told another guy that story, his friend would tell him to man the fuck up, *shut the fuck up*, and just move on.

So when the tides turn and you invert the gender roles, it's not your fault if she's not happy about your dating patterns. Never apologize to her for your pattern of interactions with other women if she finds out.

If you never overtly told her you're in a relationship, you're not in a fucking relationship.

Most of the time women will make the **assumption** that you're only sleeping with them. A lot of women will question you about your dating patterns, but you're under no obligation whatsoever to discuss your pattern of approaching/rostering with anyone you're seeing.

If a woman ever relentlessly pushes for you to be explicit about your dating patterns, you either have to drop her or be straight with her.

Once you're straight with her, she'll generally distance herself. So the best you can do is jump around her questions and make jokes until she stops asking. That's not dishonesty. Your thoughts and experiences are not her property. I've told women before that they're *not entitled* to the information in my head. If she doesn't like your degree of transparency, or lack thereof, you're not holding her there. She can easily leave.

Likewise, I'm not there probing her on her behavior. *I'm not entitled to that information either, and I don't care.*

If a woman says to you, "our relationship," or calls you her boyfriend, you ignore it. Some of them like to assume that because you don't explicitly refute their words that somehow that means their imagination is reality. Once again, just ignore it. I've sometimes had women be overly excessive about it too, either through text or in person – "Because we're in a relationship and you're my boyfriend…" Sometimes I'll joke with a guy friend that I've just discovered I'm in a relationship!

People have a responsibility for their own feelings and emotions. If a woman I like isn't committed to me and I'm all butt-hurt about it, that's my issue, not hers. She's not responsible for how I feel; I am.

You have the right to date whomever the fuck you want to date, and in the dating world, one of the inconveniences people just have to deal with is not having their feelings reciprocated all of the time.

As a man who approaches, you will continually get rejected a fucking shit-ton in order to get dates and establish relationships. You handle it. The counterbalance is that you will end up rejecting most of the women you enter into sexual patterns with. And they'll handle that.

The same way the women you approach who reject you don't need to apologize to you at any stage, neither do you to any woman you're not fully committed to or interested in.

2) The other thing you should never, ever do is tell a woman you're lucky to go on a date with her or be with her.

"I…just…I don't know how to say it. I just…feel so lucky to be with you."

Never let the word "lucky" come out of your mouth, unless it's to tell her that *she's* lucky. I will playfully and kiddingly tell women sometimes that they're lucky to be on a date with me. In reality though, I'm not actually joking; and not because I'm being some wildly self-inflated jackass, but the truth is, there are not many high status (confident and direct) men around, so for her to be on a date with me *is actually a big deal.* Guaranteed any other guy she goes out with isn't able to say hi to women.

I was once dating a South American girl who told me her father was a huge player for years. She said while he was married to her mom he used to see many women on the side, and that her mom knew. They divorced when she was young, and he continued seeing lots of women. Then, when he got to around 50, he married a woman who was 28, and he looked after her, even paying for her university. She said that, even while married to his new wife, he was still seeing a woman on the side here and there.

My response was (almost in an *"well I'll be damned"* sort of way), "She (his new wife) got lucky."

She said, "She got *lucky??*" I said, "Yeah, absolutely. We're talking about your dad here. *Your dad.* I mean, he could have married *anyone*, and he chose *her*, so she got really lucky."

And in a somewhat fucked up way, she looked at me smiling, almost more attracted to me when I said that. She knew deep down somewhere that I was right. This girl I was dating was exceptionally stunning, and she knew I was confident. She knew I *chose* my relationships, whether it be her or anyone. She had even said at different points in time that I was similar to her father and brother. So when she talked about her father's second wife, I thought of it in terms of a woman I would marry some day.

*With all of the women I've approached and dated – and will continue to approach and date – one whom I'd eventually choose to marry **must be a really big deal to me**, and in turn if I selected her above the rest, she'd be lucky.*

So when I told her, "We're talking about your dad here. *Your dad*," she probably became more attracted to me because she realized *she was lucky to be there with me*, and she was.

This same girl once had her grandmother, who didn't speak a word of English, visit Australia from South America. She wanted me to just meet up with them in the city for a half-hour or so to have some cake and coffee. When I saw them, I immediately said, "Let's go," because I had something I needed to take care of.

They followed me into a grocery store because I needed to pick up a new stick of OldSpice. They stood with me in the aisle as I was scanning for my preferred scent (original scent). When we walked out of the super market, before I put it in my backpack, I opened the cover so they could smell it, because it has a fucking awesome scent.

Yeah, that's a fucked up story, I know. And you know what? Her grandmother was giving me the weirdest looks and was smiling.

When I hung out with her the next time, after her grandmother had returned to overseas, she said to me, "*My grandmother really likes you. She said she liked that you did what you wanted to do and didn't change your behavior for us.*"

It's like, no fucking shit. I know.

In the past, I had once told an exceptionally beautiful girl through text that I'd be very lucky to go on a date with her. I was honest, so I thought there was no harm. Looking back, she probably lost all attraction for me then and there because it signified to her that I perceived myself as lower status than she.

That's essentially the equivalent of saying, "I'm reaching for you and putting you on a pedestal – I think you're higher status than I – so in turn a date with you is something I'd be very fortunate to be granted." So yeah, never fucking say that to women.

Even in a dating interaction that's *already* well-established, I wouldn't say that. You might philosophically feel "lucky" because, yes, the person you are with is such a good person and you appreciate her for her goodness, etc., but don't ever tell her you're *lucky to be with her*. If you're in a longer term pattern and want to communicate this type of sentiment, you can acknowledge that you have *gratitude* for someone being a good person and a part of your life.

APPROACHING WITH A WINGMAN / APPROACHING DUOS

The vast majority of the time you won't be with a friend when you're approaching. Most of your interactions with women on the street, in cafes, libraries, stations, etc., will be spontaneous and integrated into your day as an independent man. But I'll talk about if and when you do go out approaching with a guy friend.

The two most basic structures are singles (one-on-one) and duos (two-on-two).

Most of your approaches should be singles, where one of you breaks away from the other and approaches alone.

The reason for that is because most of your opportunities will be with single girls walking around, so if you're only seeking duos, you're passing over most girls. You need to not rely on your friend as a buffer against rejection, where you're not willing to say hi to girls unless it's the two of you together. Also, if you're slightly less aggressive than your friend, approaching a girl solo while he observes from a distance allows you to work on your own aggressiveness level, rather than relying on him to open duos for you.

The two of you should essentially take turns approaching alone and getting rejected, while your friend watches from afar. Then you return to your guy friend and laugh/joke about it.

The guy who's approaching should employ a **five-minute rule**, where he does not exceed this length of time with the girl he's talking to. In the mean time, the guy who didn't approach should, *without being seen by the girl*, watch his friend's approach for 5-10 seconds or so, in order to observe how he opened. If he gets rejected instantly, you just let him come back to you, and you resume as you were before.

Never, ever, ever fucking hover around or over your friend while he's approaching a single. That is the number-one way to cock-block your friend's approach.

I was once approaching with a classmate who only liked opening duos because he hadn't yet ripened his skills doing single approach. So every time I did a single approach he got annoyed because it "took time away from duos." I can recall one time in particular I had opened a girl in a subway station, and she was very receptive. He appeared out of nowhere 30 seconds later and was just hovering next to us awkwardly, looking right at us. In my mind I was like, "What the fuck are you doing." She got weirded out and walked away. It's like, no kidding. It completely killed my approach.

I once met an absolutely stunning Greek girl in a mall. Her skin was literally perfect and bronze, and her hair golden. She was wearing a tight, short, white dress and her body was muscular and nice. I was with my housemate and his Spanish friend at the time (see chapter: Using Facebook and Instagram). I didn't know this Spanish guy at all, and he and I were **not friends**, but because he was close with my good friend/housemate, we were "friendly through association." He had a lanyard with an ID tag because he was involved in sales, and decided to turn my approach into a comedy by acting like a pertinacious solicitor.

He then approached us "advertising something." At first, I appreciated the humor/creativity of it, but he was overly animated and wouldn't leave us alone. As I was walking away with her, he tracked alongside us. I mean, *he really wouldn't leave us alone*, and he was actively killing my approach with this otherwise very receptive stunning girl I just met.

He came face to face with me and I told him to fuck off and pushed him. The girl got freaked out by my sudden aggression and immediately left. I almost had a fight with that guy then and there. His perception was that I was an asshole who couldn't handle a simple joke; my perception was that he was an unforgivable douchebag who broke "bro rules" and tried to sabotage my approach. He and I saw each other around on occasion because of our mutual friend, and we both later on apologized to each other and shook hands, but that event always stood between us ever liking each other.

If your friend and the girl he approached appear to initiate a conversation, don't ever let the girl see you. Immediately start scanning for girls yourself in the general vicinity. It's not unusual that once your friend finishes his five minutes, he notices you're now in a conversation, and now he's waiting on you to finish your five minutes.

Even if you "hit it off" with a girl, don't be a douchebag. If you're with a friend, adhere to the five-minute rule.

The only real exception to the five-minute rule is if you truly, truly believe you have unusually strong chemistry with the girl you've encountered, and you want to turn it into an InstaDate then and there. But don't go halfway on any of that shit. Don't talk to a girl for a half-hour and then start searching for your friend again. You either adhere to the five-minute rule, or you're literally full-on going for coffee/drinks now and will see your friend tomorrow. But in general, you should never plan on going on an InstaDate; consider that option as rude to your friend.

You should discuss with your friend that if you take longer than ten minutes with any girl, he has the right to leave for good.

While my friend is in conversation and I'm scanning for women in the vicinity, if everything is uneventful and I notice he has cleared ten minutes, I just leave. I'll go approach elsewhere in the city by all means. Then if he texts me later and we're still in a position to meet up, we can arrange that, but I'll have a serious chat with him about why he took longer than five minutes.

The point being, if you adhere to the five-minute rule, you set a good pattern of being able to approach women followed by giving feedback to your friend. And you guys can use that cycle as positive momentum to build off each other. Likewise, you can turn your rejections into entertainment for each other. A five-minute limit also keeps you non-needy in the woman's eyes; that is, your day didn't just all of a sudden stop because of her. You have shit you need to do, and for one, that entails not abandoning your guy friend.

Of all of the times I've approached with guy friends, I only ever once turned an interaction into an InstaDate, where my friend left after about ten minutes. He was angry about it later because it was my first approach for that session and we had said we were going to spend a couple hours approaching together. But in all fairness, I ended up dating that girl for some time (it was the Canadian girl who refused to take the ciders [see chapter: How to keep the women you attract]), so I wasn't incorrect in my assessment that I had good chemistry with her.

When you first see a girl, in terms of "who gets the approach," it should generally follow a rule that the guy who sees her first gets first dibs, and he has the right, without negotiating first with his friend, to break away and just approach her.

If I'm out with a guy, my routine is I'll typically be in a conversation with him while walking and "scoping the terrain," and then just spontaneously break off and approach a girl, without even saying anything. He'll just randomly see me dart away toward some girl. Or likewise, I'll see him do that.

If for some reason both of us see the girl at the same time and neither one of us is immediately breaking away, we might take a few seconds to negotiate. Sometimes if I just approached a string of girls before he did, we can agree it's his turn, and vice-versa. Sometimes if I think the girl is my friend's type, I'll say, "She's yours. Go." If he doesn't go, *I'll go*. Sometimes I use that as incentive to get my friend to approach if he's stalling – i.e., "If you don't approach her, I'm going to."

Usually the friend you're out with won't have the same exact taste in women as you, so you both won't be overly eager to approach the exact same people anyway. Most women you see will fall somewhere in the middle of your interest spectrum.

My old housemate used to wear nice jeans and black shoes, and liked women who seemed a bit classy. I'm the exact opposite. I'm almost always with a skateboard and tell girls I don't drink wine because I'm not classy. I prefer those who are very casual and low-maintenance, and if they're a little skater or alternative, that's a plus. We were both probably 25-27 at the time, and I used to joke with him saying, "Basically if she's 18-25 she's mine; if she's over 25 she's yours."

So if I saw a classy-looking woman, I'd say, "Over there. Look." And he'd go. Similarly, if he saw a girl he thought was my type, he'd let me know. So the best pairing you can have is when you go out with a guy who has different taste from you.

Another good reason to approach with a friend is it gives you additional incentive to be extra aggressive for purposes.

For example, if there's a girl (let's say attractive but I'm not overly eager) who just entered a clothing store from the street, if I were on my own, I might just continue doing more street approaches rather than going in there after her. But if I'm with a friend, it could be entertaining for the two of us for me to run in there, get rejected, then run back out.

There's no better humor in the existence of human life than the real-time observation of your friend getting instantly rejected making an aggressive approach.

You can basically turn it into a little activity where the two of you take turns seeing who can get rejected more ridiculously. You can feed off each other using that energy and be extra confident running up to pretty much any woman, anywhere.

Now, for duo approaches –

When the two of you are approaching a pair, the ideal situation is **you both approach the pair together at the same time.**

The last thing you want is for one of you to approach while the other lingers behind like a complete tool. Both of you should approach together, directly, and fast. If you have time, decide beforehand which girl in the pair you want, and if you can't agree, do rock-paper-scissors (best of three) if you have to. When you walk up, position yourself next to the girl you're most interested in.

A fairly typical way to open pairs is with a simple, "Hey, what's up. I'm Michael. I just wanted to say hi." Then my friend will say his name, i.e., "Hey, I'm Corey, how's it going?" **You want to do this pretty much in unison, with no discontinuity, as the team that you are.**

If I'm ever with a guy who's lingering behind and banking on me to make the approach, it makes it slightly awkward for me and makes him appear lame. I can recall with one guy in particular, I'd say something like, "Hey, I'm Michael. I just wanted to say hi." Then I'd look back and see him still 10 feet away and say, "This is Salem. We're both studying Japanese." Or I wouldn't turn around at all and he'd then enter the conversation secondarily.

I slowly started to figure out that this guy didn't have enough confidence to open in unison with me, so his strategy was to rely on me for the approach, then he'd come in after and try to "out-power" my opening by speaking really fast Japanese and sucking up the attention. That's not a wingman. He even once did that while I approached *a single* and took her Instagram (his Japanese was a lot better than mine at the time and I didn't have the conversational ability to out-maneuver it). I abandoned him on the street after he did that. Had I not been his classmate, I wouldn't have ever talked to that dude again.

So anyway, after you open in unison with your guy friend, make general chat with the pair for 60 seconds or so getting their names, what they're doing now, and what they do for work/study.

The next step is creating two simultaneous and adjacent one-on-one conversations.

That is, break their attention away from the four-person group dynamic and into isolated, side-by-side convos. I'll look at the girl I'm interested in and just abruptly change the subject to something like, "What are your hobbies," or, "So what's your favorite movie." When I do this, my friend, *at the same exact time*, says directly to his girl, "So what do you like to do in your free time?" You should be able to tell clear as day if your friend is trying to isolate his girl, so be a good wingman and isolate yours. **And don't be fucking weak doing it.**

For the next 5-10 seconds, the girl will usually have a tendency to resist the split and maintain her attention on some form of "group talk," but don't let the girl you're talking to look away from you. Keep her attention locked on you by asking her direct questions and maintaining eye contact. Simultaneously, your friend should be asking direct questions to his girl in order to keep her attention locked.

The directness you and your friend exert should convert the interaction into stable side-by-side convos within ten seconds.

Once I've established a one-on-one conversation, the next objective is getting the contact within 90 seconds. Whilst you might be hitting it off with your girl, your friend might *not* be hitting it off with his. So if their conversation starts imploding after 30 seconds, his girl will start to look over and hover over her friend, thereby ruining your conversation.

You have to be peripherally aware that your friend is doing everything he can to force his conversation for another 60 seconds in order to buy you time so you can get the number. That's why you should be closing quickly. You don't really know

how much time you have until your friend's convo collapses.

Girls are more likely to give their numbers if they don't feel their friend is hovering/watching. That's just what I've observed in my time approaching.

If you get her number by the 60-second mark, continue small-chat while observing in your periphery how your friend is doing. If their conversation is imploding, restart group discussion. If they're still talking somewhat receptively to each other, ease back into group discussion in another 30 seconds. That's roughly the time limit you set. If your friend was hitting it off and didn't get the number by this point, he was too slow, and he has to ask for it now that you're back in group-mode.

As I'll reiterate, the reason 90 seconds is a good time limit is because some of your one-on-one talks will be really awkward and forced, and pretty much impossible to sustain longer than that. 90 seconds is enough time to get the number if you're hitting it off, but not an exorbitant amount of time to endure (or to make your friend endure) if either one of you is not hitting it off and trying to buy time for the other.

If you're hitting it off and want longer isolated chat, if you can sense your friend is also strongly hitting it off (i.e., they're laughing and animated, etc.), you can both improvise by continuing your convos. But in general, even if you have great chemistry with your girl, if you can sense your friend is having a neutral-esque conversation, definitely shift back to group discussion after 90 seconds. It's not really fair to continue your chat beyond 90 seconds, not having retrieved a number, while your friend is miserable in his chat.

After you've shifted back to group discussion, regardless as to what type of number exchange occurred, you should typically just say something like, "So it was great running into you guys. Thanks for the chat," and leave.

So in summary, the duo approach goes like this:

Guy 1: "Hey, what's up. I'm Michael. I just wanted to say hi."

Guy 2: (Immediately after, with no discontinuity) "Hey, I'm Corey. How's it going?"

Guy 1: "We're both students at the university."

Girls: "Oh hey, nice to meet you guys."

Guy 2: "What are you guys up to right now."

Girls: "Just shopping."

Then you make improvised group chat for 30-60 seconds regarding what they do for study/work. At this point, the two of you should start isolating your girls.

Guy 1 to Girl 1: "So what's your favorite hobby."

Guy 2 to Girl 2: (As soon as Guy 1 asks a targeted question to Girl 1 that seems abrupt relative to the group convo, that's the indicator to switch to parallel talk; so Guy 2 should initiate immediately) "So what do you like to do in your spare time."

During the first 5-10 seconds of isolated talk, the girls will usually have a tendency to want to maintain group talk, so keep asking them targeted questions and don't unlock eye contact.

Guys to Girls, in isolation: "Tennis? Oh cool. Do you play that often… Really, you do? When did you start playing?…Yeah? You went to tennis camp?"

You often need to get over the "hump" of her wanting to return to group talk. So whatever she says, just ask her more questions about that in order to carry her momentum into isolated talk.

Guys to Girls, in isolation (within 90 seconds): Establish age and 100% wing your conversation. Exchange numbers.

Guy 1 or 2 directed toward the opposite pair (after 90 seconds): "So she said she really likes tennis. I'm assuming you guys play together sometimes?"

The other guy will understand this is the signal to revert to group dynamic. On your friend's behalf, when he makes this attempt, don't ignore or resist it. Run with it.

Guys to Girls: "Yeah, well it was awesome seeing you guys. We should definitely hang out again some time. What are you guys doing the rest of the day?…Oh cool, well have fun. See you guys soon."
That basically sums up the direct duo approach.

That is always superior to both of you getting both of their numbers and casually saying you'll all hang out again some time. You want her to remember *you*, and the conversation she had with *you*. Also, you risk having occasional conflict with a wingman if both of you felt you hit it off more with one of the girls, or both of you were interested in the same girl, yet you're **both** in possession of her number. So that can lead to very frustrating negotiation. Deciding who the target is for each of you *before the approach* avoids this problem.

If you are with a wingman and want to approach a group of three, I view it as ideal for one of you to walk up and immediately open just one of the girls, directly and boldly, while your friend distracts the other two. He can then chat and/or close them as he sees fit (see next chapter for elaboration on this idea).

For groups of four or more, I view it as ideal (and this takes a lot of confidence) for both of you to walk up and immediately just address two of the girls (i.e., you instantly create side-by-side isolated convos), allowing the other 2+ girls to just chat amongst themselves (see next chapter for elaboration).

APPROACHING PAIRS + GROUPS SOLO (I.E., 1-ON-2, 1-ON-3, ETC.)

There are two ways I will approach duos. However there's only one way I will approach groups of three or more.

Regarding duos, the options are either 1) to open them broadly (i.e., saying hi to both of the girls at once), or 2) to pre-select one of the girls and then open her directly, while paying little, or no, attention to the friend.

If I open broadly (i.e., probably about 5% of my duo approaches and 0% of my group approaches) and both of the girls are receptive, I'll assess who's a better bet for a contact exchange by asking if they have boyfriends, what their hobbies are, and just overall getting a feel for their energy and personalities.

In these situations, I 100% improvise as to whether I'll go for one or both of their contacts. If there's a girl I'm a little more interested in, I'll ask for her contact first. If she says no, I'll ask for the second girl's contact not caring whatsoever about the impression this gives off to them.

If I open them broadly and one of the girls is receptive but the other isn't, I just focus on the one who's receptive, basically rewarding her for it.

If there's an unreceptive friend in the duo, I do not try to make her more receptive.

That is, I do not go out of my way to try and make the friend "like me" so that she'll give her friend permission to date me later on.

I just focus on the one who's receptive and let the unreceptive friend suffocate in the opportunity she's chosen to relinquish. Never try to "make" anyone like you. You're not there to qualify to anyone. If there's an unreceptive girl in a duo, it's her issue, not yours. I'm serious. Let her voluntarily writhe in her own misery.

Sometimes in a duo, one friend is very receptive and the other very unreceptive, such that the unreceptive friend *becomes more and more unreceptive* as the interaction progresses because she feels compelled to hold onto her negative frame.

In other words, sometimes one girl in a duo is like, "I've chosen to be depressed and closed off right now, and I'm going to do everything I can to take my friend down with me."

I've even occasionally had interactions where the unreceptive friend has stepped in front of her receptive friend, effectively guarding her. In these cases, I will still just focus on the receptive girl, and if she is too weak to overcome her unreceptive friend, then I just leave. I have no reason to force any interaction because there are literally new/different girls I could approach anyway.

In the past, I used to open some groups broadly. Now I never do that anymore. Regarding 100% of my group approaches and probably >95% of my duo approaches, **I do not try to start wide and work my way in.** In other words, I do not try to first make chat with "all of them" as though I give a fuck. Never play the role of group entertainer.

If I pretended as though I cared about making chat with all of the girls in a group, I'd essentially be lying with my behavior. Opening a duo/group can give you a huge opportunity to be extra-confident by literally just honing in on the one girl you find most attractive and going for it.

Directly approach your girl of interest and say hi to her *first*. You don't even need to make eye contact or acknowledge the other girls in the group. Just focus on the girl you're most interested in. This isn't douchey. This is GOOD.

The myth regarding not opening your girl of interest first (i.e., essentially trying to play disinterested early by addressing the whole group/pair and then working your way back to her) was created –

and perpetuated – by indirect, needy guys too lame to just be straight with women. The girls will sense any indirect energy you throw at them. They are hard-wired for that sort of thing.

You have to ask yourself: Why are you saying hi to these girls to begin with? If there's one girl in particular you are more interested in, why wouldn't you be anything but more direct with her. Don't worry about her friends being offended that you didn't select them first.

If your main concern is that you want to "win over her friends" so that they'll talk you up afterward, it says you're overly concerned with what her friends think. Stop caring about what others think. **They will read straight through your shit.** I've opened plenty of groups by first talking to the friends and "avoiding" the girl I'm most interested in, and I actually *feel in that moment* like I'm being indirect and needy.

In my experience, I have actually found that staying direct and bold with only one of the girls *is actually what will win her friends over.* From their perspective, there's an element of, "Wow, this never fucking happens…This guy is really confident."

As I said, never try to win the friend or friends over. You will be amazed that your confidence will actually be what "wows" the friends and, in turn, is what wins them over.

If there are guys in the group you are opening (e.g., three women and two guys), you're truthfully better off just finding other women to approach. No woman is that important, and you could literally look over your shoulder and see another hot girl right there. But, correct, if you did insist on opening this type of group, *do not bullshit by trying to ingratiate your way in with the guys first.* As I said, people will see straight through your shit. I would *still* go right up to the girl you are interested in. If one of the guys is her boyfriend, you're honestly risking a fight (or if this were Brazil, probably your life), so don't bother.

Once again, the most powerful thing you can do is to literally walk right up to the girl you are most interested in and, firmly and directly, introduce yourself to her *first*, without breaking eye contact. You should essentially view a duo/group approach as no different from a standard single approach; it's just coincidental that the surroundings this time around happen to be her friend(s).

I promise you, women will smell if you are being indirect. If you don't yet have the courage to open a girl one-on-one when solo-approaching pairs, or trios, etc., there's nothing wrong with just starting out approaching singles. No one's judging you.

If I see a girl within a duo/group whom I find most attractive, I will approach and open her first. No indirect bullshit. No opening her friends first.

I do not worry about "losing out" on the other girls in the group because I singled out one from the beginning. As I said, I view a group approach as non-distinct from a single approach. The friends are merely the surroundings, the same way nearby people at a bus stop or cafe are.

"Hi, I'm Michael. I thought you were attractive and wanted to say hi."

At this point, most of the time she will defuse tension by looking at her friends and making a face or laughing. I've identified this as hyper-predictable and normal. In fact, this doesn't even register with me anymore and I just ignore it, continuing to focus on her.

Don't look at the friends if and when she does this. It doesn't matter what you look like or who you are. She will almost always react this way, even if receptive. Just stay focused on her.

I'll always ask her age in the first 10-15 seconds, but apart from that, I will 100% wing the conversation. I have conviction that

deregulation, where you 100% improvise your conversations, is the number-one way to be your most natural and attractive.

For every approach you do, there will always be the receptiveness probability of the girl that needs to work in your favor (i.e., you can't control whether she's going to be receptive or unreceptive when first saying hi). *But then on top of that*, with duo/group dynamics, even if the girl you're directly saying hi to is receptive, *her friend(s) might not be.*

(% chance Girl #1 is receptive) x (% chance her friend/group is receptive)

The only reason duo/group approaches could be considered "more difficult" is because you're simply dealing with *two, not one,* receptiveness probabilities, which must now be multiplied together for the interaction to play out in your favor. If either one is a no-go (i.e, unreceptive), the interaction fails.

Because opening duos/groups always entails multiplying by a second %, these types of approaches *will always be* lower probability conversions relative to single ones.

I've approached plenty of girls in duos/groups who are receptive, yet the friends aren't, and they've pulled her away and tanked the interaction.

Friend/group receptiveness plays out as you merely being granted the time/space to have your one-on-one conversation.

When I directly introduce myself to a girl and her friends are receptive, they will almost always just stay quiet and/or allow their friend to walk ahead with me (e.g., if this is street approach). I'll go for the contact exchange within 60-90 seconds and then just leave.

As you start approaching increasing numbers of duos, trios, etc., you'll even encounter some scenarios where the girl you're saying hi to isn't particularly receptive *but her friends are as a collective, and in turn, they'll encourage her to talk to you anyway.* I'll refer to this as "inverse receptiveness," where you have group receptiveness but not that of the girl you're most interested in.

I call this inverse receptiveness because it's a slightly unusual variant, or even the opposite, of what most guys typically expect with group dynamics – i.e., rather than a receptive girl being yanked away by her friends, you have an apprehensive girl being pushed into the interaction with you by her friends (see next chapter, story #2). If I open a duo/group and my girl of interest is unreceptive, I will 100% wing it as far as whether I want to continue engaging her vs instead pivoting to one of the friends. I never care what the friends think, nor do I automatically assume they're not attracted to me simply because I'm saying hi to them second.

Don't worry about whether you've turned off her friend(s) just because you initially singled a different girl out.

For 1) you must realize the "state" a girl is in has nothing to do with you. Sometimes she'll just be receptive; sometimes she won't be. So on occasion, the friend(s) will just be receptive regardless. And 2) some girls are actually really attracted to the confidence you had to say hi, irrespective of the fact that it wasn't them first. It is a mistake to assume that Girl #2 will reject you just because you said hi to Girl #1 first.

There have been times when I've directly opened one girl in a duo, telling her she's cute, only for her to be unreceptive. Then I've switched my attention to the friend, who in turn is *not unreceptive*, and then closed her in front of the first girl. This type of occurrence actually isn't too uncommon. That's yet another reason why I always just open duos/groups one-on-one. *Girl #2 often doesn't care as much as you think she might.*

A FEW STORIES OF APPROACHING GROUPS SOLO

Story #1:

I was once walking in a busy, underground pedestrian passageway connecting subway stations here in Osaka. I saw a stunning girl in a trio and thought about not approaching, but then just decided to go for it anyway.

I walked right up to her, ignoring her two friends, and introduced myself firmly, telling her I thought she was attractive. She and her friends laughed. I asked her age and if she had a boyfriend. She and her friends all laughed again, but I kept my eye contact strictly on her and didn't even glance at the friends. She said she was 24 and didn't have a boyfriend. I asked her why she didn't have a boyfriend. She squirmed and said she didn't know.

I didn't change my behavior whatsoever, 100% winged it, and just kept my cool. I made typical small-chat. I told her I'm from New York, have lived in Australia, and moved here to Japan to learn the language.

I asked if she liked tea and she said yes. I told her she and I would get tea some time and that we should exchange contacts. At this moment, she looked at her friends hesitantly, half-smiling, half-nervous.

Her friends effectively gave her the OK. We exchanged contacts. The interaction start to finish was under two minutes.

I was on fire after that. Not because of the outcome, but because I had made the direct and confident approach. *Rejection or not, it was the approach itself that was the success.*

You might wonder why I chose to mention this brief example, as though you're supposed to give a fuck. It's probably because it stands out in my mind as the one where I first learned an important lesson:

Guys often worry about trying to "win over the friends." However a confident and unwavering approach, even if entails completely ignoring the friends, *is what actually what will win them over.* Never play group entertainer. Don't approach indirectly and then "work your way back" to your girl of interest. Just open her directly.

With the above example, the girl I said hi to was neutral but the friends were receptive as a collective. Their group receptiveness was exemplified by them merely allowing my one-on-one conversation to occur without pulling her away. Recognize that no matter how much laughing there is objectively – or awkwardness that's in your head subjectively – if the friends aren't pulling the girl away and are allowing you to talk to her, they're at least neutral to receptive as a group, and that's all you need.

Story #2:

I once approached a girl in a subway station here in Osaka, only for her three friends to pop up out of nowhere seconds later – i.e., so now I was abruptly confronted with a quad situation. I kept my cool and didn't even look at the three friends. I just stayed focused on the girl I had directly opened.

As I started chatting with her, however, she didn't come across very receptive. But I stuck with the convo anyway because sometimes a girl's nervousness and/or apprehension in front of friends can on the surface appear like unreceptiveness.

Deer-in-the-headlights neutrality can often be misinterpreted as unreceptiveness.

If she outright ignores you, shakes her head no, or waves her hand at you, she's certainly unreceptive. If she's simply "stunned," or taken aback, by you abruptly engaging her, she may seem unreceptive even if she's neutral or receptive.

I asked her hobbies and she didn't respond. She just looked at her friends, one of whom then said to her (in Japanese), "He just asked you your hobbies. Answer him." And she said it in such a way that she was essentially insinuating, "Talk to him. We're giving you permission. Yes, have the conversation."

Then as she started to answer my question about hobbies, the friend who had just said that to her put her arm around the other two girls and walked away with them, leaving us in a one-on-one convo.

I was like, "Wow, that's amazing group receptiveness."

As I was now engaging in this one-on-one convo though, the girl *still* wasn't receptive toward me. I made small-talk, and then she declined the contact exchange twice. I believe the reason I pushed for it twice was because *I wanted to believe* that she should care that she effectively received her friends' permission to have a chat with me. I mean, that's huge points right – getting the friends' assent?

(Once again, never try to make friends like you. I'm just making a general statement that *it at the very least can't hurt* to have the friends' permission.)

I mention this story for two reasons: 1) this is a perfect example of inverse receptiveness, where the group was receptive but the girl I said hi to wasn't; and 2) despite receiving the friends' permission, that didn't convert her from being unreceptive into receptive – i.e., a girl will often just be in her "state," where she's not going to be open to male encounters – you, me, anyone – at certain moments. There's nothing to take personally.

Story #3:

I was in a cafe here in Japan and saw three absolutely stunning Japanese girls, "dressed to the nines," who came in for coffee. It was probably around 9:30pm and they sat roughly six feet to my left, two tables over. They were heavily animated, taking selfies and in loud convo. I could tell they didn't speak English.

About ten feet to my right, there were two guys who I could hear were speaking Korean. One of the guys had a big diamond in his ear. The other was wearing a long, burgundy trench coat. This second guy, in particular, was really going out of his way to peacock his appearance.

Now, across the cafe, probably about 20 feet away, there were two Korean girls looking over at the two Korean guys. They were exchanging glances. I could see the guys debating whether or not to go say hi. Finally, they stood up and walked across the cafe to the girls and said hello. The two girls rejected them instantly and the guys returned to their table alone. I was impressed at their initiative, as I don't often see guys approach in cafes. I actually felt a little annoyed on behalf of the guys, because truthfully, the girls were very plain-appearing and they turned down a good opportunity probably because they were too scared of the tension.

At this point, I was still caught up with the animated, stunning trio to my left. One girl in particular really stood out to me. *I decided I was going to say hi to her no matter what.*

I thought I would first experiment by creating a makeshift group and seeing if the two Korean guys wanted to go in together as a 3-on-3. The timing couldn't have been more opportune. I got up from my chair and walked over to the guys. I said, "日本語が話せますか (Do you speak Japanese?)." They said yes. So we continued the conversation in Japanese.

I told them that because there were three stunning girls right there, my thought process was that we should approach and open them together. The whole situation was pretty outrageous actually. Here I was in a cafe wearing a Michael Jackson-esque Thriller jacket, talking to a guy wearing a burgundy trench coat, and another guy with diamond bling, about to direct a makeshift 3-on-3.

Now these two guys had *just* approached a pair a moment ago, but when they looked over at the super-stunning girls, seemed hesitant and nervous. I reiterated that we should just go approach them together. Let's GO, I said. They said they'd think about it.

I returned to my seat. About 30 seconds later, the girls started getting their belongings together. I was like, "No fucking way is this situation getting ruined."

They stood up from their chairs. I walked over and right up to the girl I was most interested in. All three girls stopped to look at me.

I told her, "俺はマイケルです。こんにちはと言いたかっただけ (Hi, I'm Michael. I just wanted to say hi)."

She was in an unreceptive princess mode and just laughed condescendingly with her friends, that stereotypical, "I'm with my friends and the three of us are so high-status that we are above all guys"-type of state. I have experience so I didn't flinch or waver whatsoever.

*This type of response I got from them was **exactly the reason** the two Korean guys were scared to say hi.*

Next I just directly asked her age (何歳ですか). She said 29. I thought, "Wow, she looks 19 at most." I told her I was 30, which I thought would give me points in that situation. She said I looked young.

I told her, "俺は日本語勉強してるぜ. 一年半ぐらい前に日本に引越しした (I'm studying Japanese. I moved here about a year and a half ago)."

She laughed and said "頑張って (Ganbatte; which means "good luck"). That is probably the number-one fuck-off thing a girl can say to you in Japan. Any time I introduce myself to a girl and she says "ganbatte," I immediately lose all interest. I'll just leave. Imagine introducing yourself to a girl and she gives you a fist pump and is like, "Good luck!" You'd be like, "*Good luck*? How about *shut the fuck up*."

Her friends were equally in princess mode. So I said bye and they left the cafe. I looked over at the two Korean guys who were watching in amazement. I was thinking, "How was that any different from what you just did with that pair a moment ago." These guys could have easily said hi to these girls with me. And truthfully, had we gone up together and initiated group discussion or three parallel conversations, it may have gone somewhere. And they were HOT.

I noticed that roughly five feet away, there was another Japanese girl who observed what I just did. When I glanced at her, she looked down at her phone. I spent another 60 seconds or so finishing my coffee, and then I approached her one-on-one. She was slightly cute but also extremely weird. She was waiting on a friend she said. I told her we should exchange LINEs (Japanese messaging app). She declined. It's like, have a good life. I walked out of the cafe and approached another cute girl walking. She had her headphones in and ignored me.

But I was on fire after that.

BIG APPROACHES IN A SMALL WORLD – A MIX OF SHORT-STORIES

On a few occasions, I've received texts from numbers I don't know saying, "That was my friend you hit on you asshole. Do you just go up to every girl saying 'Omg you're the most beautiful girl I've ever seen. I just had to talk to you?'"

As you do more and more approaches, expect to inadvertently approach the same girl more than once, as well as the best friends, housemates, and siblings of girls you've already approached. You'll also sometimes approach, and even hook up with, people whom your friends had previously hooked up with, and vice-versa.

I once cold approached a Vietnamese girl in the city and we walked around and chatted for a bit. We kissed and said bye. We ultimately never met up after that.

Fast-forward 3-4 months. I was on a train and sat down next to a really cute girl. She said she was Vietnamese. We chatted for a good hour. She lived in a far suburb. I was going to see a friend in that suburb. As we disembarked, I told her we should exchange numbers. She said she had a boyfriend. That was the end of it.

Within a few days, I got a text from some number I didn't know saying, "Just so you know, you hit on my sister on the train the other day. I doubt it was a different American Michael with a skateboard." And I was thinking, "Who the fuck is this? What other Vietnamese girls have I met?" I approach so many women I would have had no clue. I finally made the connection it was the girl from the city months earlier. I texted back, *"We should meet up for a date."* She declined. I just blocked the number.

Occasionally, you will approach the same girl by accident more than once. Some girls even three or four times. After all, before you say hi to girls, you might first see them from the side, or from behind while skating/walking, or you'll be mainly focused on the body, or hair, etc., and you're really not analyzing, out of the thousands of girls you've approached, if she's in your history of previous encounters.

I once chased a girl out of a campus library and told her, "Hi, I'm Michael. I thought you were cute and wanted to say hi." She looked at me and said, "Do you realize that this is the *third time* you've done this exact same approach to me, in this exact same location? I told you I have a boyfriend."

Another girl I approached at a library computer. She turned to me, with a hostile facial expression, and said, "This is, not the first time, *but the second time*, you've said hi to me like this." I told her it must be a shame getting approached by a confident guy, then I left.

On occasion, if I approach a girl and then realize at the very last instant, after it's already too late, that I've already done so in the past, I will basically just say, "Heyyy, I just wanted to say hi." And then we can make awkward/improvised chat. I once sat down in front of a girl at a cafe and then realized right away that I had already done so in that same exact seat, with that same exact girl, probably about two months earlier. I told her, "Hey, I just wanted to say hi. How have things been going?" I recalled that she had a boyfriend and was really boring anyway, so after about 30 seconds or so, I said, "Well anyway, I just wanted to say hi. Good luck with everything."

One time I was skating to campus and stopped a cute girl on the road. I told her she was really pretty and we talked for about 60 seconds. I just kissed her on the lips then and there and exchanged numbers with her. Soon after then, I ran into one of my acquaintances at the gym (not a friend, but someone I had "see around" now and again, just at the gym). He said, "Hey, you realize Ellie and I are together right? She told me she was approached by an American Michael the other day and that he kissed her on the spot. She said he was skateboarding. I told her I know you." I was like, "Oh shit, sorry about that man." And we both just let it go.

When I was 25 and still dating the 18-year-old as the lame beta I was at the time (see chapter: End of the beta male), my Italian housemate had a beautiful blonde girl named Catherine over for dinner one night. She was really cute. The two of them were having pasta together, and I came out of my room with my girlfriend. The four of us talked in the kitchen for five minutes or so, and then my girlfriend and I left. My girlfriend said after the fact, "Wow, that girl is really pretty."

Later on, he told me they didn't fuck, but that he went down on her. He also said it was an incredibly weird hook up because she was panting and moaning excessively, even at times when he wasn't really doing anything. He went on to hang out with her a second time. Once again, they didn't fuck. After that, they didn't hook up again.

Fast-forward six months. I was now single and hooking up with different people. It was summer vacation for the majority of University of Queensland, but my medical program had a slightly different calendar, so I was in the library on occasion. This particular library closed around dinner-time every day, and the staff would come around telling people they needed to clear out. One day, a beautiful blonde girl came by my study room and said they were closing. I didn't recognize her. I said that was fine and then left.

The following day, when she came to clear me out of the library, I asked her name and she said Catherine. Once again I didn't recognize her, nor did she recognize me. I asked what she was doing now. She said she didn't know. I told her she could get dinner with me. We got pizza and I walked her home. I made out with her in front of her house.

For one reason or another, I didn't get her number right away. I think there was something about the spontaneity of our interaction, where we were bumping into each other at the library, that was exciting, and I just wanted to run with it. I figured I could just go to the library in the coming days to see her again.

Maybe a few days later, I went back to the library. This time I chose a very secluded, private study room without windows in the back corner of a quiet corridor. Especially since it was summer vacation, absolutely nobody was studying in this part of the library.

When she came to clear out the rooms, she saw me in the study room and came in. We started making out then and there. I laid her down on the floor and we both started taking off our pants. She asked if I had a condom. I said no. She said, "It's my period. Is that okay?" Without saying anything, I decided I didn't want to then and there. She was fine with that. We walked down together and she closed the library. Outside I said bye to her and we made out for another 30 seconds. This time we exchanged numbers.

A week or two later we got dinner. I went back to her place and we had sex. But the sex was really fucking weird. Basically she was panting and moaning really loudly and excessively, even when I wasn't actively thrusting. It was just way too over-the-top.

I realized, holy shit, this is the same Catherine.

After we fucked, we walked to my place, and I slept with her there as well. Now I had just moved into a new unit at the time, and the layout was really bizarre – when you walked in the front door, the first thing you immediately saw was a *bed*. We didn't have a couch. Just a bed. Whenever I brought someone over, I'd essentially say to them, "Yeah, I know, my house is weird. I don't know why we have a bed there instead of a couch, but just handle it." So that's also what happened with Catherine when I brought her over. She saw the bed and was like, "Yeah that's weird."

I didn't hook up with her again after that day, as the sex was too over-the-top.

Now in the mean time, my Italian housemate was currently home in Italy and impossible to get a hold of (he never checked his Facebook and had like 350 unread messages), but he was coming back in a about a month's time and would be moving into our new place. He was involved in various leadership projects on campus, some of which involved activities with incoming students. As it turns out, that is how he had originally met Catherine. They were both group leaders together.

When he returned from Italy, we had different schedules, and I didn't see him right away. I just saw his luggage for about a week as evidence that he had returned. He immediately started doing his leadership projects again. For one of the events he did, he was speaking to a circle of about 50 new students on how to find cheap housing, etc. He and Catherine were co-leaders of that group. According to him, he had said at one point to the group, "Yeah, so you can find pretty much any type of cheap housing around here. For instance, I just moved into a really cheap unit a five-minute walk from here, but the layout is really bizarre. When you walk in, the first thing you see is a bed."

He said her facial expression got really red and weird when he said that, but he didn't know why.

I told him the story and he put the two puzzle pieces together. I mentioned her crazy panting and moaning. He was like, "What the fuck did I tell you! I know!" Then I joked with him saying, "So…how come *you* didn't fuck her?"

But in all fairness, he had actually approached and slept with a Colombian girl later on whom I had gone on a date with but never fucked. So these things have a way of cancelling out. But it's always good to have a laugh with your friends.

WHEN DAY GAME MERGES WITH NIGHT GAME

In 2016, after I graduated med school, I went on a road trip from Perth, a city located in southwestern Australia, to Darwin, the northern-most city in Australia. I was with one of my guy friends. We drove the coast all the way there.

One evening, as it was nearing dusk, the two of us approached a tiny port town in northwestern Australia called Port Hedland. We had picked up some food earlier in the day and were looking for a place to just chill and eat our dinner.

Coming into the town, we passed giant salt dunes and rusty railways. This town was absolutely dead and seemingly deserted. There was nothing going on. We had thought that if we were lucky, we might be able to find *a bar* to go to, and maybe have some beers with fisherman or salt miners who were in their 50s or 60s.

As we were driving in, I literally told my friend, because it was so ridiculously obvious that we weren't going to meet any girls tonight, "LET'S GET LAIDDDD!" I was trying my best to humor us. I said a few times, "We're gonna get LAIDDDD tonight."

Had you given me the opportunity to place a 50,000-to-1 bet on the spot regarding whether I'd have sex tonight, I would've said fuck off and saved my dollar. Maybe I could find a 99-cent pack of Chiclets at our next gas station.

There was a giant ship that looked like the Titanic slowly making its way into the port. We found a parking spot with a nice view and the sun was going to be setting within a half-hour. There was a small patch of grass with a picnic table, and we got out of the car and brought our food over to it.

I noticed about 200 feet away from us there was an Aussie-looking guy, who appeared about 30-35 years old, walking toward the port, but not toward us. There was a girl, who looked early-20s, about 15 feet behind him, walking in the same direction as he. I told my friend it looked like they were probably together. After all, there were literally no other people around, so I assumed they were a couple going to watch the sunset together.

The guy went to look at the water and sunset for a couple minutes. The girl came closer to us, probably within 100 feet, and was taking pictures of an old sign. She was really beautiful and had long, blonde hair. She was wearing a short, white dress that fluttered in the breeze from the port.

She squatted down to take a picture and, with a gust of wind, I saw her legs in full for a split-second and they were amazing. She then turned around and sat at a picnic table near the sign. The guy I thought she was with disappeared.

She was just there on her own. She took a book out of her knapsack and started reading.

Now my friend and I had absolutely no logistics at the moment. We didn't even know of a hostel or hotel we could go to. We were probably planning on just sleeping sitting up in the car, like we did most of the time.

Even if I said hi to her, where would we go? What would we do?

I had zero reservations about approaching her, but in a way, preferred to just chat and relax with my guy friend rather than starting to entertain some girl with superficial conversation when it wasn't going to go anywhere anyway. I told my buddy that. His reply was, "That's not the Michael I know." When he said that, *now I had to approach*. But I warned him, "Just letting you know, if we start chatting with her, I'm not going to be the one who's entertaining her for the next 20 minutes."

I walked over to her picnic table. I said, "Hi, I'm Michael. I thought you were cute and wanted to say hi." She looked up. She was even more pretty up close. She was from Sweden and 22. She was on some working holiday visa and had just moved from Perth to Port Hedland a day earlier to start bartending at a hotel for the next few months. The hotel was giving her free accommodation, but she didn't start work until tomorrow night.

She was traveling with a friend from Sweden, but she said her friend had really bad menstrual pain and was seeing a doctor in Perth, and wouldn't be up for another couple days.

I told her I was traveling with my friend and that she could come over and chat with us while we were eating dinner. She stood up and was my height. She came with me and the three of us started talking.

Now the guy I was traveling with was, on average, a lot more socially lively than I. He had a tendency to get animated in his conversations with new people and make friends more quickly. Compared to him, I was a lot more quiet.

In that moment, I remember specifically thinking to myself, "If I were here with just him right now – just the two of us – I wouldn't be saying jack-shit. I'd be fairly quiet like I normally am and would just be chillin' out, eating my dinner. So I'm not going to change my behavior whatsoever just because this girl is here. I'll let him be the one who entertains her if he's really keen on having conversation."

And that's what he did. He entertained her.

Now my buddy is an absolute champion of a wingman. Even though he was doing all of the talking, he's more of a relationship guy, and he knew that because I approached this girl, I had dibs.

We ate our food. After about 20 minutes of the superficial conversation that I had predicted, I told her we had an unopened bottle of really good tequila we could drink together. She thought this was a good idea. After all, the three of us literally had nothing else better to do.

We all walked to the car and I showed her the tequila we had. My sentiment was that because it was legitimately high-quality tequila, we couldn't drink it without lime and salt, so I told her we could drive to the town's supermarket to see if we could find some.

That was the truth, but my thought matrix was that if I could establish positive momentum and trust on her end in terms of doing "little activities" with us (i.e., coming in our car, going on a scavenger hunt for lime/salt, etc.), she would be more inclined to submit to the pattern of taking my lead.

I pointed out to my friend that because we just ate, we should wash our hands at the small public bathroom before we leave. He knew, as the good wingman he was, that I wanted her isolated for a minute. He walked off to the bathroom.

I looked right at her. The next thing out of my mouth was, "Do you like forward guys?" She said, "Umm, yeah, I guess I do." So I just walked two steps toward her, placed my right hand behind her head, and kissed her on the lips. Then I took two steps back and continued small-chat like nothing had happened.

My thought process was this: If she was receptive to my escalation then and there, when my friend came back from the bathroom, we would move forward with our plan and take her with us to go on a scavenger hunt. If she rejected my advance, I would tell her, in front of my friend, that he and I are taking off and that we wish her luck.

I wanted to establish a point of inflection then and there. I was not going to waste any time on a girl if she wasn't going to be sexually open to me. Not just my time, but also my friend's. If my friend was going to play wingman, I didn't want him to waste his energy, so I had a responsibility to push for a conclusion every step of the way. In addition, I could save our alcohol by not having to split it three ways with an unreceptive girl.

After my friend came back, I then went and washed my hands. I was aware that he didn't realize I had kissed her. Although he was already playing wingman and had my back, what I had done was established in her mind that I, not he, was her potential sexual partner that night. And I knew that leaving them to be isolated for 60 seconds while he entertained her more with his social and lively talk was OK and would further increase her trust and comfort in us.

The three of us got into the car, found a supermarket, and bought some limes and salt. I told her, "Do you think we could just use your room or something to just chill and drink." She said that would work. So I said, "Okay, well let's just go there." She said okay. We drove to the hotel she was working at and started walking up to her room. The building was made of wood and looked like a saloon out of the Wild West.

As she was walking ahead of us, I said to my friend, "After a half-hour of us being in her room drinking, you're going to leave because you have to make a 'phone call.'" He then said, "Actually, what I can do is set my alarm as a ring tone for a half-hour from now, then I'll just 'take the call' and disappear for 45 minutes." It was a great amalgamation of our ideas we had, which was basically conceived as we were walking up the hotel staircase.

We got to her room and started drinking. We took three shots each. It was great tequila. She sat in a leather chair and crossed her left leg over her right, showing the entire length of her left thigh for the most part. It was definitely a sexual gesture.

I noticed she started testing me.

She made a slightly serious face and raised her chin. She asked if I knew the capital of Sweden. I was like 90% sure after three shots that it was Stockholm. Cool, I passed her junior high school-level question so far.

Then she asked if I knew what the flag looked like. I told her it was blue and yellow. She said, "But yeah, what does it look like." I said it was a cross. Then she said, "Which colors are which." I said the flag is blue and the stripes are yellow. She said, "Yeah, that's right."

My friend's phone went off. He had to "take a call." My iPhone had gotten run over by a road train in Useless Loop, Western Australia a few days earlier, so he had no way of getting a hold of me. I knew he was going to be coming back in 45 minutes.

My phone really did get run over. I rarely take photos but had the best ones of my life on there. They couldn't be extracted.

After he left, I got forward with her again. I told her to sit on the bed next to me. We kissed a little. I started going for her clothes and she said she wasn't going to have sex because we just met. I continued being forward with her anyway. She wasn't taking my advances.

In other words, my fast and forward game worked at the port when I kissed her, but her bedroom reception was slightly more demure. Through my experience, however, I knew to be persistent. I stayed aggressive, alternating between kissing her/going for her clothes and talking with her. After 20 minutes, I wasn't getting any closer. I knew whatever game was required to bed her needed a change of tactic.

So what happened next is: I was genuinely willing to walk.

I knew my friend was probably walking around by himself in the dark with nothing to do. That wasn't fair to him. If this girl wasn't going to have sex with me, despite the fact that I was aggressive and doing everything I could, I ultimately had to accept her wishes and be willing to return to my friend. It's not like I wasn't trying. *I was fucking trying.* But if it's a no, it's a no.

So I calmly stood up and said, "I'm going to shower." I decided that a short "intermission" could 1) serve to let her mentally regroup and become more receptive, and 2) serve as a counterbalance to the straight 20 minutes of aggressive tactics I had just implemented.

In terms of being there with this girl, if she wasn't going to sleep with me, then I could at least get a shower out of it. I thought it would make for good humor after the fact. That is, upon meeting up with my friend again, I could tell him, "Well ya know, I didn't get laid, but I had an awesome fucking shower." (When you're on a road trip, a good, hot, proper shower can be hard to come by.)

While in the shower, I knew if I didn't change tactics, I would lose her. She was playing a little game with me to see how needy I was for the sex. I had to demonstrate to her that I was able to balance my aggressiveness with a little restraint. So after I got out of the shower, I *talked* with her and didn't make a move on her for the next ten minutes or so.

Then my friend came back. He was in the room for about 40 seconds dithering and not sure of what to do. He didn't know if I had slept with her or not. But if he didn't leave this second time around, I 100% had no chance. I was point-blank with him and told him to politely step out. I said I would meet him downstairs in 30 minutes. And I meant it. I was going to leave no matter what. It wasn't fair to my friend. So this girl had 30 minutes to decide whether she wanted to have fun with me. Otherwise I was gone.

When my buddy left, I took a more "cuddly" approach to being forward. I stroked her hair a little bit while I was talking to her. And I didn't try kissing her. I just kept touching her hair, and her ear, and her cheek a little, while having straight convo with her about life for another ten minutes.

During these ten minutes, I was willing to walk. I truly didn't care at this point if this girl was going to be unreceptive to sex. I genuinely thought that. She must have been able to sense that.

We started kissing spontaneously and had sex twice in the next 20 minutes. It was awesome. It was one of those sexual encounters where in the middle of the sex you're thinking, "Is this really going down right now?"

I would say out of all of the approaches and sexual encounters I've had, this one ranks as one of the highest in terms of the *diversity* of different game tactics I had to implement to get from start to finish, all of which I had acquired over the course of years of different experiences with women. I believe had I been even 1% less experienced, it wouldn't have happened.

This also serves as a good example of how day game can be used to generate same-day sex, as well as how it can fuse with night game. If you have good day game, you always have good night game, but not necessarily the other way around.

NO LONGER BETA BUT NOT AN ALPHA – OUTSIDER STATUS

I'm absolutely not an alpha male. I don't have the physical presence of one. I'm muscular, but I'm 5'8". It's an easy contention that size isn't necessary to be alpha, and I completely agree that it's only one facet, but regardless, I don't have overwhelming physical presence, and there are plenty of guys bigger than I am.

At the gym, guys will occasionally look at me when they think I don't see them. Not because anyone is jealous of me in the slightest. Guys don't want to be me. No one wishes they were me. The ones who look at me probably find me slightly peculiar for my mildly alternative appearance in conjunction with the confidence I exude.

The evolution of my personality over time has manifested greater assertion prowess, although I don't command or direct groups unless doing so accomplishes a very transient or fleeting interest. And that interest almost invariably involves picking up a female. If that possibility isn't present, I have no reason to be there. And I won't be there.

Other males in a group don't see me as a leader, and they don't really look to me. There's usually someone else people are looking at during standard group discourse. It's very rare that I'm the focus of attention during normal conversational flow. If I am in that position, it feels unusual and unstable. That is, I have a cognizance for it and its ensuing evanescence. Group members' passive attention might fall on me if the topic of conversation becomes about women.

I'm not ever mentally attached to a group, nor do I care if anyone wants me there. I don't like contemplating the notion of group cohesion or the tacit responsibility leading anyone entails. I'm never there to entertain anyone. I'm quieter than most people. If a group is pre-assembled and I show up, I draw attention as the slightly alternative "weird friend," or the guy people can't quite read or understand. They know I'm not a leader, but they know I'm not a follower.

Group members have seen me effortlessly talk to attractive women outside the group before. They may or may not also have knowledge that I've already hit on their friends or other women they know, sometimes in weird places like stairwells. They've also witnessed me get women's numbers, as well as introduce attractive women I've met on the spot to the group. I never introduce women I'm already seeing to a group unless it's to use them as bait to court an attractive female within the group who is otherwise resistant to my advances.

Women in a group understand at the very least that I am able to pick up women *outside* the group, while they themselves might not have a singular interest in me. My interaction with them is very brief, direct, and confrontational. I will quickly escalate and evaluate the dynamic I hold with any woman within a group who interests me, and if there's nothing suitable for me, I leave the group.

Most women seek out some form of ostensible social structure. I only seek out women who prefer to abdicate it. Women who are seeking that abdication see me as their rock star and a huge relief. I'm aware that sounds absolutely outrageous, but I've been told that.

Group members will never consider me as being part of their "inner circle." I'm that guy who appears sporadically/rarely and isn't really part of the group. I have high success picking up women as an autonomous male and don't rely on, or benefit from, any group structure. A guy with a tendency for leadership initiative interprets me as not really someone he's trying to lead anyway. He knows I'm not interested in his leadership. If he pulls the group in a direction that doesn't suit my liking, and there's no female in the group whom I'm courting, I leave. That is truthfully in the best interest of both the group leader and myself. And I'll usually abscond. I never promulgate my farewells.

If there's anyone who challenges me, even if it's friendly camaraderie, I will become somewhat targeted and intense toward that person. I never let anyone off the hook for being condescending toward me.

My natural equilibrium point is tangential to social structure for the most part. I loathe societal constructs because they necessitate conformity among the majority. Even if there are conceivably many subgroups to choose from, you're either at the top or you have to follow. I'm not at the top, nor do I seek it, and I certainly will not follow anyone. I will only ever do my own thing. Those who are strong conformists and heavily entrenched within social structure will view my personality style as contumacious and juvenile. I view those who are heavily entrenched as victims and slaves of external pressure and expectation.

If guys "follow" me, I tend to mentor them. They'll observe me approach and get "coaching" on how to do the same themselves. I'm never not approaching, so any guys who are with me naturally fall under my wing. They sometimes adopt my habits or way of speaking. They'll often acquire my slang. They'll question what my life was like in the past and how/why I came to be this way.

I'm very open to the viewpoints of others, but I practically never learn anything new about women from other guys. I'm always the one teaching guys about women. The things I could learn from other guys only involve being *softer* in some way. I'm not interested in being a soft piece of shit. No guy could help me become more forward, confident, or direct with women.

I view most guys as too readily willing to enter commitment. They choose that route because it makes the most sense for them sexually and logistically. When they find someone who's "cute enough" who shows a little interest or emotion toward them, they'll jump on it. Most guys aren't incorrigibly tethered to this mindset – I was once there and escaped it myself – but they live bound by varying degrees of fear.

I couldn't imagine that every guy reading my content could or would adopt the principles and viewpoints I lay out. I believe the most important thing is having a good mentor. The guidance you have means everything. I believe I've grown to be one of the best day game male mentors in the world for guys looking to approach and date many women.

Yeah, I know. That probably comes off as a wildly self-aggrandizing and pretentious statement, but I just know.

I've already made a point though that I'm not inherently special. Had I not met my housemate years ago, I never would have experienced the changes that made me who I am today. I think about that a lot actually. There's not a day I don't feel grateful for the mindset I hold.

Had I stayed beta, I wouldn't have had the awareness for my situation either. I probably would have built resentment toward whatever partner I had for my sexual restriction and lack of control in the relationship, but at the same time not feeling like I could do any better. It's crazy to think that the summation of low-probability events having incidentally coalesced was the basis for what freed me from the beta mindset.

Guys just need a good mentor to help them see that they can get any woman they want. That's probably the biggest reason I started writing. It's to help you change your mindset to bring out the most confident you that can exist. We're all different people. And the most confident version of you isn't and won't be like the most confident version of me. That's a really cool thing actually.

COMPLACENCE

It's important I reiterate that in order to sleep with lots of women, you have to accept and enjoy getting rejected a lot. You have to see your rejections as successes. You have to see them as strong contributors to your confidence. Sounds paradoxical, but it's true. You should be getting rejected light-years more than you're sleeping with new women.

You'll develop mechanisms to own your rejections, take pride in them, and use them to propel you into bolder subsequent approaches. And ultimately, it's how you interpret what it means to get rejected that determines whether you'll be able to integrate your approach skills into general life. It's when you achieve integration that you don't think about your approach prowess as actual game anymore; it's just you being the confident guy you are unabated.

In the beginning, meeting attractive women and sleeping with them is undeniably rewarding and exciting. It's just what you do as a guy. There's nothing to think about. In other words, early on, when this is the main objective, it's unquestionably worth it to tolerate lots of rejections and female games in order to get the outcome you're looking for.

But over time, after you've slept around a bit, it'll start to feel like getting laid isn't such a big deal anymore. It'll actually start to feel like you don't **need** get laid so much. And I'm not talking about apathy or laziness; I'm talking about a genuine lack of need, in the sense that you have nothing to prove to yourself anymore.

In other words, since you already know you're capable of approaching women and getting laid if you really want to, what are you still trying to prove? And to whom?

You'll become a little "philosophical" with yourself as to what's driving you to get laid so much in the first place. Is it compensatory in some way for feeling inadequate? Is it validation I'm seeking (internal vs external)? Is it reactionary because I was a lame beta in the past and am now making up lost ground?

When you start to feel like you don't need to get laid anymore, it can inadvertently attenuate your drive to continue making aggressive approaches at high frequency. There's a growing sense of complacence, and you'll ask yourself what the incentive is to continue being as bold as you know yourself to be.

Simultaneously, you'll also start to get sick and tired of dealing with the rude rejections many girls give, as well as their repetitive and predictable games, and wonder why you're willing to put up with the constant negativity stream just to get laid more. Is it really worth the time and mental energy for an outcome that doesn't matter so much anyway.

I went through a few-month phase during the latter part of when I was living in Australia where I was asking myself these types of questions because I was able to identify a degree of complacence in my behavior. I began to see that I was sometimes forgoing aggressive approaches because I didn't feel like dealing with the constant rejections and gameplay getting laid an additional time entailed.

*I would basically say to myself, "Okay, well I would actually rather **not** get laid one extra time if it means not having to deal with 99 additional flaking women and rude rejections just to get there. It's not worth my time and energy to deal with at this point."*

But in a way, this was unacceptable to me. Then I thought about *why* this was unacceptable to me.

It slowly started to occur to me that approaching women did not just serve the mere purpose of getting laid. I saw that the process made me more driven and less needy in all other areas of my life.

When you're a go-getter and very direct with women, you're already ticking off the box for the boldest thing there is to do. That bold behavior feeds into making you much more forward and confident *in all other areas of your life.*

The approaches you make on women day in and day out don't just give you the confidence to make subsequent approaches. They give you the confidence to finally approach your scary research supervisor about inconveniently changing the direction of your project at his dismay. They give you the confidence to admit to yourself that a change of career and country you live in is OK. They give you the confidence to take an abeyance from a class that's supposedly so important and linked to your student visa so that you can start writing a blog on socially contentious topics.

Honestly, they give you the confidence to just live out your life however the fuck you want to live out your life.

Confidence is something that oscillates above and below a baseline. The summation of your approaches will make you much more direct, forward, and non-needy in the long run, as well as better equipped to tackle obstacles in life completely unrelated to women.

As I talk about in more detail in the later chapter, The Five Stages of Approach, I view repeated rejections through dating/approach as essentially akin to daily, "mini-adversities." And it is the process of overcoming repeated adversity – not a lack of it – that builds one's confidence.

This is why I'm never complacent anymore. I'm never lazy. I'm aware that the daily rejections I seek out make me a much more confident person. It doesn't mean that daily approach *must be* the only way one can achieve confidence, but it happens to be the way I've been able to grow mine.

Hooking up with girls you meet is always great, but I'd say, with respect to daily approach, what keeps me "in it" is the pellucid awareness that **one is never entitled** to always having a high confidence level, and if you strip adversity out of one's daily life, you remove the mechanism for continuous confidence augmentation.

Non-neediness and confidence are reversible. Whilst the summation of your approaches will increase your baselines with time, there are still short- and medium-term reversibility elements that entail an inadvertent return to neediness if you curtail your approaches.

My confidence has far less to do with any "positive outcomes" I've had through dating. It's all of the **rejections** I've received that compose my core and make me resilient. No one can take away the rejections I've received.

When you overcome repeated adversity, many of the quotidian frustrations, annoyances, and inconveniences in life just don't seem to matter as much anymore. In fact, you start to view them as a positive. If rejection improves confidence, then adversity and setbacks in *non-dating* life contribute to general resiliency and happiness. I talk more on this topic later in the book, but the bottom line is:

Don't be complacent with your approaches. Don't get lazy.

If you do, you will experience the repercussions and a gradual return to neediness. We are never entitled to a high confidence level. Recognize that daily, mini-adversities (i.e., rejections) are a tremendous source of confidence and resiliency. This does not mean confidence must only be derived from ongoing approach, but subjecting yourself to constant rejection is a tremendous way of getting there.

"MONEY'S IMPORTANT TO ME. I HAVE HIGH STANDARDS."

In 2017, I went to Guam for the first time for a weekend to free my head from various frustrations. On the flight back to Japan, I was sitting in an aisle seat studying kanji, and an attractive Japanese woman in her late-30s in the adjacent aisle seat looked over and said to me, "Oh you're studying kanji! That's great!" We started talking in a mix of Japanese and English.

She said she had lived in the United States for ten years teaching Japanese but had just moved back to Japan because of difficulties maintaining her US visa. She was visiting Guam because her ex-boyfriend lived there and they had been vacillating as far as whether to continue their relationship. She said it was over between them.

In case you don't know where or what Guam is, it's a tiny US territory in the Pacific. It's a huge hotspot for tourism from the Asian countries.

I was attracted to her, and because she was a Japanese teacher and in the midst of telling me she was single, this was a fortuitous encounter. After the flight, we exchanged contacts.

We went on a couple of dates together, and on the second date, she told me that because I hold a medical degree, there was no reason for me to be in Japan and that I should go work in a hospital in America. I told her I wasn't interested in that. Had that been something I wanted to do, I wouldn't have moved to Japan. I said there was a zero-percent chance I would go on to practice any form of medicine.

She seemed disappointed, but I didn't think too much of it. My impression was that she most likely viewed it similar to the way my family and some of my friends did, which was that I was throwing away my potential for doing something "worthwhile" with my life. But either way, I wasn't really interested in getting into a heavy conversation about it at that particular moment.

Mottainai is a Japanese term conveying a sense of regret about waste. If you finished med school but don't practice medicine, one might think your situation is a bit of mottainai. Fortunately I couldn't care less what anyone thinks.

We went to some yakitori place. She told me she wanted to move back to the United States. I told her I had no interest in ever living in the US again.

Yakitori is grilled (yaki) skewers of different types, all coming from chicken (tori).

While we were eating at the counter, we were chatting with the chefs in Japanese. I made light jokes, telling them that she and I were incompatible because I wanted to stay in Japan and build my language skills, while she wanted to move back to the US and use her English. In reality, that was the truth.

After that date, despite our difference in goals, I was still attracted to her and wanted to learn a bit more about her.

But she wasn't interested. I could tell through our texts she wasn't. She was "busy" the next one or two times I attempted to hang out.

I hadn't really analyzed it prior, but it sort of slowly occurred to me that even though I would text and speak to her in Japanese, she would usually text and speak back to me in English.

I decided to switch gears and started texting her exclusively in English.

I asked what about a guy turns her on. She said doctors, the army, and big muscles. She told me, once again, that I should move to the US and be a doctor.

So I texted her a photo of me in surgical scrubs from my final year of med school. After I sent her that pic, she became more interested.

In order to further discern what her thoughts and intentions were. I said, "Well you know there's no way I would date you if you're just after me for my career and money."

In reality, I don't have a lot of money, and she knew I wasn't a practicing doctor, but I said it anyway because I was curious as to what kind of response it would elicit.

She then sent me back an emoticon of an excited face with lips sealed shut.

I said, "What's that supposed to mean?"

Her response was, "Yesss, you should be a doctor. I really like that."

I decided to roll with it. I began back-pedaling and pretending that I was now slightly less conclusive about not wanting to live in the States to practice medicine. I said I actually didn't know how much longer I'd be in Japan and that the two of us should move to the States together where she can live in my "big house" while I'm a practicing surgeon (an obvious joke from my end).

She agreed to meet up again.

When we met up for our third date, I made sure to be straight from the gym, wearing a fitted shirt and my army cargo shorts, and I spoke to her the whole evening exclusively in English.

I talked up the idea of leaving Japan and going to the United States to be a rich surgeon, and she could live in my big house.

She came back to my place and slept with me.

"Yesss, let's live in a big house and speak English. I like that."

Now the thing is, I completely understand that some people have various criteria that they want met when they start dating someone, but I just couldn't get past how obvious she made it that she wasn't into me whatsoever apart from the idea that I could offer her English, US residence, a "big house," and the supposed status of being with a surgeon.

I continued rolling with her superficial prerequisites for a relationship because the bedroom aspects of our interaction were good, and I felt that if she began generating an emotional connection for me then she would loosen up and not ultimately care about those things anymore.

Because she was in her late-30s, I didn't want to waste her time, so after sleeping with her a few times, when we were out at dinner one night, I asked if she wanted children.

She told me, *"I'm desperate. I really want children but don't have much time left. If my conditions aren't met, I don't want them though."*

I made an obvious, over-the-top joke and said, "If what conditions aren't met? You have to marry a rich doctor in the United States, where you can live in a big house, have a nice car, and speak English?"

She then smiled in such a way that I could see, with unequivocal lucidity, that she was serious, and said:

"Money's important to me. I have high standards."

Here you had this woman, in her late-30s and still single, talking about how she was "desperate" to have kids, yet meanwhile she wouldn't ever have any because she was too caught up in her own superficial criteria of what she believed were "high standards."

She refused to be with someone who didn't fulfill her requirements for money and career, probably to satisfy her perception of ideal biologic support, but in reality, it was actually to her biologic *detriment*. If she couldn't have a rich family, she wasn't going to have one at all.

By all means, no one is to judge what dating criteria are genuinely necessary for any one person except for that person him or herself, so my dislike and/or disagreement for her conditions and values was, truthfully, not relevant.

She was lower status in my eyes for believing money and career were somehow so integral to "high standards." Those were the two biggest things I had abdicated by moving to Japan, as I didn't see them as important in life, so I viewed her outlook on existence as completely devoid of depth.

The extent to which I viewed her as unattractive for thinking those things were important was the same degree to which she found me unattractive following our second date, when I told her I had no interest in those things.

I didn't blame her for her way of thinking. I asked her general questions about her parents and could gauge they had likely imbued those values into her as important. They believed that for their daughter to be "happy," she needed to have that type of life. And her parents had probably received that message from their own parents. So the chain continued.

After all, my family is the exact same way. The difference is I broke the chain. My family still doesn't get it, and probably never will. I've stopped caring.

After that night, she began discussing her thoughts as far as us taking vacations together across Japan. I had no interest.

When I thought of her, the only thing that came into my mind was her smile, followed by, "Money's important to me. I have high standards."

So how did I start pushing her away? By just being myself and speaking the complete truth.

I started texting her in Japanese telling her that I was stressed out because I really wanted to improve my communication skills but didn't get as much practice as I wanted. She told me it wasn't a big deal and not to worry about it. But I told her it was important to me and that I really wanted to improve my Japanese. I also told her I wanted to stay in Japan longer and didn't want to leave before hitting proficiency.

She was basically like, "そっか, or sokka," which means "really…" or "I see…"

"そっか… *I'm not interested in your goals.*"

She wasn't interested in my goals. She didn't care that I had aspirations to learn Japanese. She saw my interests as antagonistic to her own. As far as she was concerned, the only thing my words meant to her was: "I'm not going to be your English-speaking, rich doctor who will buy you a large house to live in." I was aware what I was saying was a turn-off to her. I didn't care.

A short time later, she said she needed an umbrella she had forgotten at my place because it was actually her sister's.

She said I could bring it to her in the city.

Now I knew right away she didn't plan on coming back to my place after meeting up, because if she had been planning to, why in the world would she inconvenience me into bringing the umbrella out to the city. She could easily retrieve it from my place after coming back with me.

I definitely wasn't going to be her umbrella delivery guy.

Although I wasn't interested in her anymore, I thought it wouldn't be the end of the world to sleep with her one last time. I told her she could get it at my place.

She texted saying she'd be arriving in 45 minutes at my train stop. *She told me to bring the umbrella with me to the station.*

Despite her text, my plan was to "forget" the umbrella at my place so that the two of us could walk back there together.

She then texted me a few minutes before she arrived, saying once again, "I'll be there in a few minutes. Please don't forget to the bring the umbrella to the station with you."

I joked with her and replied, "Wow, this must be one very important umbrella."

She said, "Yes, it's my sister's. Please don't forget to bring it to the station with you."

I was thinking (but didn't reply with), "Yes, we get it, you've made your point about wanting me to physically bring the umbrella to the station. Thank you for stating that three times just in case."

*In my mind, our interaction wasn't going anywhere anyway, but I resented that she too now felt that way **strictly because** I had communicated the truth about my goals. And in turn, **she now didn't want to sleep with me either, strictly for that reason.***

If I wasn't going to be the English-speaking, rich doctor in the States she was looking for, she wasn't interested in me, as a person or sexually. It was either that Mike or no Mike at all.

She texted me saying she arrived. She said, "Please bring the umbrella and come into the station."

That's the fourth time she said it.

Once again, "Yes, we get it, you're not interested in coming to my place. Thank you for the reinforcement."

I took the umbrella with me to the station. I walked down the stairs to where the electronic turnstiles were. She hadn't exited and was standing on the other side.

As I approached the turnstiles, I didn't even make eye contact with her. I just handed her the umbrella and turned around and walked away. I didn't look back.

I thought to myself, "Take your fucking umbrella."

I never heard from her again after that. The lack of subsequent communication from either of us reflected the tenuousness of the interaction. There was never anything there to begin with.

She wasn't looking for a relationship with me. She was looking for a relationship with English, a big house, a car, and the idea of an occupation.

We all have conditions we put on a relationship whether we consciously realize it or not. Maybe you wouldn't date someone who doesn't have decent teeth. Maybe you wouldn't date someone who isn't of the same religious faith as you. Regardless as to how superficial or meaningful you believe the requirements are, we all have them.

A woman doesn't have to be interested in me for any number of reasons. I'm not entitled to every woman's interest. If she's not interested in me for who I am, that's her issue, not mine.

Rarely in life will you encounter a woman who swings between on and off states so drastically based merely on the aspirations you communicate.

With all of the women I've courted and dated, I write about this example because it stands out to me as probably one of the most clear-cut, conspicuous ones of when I had to stop seeing a girl because of how superficial I perceived her to be. In addition (and as I already said), I probably resented her for not actually liking me as a person, despite the fact that she had hung out with me several times and had a chance to get to know me.

If you meet a woman where you feel her conditions for the relationship rely on you being someone other than yourself, she's not someone you should date.

She can take her umbrella and vanish forever.

HANDLING PEOPLE WHO ARE UNRECEPTIVE

It was late-December 2017. I had just landed in Athens. The first thing I did was buy a small chocolate pastry and full cream milk. I then boarded an hour-long bus to Piraeus port in order to catch an overnight ferry to a small island called Amorgos.

Amorgos is a Greek island about 8 hours by ferry from Athens.

I wasn't 100% sure which stop to get off at, but saw the final one was called "Piraeus gate E1," so decided to get off there.

It turns out I had gone too far and had to walk about 25 minutes back around the port in order to get to E7, which was where my ferry would be leaving from. I had no qualms about doing a little cardio, considering I had just spent 17 hours in the air flying from Osaka, Japan, which is where I live.

However, the walk quickly turned into an escapade of me eating. I had about 3 hours to spare, and since I was in Greece, it would have been asinine to not eat as much authentic food as I could.

As I was standing and eating a sandwich at a table out in front of a store, I noticed a slightly heavy blonde girl in my periphery engaging in short exchanges with passersby, clearly selling something.

When I first saw her, she didn't see me. But I was thinking, "Please don't even come over here."

That is, I was just in a "state." *I was unreceptive.*

She walked over to me and said hi. She immediately put out her hand for me to shake it. I didn't reciprocate the gesture because I was eating and didn't need her microbes.

She asked my name, then immediately threw a small box of perfume down on the table and asked if I wanted to buy it.

I replied, "I'm a guy. I'm not really into that sort of thing."

Truth is, I wear cologne, but I just wasn't interested in buying anything.

I asked her name.

She then asked my name again.

I looked at her and said, "How old are you?" She said 22.

She looked slightly aged, with mildly visible nasolabial creases. I thought she may have been a smoker for that reason. She struck me as someone who probably had the potential to be cute had she taken better care of herself, but instead came across slightly desperate, using the minimal level of fleeting attractiveness she had to try to generate street sales.

I told her I'm 30. She didn't respond to me saying my age apart from asking once again whether I wanted to buy the perfume.

I told her the only money I had was for a boat ticket and food. I looked and saw she was wearing a ring on her left ring finger. I asked why she was married at 22.

She said she wasn't married. She showed me the ring more closely. It looked like a 5-dollar piece of junk you'd buy at a teens jewelry shop.

I had already made it clear I wasn't interested in her perfume. So if she insisted on continuing to hover next to me while I was eating, I was willing to make genuine conversation insofar as it was about something else.

She didn't ask why I was in Greece or what I thought about it. There was no attempt from her to understand who I was or why I was there. She remained exclusively fixated on the perfume she was trying to sell.

So instead, *I* attempted to generate a little context and rapport.

My mind was free to do as such because I didn't need anything from the interaction. I wasn't trying to get sex or money from her. I was just engaging in a very short conversation while eating to maybe learn a little about someone. That was it.

I began by saying I live in Japan and was only in Greece for three days. To that, she responded by asking if there was someone in Japan I wanted to buy perfume for.

As I was talking to her, I could see her attention drifting. She eyeballed a Chinese guy walking by, probably wondering if he was a potential sale instead. She knew I wasn't going to buy her perfume, and in turn, she was losing interest in the conversation.

In reality, I didn't blame her. If I wasn't going to buy what she was trying to sell, then why would she want to waste any additional time talking to me. There's nothing wrong with losing interest in a conversation. She had the right to lose interest in talking to me.

I saw it as similar to when I meet women who sometimes talk about their husbands or boyfriends, where if there's no avenue for pursuit, I lose interest. The act of me leaving saves everyone time.

In other words, when the direction of an interaction doesn't necessarily align with what we want, *i.e., with our self-focus,* then our interest starts to wane.

The only difference is I truly don't view dating/meeting people as any kind of sale. You never *need* anyone you meet, nor do you need to sell/qualify yourself to anyone. It's when you *try to sell because you're so fixated on what you want* that you lose. This girl was showing her *need* for me to buy this perfume from her. That's where she was failing.

She carried the mindset that she really needed my money. Sure, she was trying to generate an income, but integrity has to supersede that. A more effective and healthier mindset from her could have been, "I want to make some money here, but I don't *need* any one particular sale. If he's not interested, he's not interested, and that's the end of it; I'll find someone who is."

And I recognize it might not be the easiest thing to just flip on a "non-needy switch." However I would say the crux of how someone in her position could transition to a non-needy state would be to acknowledge that most people are *not* going to be interested in what you are selling no matter what it is, *nor are you entitled* to make a sale most of the time. By internalizing that, you'll never try to force your interactions and will come across (and be) a lot more genuine.

Like with approaching women, where the majority of interactions result in rejection no matter who you are or what you do or say, it is therefore an **expectation** that the vast majority of people will simply not be interested in any product you will ever sell. Doesn't matter what it is. And for that reason, walk immediately if they're not keen. There are plenty of other people out there who might be neutral or receptive. With *these* people, invest your time and effort.

Interesting how I have zero experience in sales and yet I can say with conviction that, because of my approach experience, the time you save by not forcing interactions with people who are unreceptive you can instead use to strengthen rapport, and forge positive outcomes with, people who are neutral or receptive.

In other words, don't waste your time with people who are unreceptive. Be efficient and move on quickly. Rather than spreading yourself thin and desperate across all of your interactions, by using the same amount of time, you can invest more efficaciously in the select interactions that actually matter.

If you've ever seen the movie *Boiler Room* (a movie about a fraudulent brokerage firm selling fake stock), there's a scene where Ben Affleck says:

"There is no such thing as a no-sale call. A sale is made on every call you make. Either you sell the client some stock, or he sells you on a reason he can't. Either way, a sale is made; the only question is, who's gonna close? You or him?"

Yeah, quotes/scenes like that are awesome. But in real life, I would say the notion that you need to make a sale on every person (i.e., try to force those who are unreceptive into being receptive), *actually reflects lack of other options and a scarcity of competition for you.*

An important question is, "Why do you feel the need to try to sell to a client who isn't interested. Doesn't your business do enough sales otherwise?" So whether it's dating or sales, anyone trying to fight against someone else's unreceptiveness emanates a *lack of other options.*

And I'm not talking about people who are neutral and are potentially persuadable. I'm talking about people who are actually unreceptive and uninterested.

When I am meeting new people, why would I waste my time with anyone who is unreceptive toward me. What would that say about my integrity. If it's money or dating, who cares? It's when you feel you actually **need** something from someone that you try to force people who are unreceptive into being receptive.

In the world of dating, it means you don't have other options, or it means you *don't think you could get* other options. In terms of sales, it says you are desperate for money, or it says *you don't think you could get* sales from other people. Otherwise, there would be no reason to bother with those who are unreceptive.

Random, but ever been to Mexico? Some of the merchants there will actually chase you down the street trying to sell you stuff. The idea is to feel bad for them so that you'll buy something. It can be cute/humorous, but it's also sad. If they actually had real options/other people buying, do you think they'd even bother?

You might think pertinacity in dating or sales is a good thing. It's not. People who engage in such behavior actually suck at what they do, which is why they have those pursuit mechanisms in the first place. The people who are truly the best at what they do never have to force anything.

If you feel the need to sell no matter what, then it means you aren't able to accept the idea of rejection. And if you can't accept the idea of rejection, it says you think you *need and are entitled to* every single person's business. And the problem with a sense of entitlement is that it always results in *self-focused thinking and behaviors*, because one's primary aim then becomes *obtaining for him or herself* what he or she feels entitled to.

In other words, a sense of entitlement breeds a sense of requirement. And if we hold requirements, we engage in circular, self-focused behaviors in order to satisfy whatever it is we think we need.

With dating, it is the inability for the vast majority of guys to accept rejection as a normal part of meeting people that reinforces their neediness and leads to them changing their behavior in their interactions. That is, they have a *requirement* to not be rejected, and they'll do whatever they can to avoid it, including putting on façades, or just avoiding new people altogether.

It's when you say, "I'm going to get rejected way more than I'll be accepted," that you don't feel the need to change who you are or force any interaction, and as a result, that actually *increases* the chance that subsequent interactions will pan out favorably.

If an entitlement to lack of rejection results in self-focused behavior, then more genuine behavior must be generated by a mindset that is accepting and tolerant of rejection.

It is the understanding that rejection is normal which allows us to approach our interactions in a direct, honest, and non-needy manner.

Similarly, moving toward generating a little context and rapport goes a long way toward showing the person you're talking to that you're not just about yourself.

Had the girl at the port approached me from a non-needy mindset, she would have left immediately when she could see I wasn't interested. She wouldn't have lingered. And even if she had misinterpreted me as being neutral or receptive, it would have been helpful had she attempted to establish a little rapport.

If I were to convert the way I'd say hi to a woman into how this girl tried to sell me perfume, I would not have walked up and thrown the perfume in anyone's face, but instead would have said upfront, "Hi, I'm Michael. I'm selling perfume and wanted to say hi."

If the potential customer said, "Hi, sorry, not interested," I would leave immediately, as this girl should have done with me.

If you don't *need* my sale, then why are you talking to an unreceptive customer. There are plenty of people out there. Don't feel the *need* to try to overturn anyone who tells you flat-out that he or she isn't interested.

Same as with approach, if a woman tells you she's not interested, you just leave. It's pretty simple.

*This is less about any one particular interaction and much more about the **mindset** you carry. People can smell how needy another person is.*

If you carry the mindset that you *need* something from someone, he or she will be able to sense that and it's a turn off. I would imagine that the ideal mindset is being aware that we'd be fortunate for someone's time and conversation, but if he or she isn't interested, we're okay with that and can simply walk.

Being needy with one customer decreases your chances of making a sale with the *next* one because the momentum of your behavior and attitude is carried through. The same is true with girls you approach. Needy/indirect approaches foster subsequent ones that are also needy and indirect.

If you feel entitled to every girl's interest in you, then you'll engage in needy behaviors to avoid rejection.

Any time I say hi to a girl, I always 100% wing my conversations and genuinely attempt to learn a little about her. It's not a mystery as to why I'm there. She knows I think she's attractive because I've told her so (see chapter: The direct approach).

It is the genuine, no-bullshit attempt to actually learn a bit about the person you're talking to that is the outward manifestation of your non-neediness.

Needy tactics might occasionally win you an additional sale/date or two, but they will, over the long-run, **actually lose you more than they will win you.**

So that's a short story about one of my experiences in Greece. My main driving point for this essay is: Not being needy in your interactions goes a long way toward achieving positive results.

If you carry an abundance mindset that you don't *need* any one dating prospect, that in turn will help you achieve greater efficacy in regard to the outcomes you're looking for.

Walking away from girls who are unreceptive will free up your time to approach others. It also saves you mental energy so that you can double-down on building rapport with, and learning about, those who are neutral/more receptive.

THE SERIAL COMMITTER

"I love you. But in 3-4 years, we'll see."

This isn't particularly a life-changing essay as much as it is a random mention of something I'll refer to as the ***serial committer.***

The serial committer is *usually, but not always,* a female who jumps from relationship to relationship because of an inability to be single.

This inability to be single stems from a lack of autonomy, or the state of having emotional independence, where one doesn't rely on anyone else for mental stability and buttressing.

The serial committer can't quite pinpoint to you when she was last single. Or if she was single at some stage, it was an "accident," because when she tried to hop to her subsequent relationship, it didn't quite work out for her, or there was an unexpected, transient perturbation of some kind.

If you ever have a conversation with a serial committer and ask her when she was last single, she'll almost always get defensive about it, and she'll enthusiastically use any prior accidental gaps as "proof" that she doesn't just hop between relationships.

Serial committers tend to average 3-4 years per relationship. When they start getting bored, they demonstrate roughly a 6-month **transition zone** where they'll begin dating another guy simultaneously in some capacity. They won't admit that they're cheating on their boyfriend and will justify the break in commitment in some way, but the co-dating transition period always exists.

This transition zone is also essentially a "trial period," where the girl tests out guy #2 and assesses the probability that he will commit if she terminates her relationship with guy #1. In other words, she wants to be very sure guy #2 is definitely on board before ending things with guy #1. If he's not definitely on board, she absolutely will not terminate the relationship with guy #1, and all guy #2's ambivalence serves to do is indirectly protract the time guy #1 is strung along.

In essence, the girl abdicates her decision-making when it comes to her relationships. Any subsequent guy willing to commit to her – his mere willingness to commit alone, as the guy himself is interchangeable – functions as the proxy that is the on/off switch for her choice to jettison guy #1.

Her decisions are passive *and* there is no active decision-maker either; the serial committer uses her need for emotional buttressing as the sole driving force for relationship change. Guy #1 may support her emotions just fine, but her concurrent desire to pursue infatuation pushes her into recurrent states of seeking a second guy to replace the first.

The more serious the relationship supposedly is, the longer the transition zone will be. For instance, if the serial committer wants to end a marriage, she might require a longer time period to transition because a divorce would be a *really, really* big deal.

The notion of a transition zone while being **married** is a difficult and interesting task for the serial committer because of the obvious social stigma against marital affairs. If she's lucky, the beta husband she has might acquiesce unknowingly to an "open marriage" of some kind, when in reality the girl is relieved that she now has an excuse for the initiation of a transition zone.

Give an inch and they take a mile. There's no such thing as an open marriage from a female's end. What that concept is really synonymous with is: "Let me start shopping around for someone else. Once I find a second guy willing to commit, and I'm 100% confident I can transition without perturbation, I'll file for divorce, but for the time being, I couldn't bear being single, or better yet, trying to fight through an actual marriage, so just agree to my terms."

There can never not be a transition zone because the serial committer is unable to end a current relationship and bear the uncertainty of what being newly single, and not having someone "there for her," might actually entail. If someone isn't there for her, the serial committer is all of a sudden in a state of emotional turmoil.

This means, for example, that if she has just ended a transition zone and is now freshly with a new guy, she will drop all standards in terms of this new guy even if she suddenly/unexpectedly realizes she made a big mistake.

In other words, if she just finished a transition to guy #2 but then makes a discovery that he's a druggy or alcoholic, for instance, or perhaps if he demonstrates an acute display of gross immaturity (e.g., shouting abruptly at her in public, or leaving her alone on the street at night following an argument), **she will drop all standards she supposedly has because her need for emotional buttressing is superseded by nothing else.**

The situation she's posed with is:

- Maintain supposed standards, but reluctantly return to a state of being single. Or,

- Find an excuse to justify the new guy's behavior (i.e., dropping standards) in order to ensure there's no period of being single. This option reveals that prior supposed standards were just a facade.

The more serious a relationship supposedly is, the longer the transition zone will be, and the lower the standards the girl will tolerate if she's already severed her prior relationship and is aware she can't bear testing out being single.

Guys can absolutely be serial committers as well, but the vast, vast majority of them have a tendency to be this way for *sexual reasons*. Girls tend to engage in this pattern for *emotional reasons*.

That is, a guy who lacks confidence and feels he can't meet new partners might be overly apprehensive about ending a relationship he's not happy in if that entails losing out on consistent sex.

Most guys will do anything they can to *merely maintain consistent sex*, even if that means abdicating their integrity as an actual guy in their relationship. This is why most guys are always trying to please their female partners, making sure they're happy at all times.

Women who are able to control guys in their relationships achieve this by controlling the frequency of sex. Beta males often won't stand their ground because doing so might result in the woman leaving. And god forbid she leaves, because if she does, he might be left without sex, and he doesn't know how long it will be before he can get it again.

Men are, more often than women, able to be single from an emotional standpoint. You can get all disgruntled and protest that men and women are exactly the same, but they're not: men are more likely to stay committed for sexual reasons; women are more likely to stay committed for emotional reasons. My evidence in life? Being an informal dating couch for tons of guys, and my simple observations and conversations with respect to tons of women and their interactions.

My advice to guys who fear ending a relationship for sexual reasons: absorb my content and realize you can get any woman you want. If you're afraid to be single for emotional reasons, your various options are:

Talking to your partner. It is possible you can improve your relationship through mere communication. Relationships fluctuate. No matter whom you're with, you will *always* go through times when you *don't* want to be with that person. So first execute the mentality that you really can make things work if you want, and you'll be stronger if you can traverse whatever perceived low-points you enter.

Going cold turkey. If you want to end your relationship, try going cold turkey, and literally accept a withdrawal phase of "Omg I'm single and this is what it feels like. Wow, those are trees; that's the sky; that's a guy on a bicycle passing by." Ya know, just feel out life, walking down the street as a single person. It might be an interesting experience for you. Try meeting new people.

Talk to friends, or even a psychologist. No matter what relationship you're in, you'll always go through periods in which you lose interest and attraction for your partner; that's called normal fluctuation. Whether you choose to stick it out is up to you.

So that's it for this short essay on the serial committer. If you know a chick who falls into this category, maybe you can go up to her and be like, "Hey I'm reading this dude's book and he fucking describes you to a T."

(She'll like that. Yeah…)

HOW TO COMMUNICATE YOUR HIGH LEVEL OF STATUS

Toward the end of 2016, I was at a cafe here in Japan and saw an attractive half-Brazilian-half-Japanese-appearing girl, likely mid-20s, so I decided to walk over and start talking to her.

When I sat down across from her, I introduced myself in Japanese.

She didn't even look up. And she definitely heard me.

That's right, she ignored me completely. Nice.

Because of my level of experience, I didn't even flinch or change my facial expression in this setting. I just calmly and quietly stood up from my seat. End of interaction.

As I was standing up, I saw another attractive girl at a different table. In the direct line of sight of the first girl, I walked over just seconds later and sat down across from this second girl. I introduced myself the same way.

She was doing homework of some kind but looked up and started chatting with me anyway. She was 30 and from Seoul, Korea. She was in Japan on a student visa, attending a Japanese language school.

At this stage, I had only been in Japan about 5 months, and her Japanese was far ahead of mine. We carried the conversation in probably 80/20 Japanese/English.

As I was speaking with her over the course of the first few minutes or so, two thoughts crossed my mind:

1) She didn't seem like she wanted to talk to me at that moment. My perception was that she was actually intent on getting her homework done, and although she was being friendly, she didn't have a desire to continue the conversation much longer. (And just for the record, this should **never** be a reason not to say hi to someone – i.e., not wanting to "disturb" her is *never* an acceptable excuse to not approach.)

2) Truthfully, I just found her a bit boring and stiff. It was nothing negative, but one of those situations where after the first few minutes of meeting her, I just wasn't moved by the conversation at all.

So the combination of finding her boring + sensing that she wanted to get back to her homework, after about five minutes of chat, I lost interest and just calmly said, "Ok, well anyway, it was nice to meet you." And then I got up and returned to my table probably about 15 feet away from hers.

There was no real deep analysis of any kind. As far as I was concerned, I was back to working on my homework as well, and I didn't plan on saying bye to her at any stage, or even getting her KakaoTalk for that matter. (KakaoTalk is a messaging app used by Koreans)

Maybe about two hours later, she got up to leave. She looked over at me, then walked over and sat down in front of me. We talked for another hour or so.

At this point we exchanged KakaoTalks. It was just a natural and friendly way to close out the conversation.

Bottom line was: she was physically attractive but I thought she was slightly boring.

This early, however, I didn't really know her, so decided I was open to meeting her again.

Probably about a week and a half later, we met up at the same cafe. She brought me tea. I was surprised by the gesture, but didn't make too much of it.

Once again, I wasn't really interested. She was a bit *too well-dressed and classy* for me. I could tell her long coat was a high-quality wool that probably cost at least $500.

She looked nice, but I'm the kind of guy who prefers beer over wine, and hostels to hotels. I tell women I'm not classy. It's true.

Apparently her father owned some big company in Korea. They had a lot of money and she was working as an executive assistant to him. She was in Japan solidifying her language skills because they had a big Japanese clientele. She was very career-driven.

In contrast, here I was with my skateboard and wearing a bandana. I was like, "Correct, I finished med school but abdicated the career in order to move to Japan, bum around, and just eat and drink stuff. And no, I have no idea what I'll be doing with my life."

My point being: I just didn't feel like her type at all. And likewise, she wasn't my type either.

At the end of the date, I tried kissing her anyway.

She resisted, but I could tell this made her more interested in me.

The next time we hung out, I told her what I was thinking when we first met. I said I thought she was slightly boring and that she seemed too busy to talk to me. For those reasons, I had lost interest and returned to my table.

And even now, on this third meeting, I still wasn't really interested in her. So I told her that. I wasn't playing games with her.

There's nothing that leads to more natural behavior than living/speaking the truth.

I said, "Plus, we haven't even had sex yet. So of course I don't feel anything for you."

That was probably my flirtatious way of telling her that although I wasn't moved by her personality per se, I thought she was physically attractive.

Then we had a bit of a discussion about how sex relates to emotions. I told her that a relationship shouldn't be dependent on sex, or any feelings generated through it, but that I thought sex is important to relationships nevertheless. I said I would never consider a relationship with someone I haven't had sex with.

After this third encounter, I'm not sure why I continued meeting up with her. I think it was because I didn't mind practicing Japanese with her. In addition, if she finally ended up coming back with me, I definitely wasn't opposed to fucking her.

The next (fourth) time we hung out, she told me she liked me because she could tell I wasn't interested in her.

She said guys always threw themselves at her in Korea but that she always rejected them.

I asked her if she thought she was pretty. She said yes.

I said, "So in Korea, would you say you're considered attractive?" She said yes.

I said, "How do you know?" She was like, "Because people always tells me I am."

She went on to say that had I met her in Korea, she probably wouldn't have been receptive toward me. She said she was more willing to branch out and meet new people because she was abroad in Japan, but that in Korea she was typically more closed off.

It was weird. I had an awareness she was very physically attractive, but I just wasn't moved by her whatsoever. From an emotional and personality standpoint, she was incredibly plain and vanilla to me.

She came back to my place and we went to third base but didn't have sex (Yes, I know, I'm 100% a 7th grader for writing that sentence, but you'll see where this leads).

Because she didn't want to have sex, I lost even more interest in the interaction. She obviously had that right to not want to, but my feeling was, "If you're going to come back to my place and not be interested enough in me to have sex, then I'm not interested either."

In other words, why would I be interested in someone who didn't have a desire to have sex with me when she had the chance? I don't waste my time with people who are lukewarm toward me.

At this stage, she was due to return to Korea in about a month's time.

She talked about potentially extending her visa in Japan if I wanted to spend more time with her. I told her I didn't think that was a good idea, but that if, independent of me, she wanted to extend, that was her prerogative.

Two weeks later (and two weeks before she left for Korea), we had tentatively floated the idea of meeting up for dinner. It was nothing set in stone. I didn't have much interest, so I just let the time pass without confirming with her.

About a half hour before the tentative meeting time, she messaged me on KakaoTalk asking if we were still meeting up. I wrote back:

会えない。漢字を勉強してるから. *"I can't meet. Because I'm studying kanji."*

Now it's a little hard to explain because the nuance transferred over in Japanese is not the same as in English, but the rejection I issued was completely ridiculous.

For one, the vast majority of people who study Japanese hate kanji because of how hard it is (except for me; I like it). So my message to her came across as: "I'd rather spend my time doing something most people loathe as opposed to hanging out with you."

Second, the casual grammar I used comes off extremely cavalier in Japanese, as if she were a level-zero on my priority list (which she was).

She didn't respond to my text immediately.

About a week later, while I was studying at another cafe, she texted asking if we could talk. I said sure.

When she came to see me, she was blushing and somewhat emotionally charged. She asked why I didn't want to meet up with her a week earlier.

I told her it was because I had very little interest in her and that I found studying kanji more exciting than talking to her.

I was serious. I didn't care if I came off like a complete jackass. I was speaking my truth. And the truth is liberating. Why would I censor my thoughts and lie? She had the right to walk away if she didn't like what I was saying. But she didn't. She stayed by me.

We chatted for maybe a half hour, then she left.

She went back to Korea.

Now we know life is all about timing. Well that certainly applies to what happened next.

Probably about two months later, I randomly decided I wanted to go to Seoul for the weekend by myself. So I booked a flight on a Thursday. She hadn't even crossed my mind. I was literally just in the mindset of: "Yeah, I'm gonna go to Seoul this weekend cuz I haven't been there before. Coolz."

The next day, on Friday, she randomly texted me out of the blue asking why I had gone so long without messaging her. I told her I thought we weren't going to speak again.

Then I mentioned that, interestingly enough, I was actually on my way to Seoul, and that I'd be staying the weekend.

She asked why I was coming to Seoul.

I said I just wanted to go.

She asked if I wanted to see her.

I didn't really answer her question but told her I wouldn't mind meeting up with her. It was 100% true that I hadn't booked the flight to Seoul to see her. In addition, I hadn't slept with her prior anyway, so I couldn't have cared less about whether I'd be meeting up with her or not.

I think I had said something along the lines of, "Well I suppose it wouldn't be the end of the world seeing you again."

So I met up with her on the Friday and she showed me around to some really good Korean BBQ. It was a great time.

At around midnight, we were out on the street in front of a convenience store and were approached by a Canadian-Korean girl asking for directions. When she said hi to us, she said to my Korean date, "Excuse me, can you help me with directions to…wow, you're really pretty."

"I told you. People think I'm really pretty."

I had already booked a hostel for the weekend for probably $18 USD/night. I was staying on a bunk bed in one of the shared rooms. She walked me to the hostel and said she couldn't come in. I told her to book us a hotel for the next (Saturday) night. She did.

I spent the next day walking around with her seeing temples and eating good food. She took me to some restaurant her family frequented in a distal part of town. Like the night before, it was an awesome time.

When we got to the hotel that night, she showed me some condoms she had purchased and told me, "I have a secret to tell you."

I was like, "Alright…"

She said she actually hadn't had sex before and that I'd be her first. She said she wanted me to be her first because I was different from other guys she had met.

She said she liked that I wasn't overly crazy about her.

She was sick of other guys always throwing themselves at her. She said she didn't know why I didn't like her, but that she liked me, and that was good enough for her.

She also said that her parents were aware she hadn't had sex before, and that she had told them that many times. She had explained to them she just hadn't met the right person yet. Her parents told her something like, "It's okay ya know…to just…try sex out…it doesn't have to be with a 'one and only' or anything like that." But she had insisted to them that she was going to hold out anyway.

It occurred to me she had repeatedly told her parents she was abstaining in an attempt to have her value increased in their eyes, as though she was satisfying and upholding an arbitrary social standard and expectation.

In other words, by holding out until she was 30, and by insisting to her parents that that's what she wanted, she felt she was "proving" somehow that she was a crown jewel and of high value.

Right or wrong, that's just what I perceived based on the hotel room conversation with her.

This girl placed her virginity on such a high pedestal, as if it had so much meaning. And meanwhile, here she was *telling me she wanted me to be her first because I wasn't crazy about her.*

I mean, think about that for a second.

You could follow a lazy line of argument that she was of weak character and just willing to give herself to someone who didn't like her back because she lacked confidence and self-esteem. (Which I don't believe to be honest. I actually think she had very high confidence and self-esteem. Truly.).

Or,

You could posit that she perceived me as very high value because:

I didn't need her and was always honest with her. I didn't change my behavior because of her. All other guys she had ever come across changed their behavior for her.

It's the act of not changing your behavior for a woman, in combination with being forward and confident, that communicates to her your high level of status.

Yeah, she was pretty, and I was very aware of it, but I just didn't really care. Her personality just didn't really do it for me. I don't know what to say.

That weekend was a good experience with her, however I went back to Osaka thinking I probably wouldn't see her again.

Maybe two months later, she came to visit me in Japan. She asked if she could stay the weekend at my place. I acquiesced.

I would say one of the major areas of personality clash we had is that we were both very dominant people. I learned this especially on this visit.

She was flying out on Sunday evening and we were getting lunch beforehand. The weekend had progressed up until this point somewhat uneventfully.

I went to my favorite restaurant with her and ordered us both a lunch special. I said in Japanese, "Today's curry is good. Two please."

Now what I'm about to talk about is going to sound extremely fucked up to a lot of people, but I don't really care. So handle it.

After I ordered, she immediately intercepted my request and said, "いいえ、鶏肉カレーをください," which means, "No, I'll have the chicken curry."

She didn't notice my reaction because I was fairly good at concealing it, but I was so turned off I could barely talk to her. I got up to go to the bathroom.

After the meal, we went back to my place. I told her that today was going to be the last time we'd see each other. I said I felt our personalities were too dominant for each other, and I preferred a woman who's a little softer and more submissive.

She asked me to elaborate.

I told her she was a great person, and that it was nothing negative whatsoever, but that she'd probably pair much better with a Korean guy who didn't mind how strong her personality was.

I told her it was a huge turnoff for me that she negated my lunch order and asked for the chicken curry.

She was essentially like, "You've got to be kidding me. You think that's a big deal?"

I said, "It's not just about the lunch order in isolation. That type of thing translates over into a spectrum of other scenarios."

She replied, "So you don't want to see me anymore because I ordered the chicken curry?"

And I said, [raising an eyebrow]:

"Look…you shouldn't have ordered the chicken curry."

She was dumbfounded. Although I said it somewhat kiddingly, my message was nevertheless serious.

She didn't have to leave for the airport for at least another four hours, but she asked if I wanted her to leave now. **I said yes.**

She asked again, "Wait, you want me to leave?"

I closed my eyes this second time and said yes. I didn't want to be rude to her, but it was true. I didn't want her there. And if anything, it was a *good* thing that she had a clear, no-bullshit message as to how I felt.

She left. And I felt *relieved.* Weird, I know. But I was just glad she was gone. And that was the end of our interaction.

We texted a few times over the following six months or so, but I never saw her again.

Here I was, as the guy she had chosen above all others to give her virginity to, and the interaction ultimately culminated and ended when I told her to leave because she ordered the chicken curry.

I mean what the fuck is that.

Some general reflection:

Women in society (in Korea, Western countries, wherever) are often inculcated with the belief that a reluctance to engage in sexual activity coincides with greater social value or status.

This is the typical, "I can't sleep with you on the first date cuz I don't wanna be a slut" mentality. In reality, nobody cares. This girl missed out on sex her entire 20s because she pandered to her parents' judgment.

I'm flattered. But doesn't reality hit you like a fucking bombshell sometimes.

The other thing is: two genuinely dominant personalities brought together are set up for a clash. This isn't about being an intransigent, unremitting asshole. But sometimes it can take a variable as trivial and nonsensical as a chicken curry to realize the degree to which you're not willing to have a woman you're with be the decision-maker in the relationship.

I'm not opposed to the broad generality of a woman making decisions. That's not what I'm saying. I'm more than okay with a woman making her own decisions and being autonomous. I'm talking about the degree to which a man is willing to tolerate a woman *overriding or disagreeing with his decisions. That's totally different.*

You actually need to have a fucking backbone as a man. Never be with a woman who overrides your decisions.

I would probably say challenges to this power dynamic are the one thing that, above all else, allows me to effortlessly sever an interaction without thinking twice about it.

If you make a decision and your female counterpart overrides it, you need to put her in her place and not tolerate it.

Women actually like that. They want to be like, "Oh wow, I'm actually with a confident, strong guy I can't control."

If you're a guy and disagree with me, I can guarantee you don't maintain the attraction of the women you meet. And if you're with someone now, you'll probably lose her (just think about how high divorce rates are).

If you're a gal reading this book (for whatever fucking reason) and disagree with me, ask yourself (I'm serious) if you *really want to be with a guy whose decisions **you are able to** override.*

Any time you make a decision as a guy and allow your female counterpart to override it – or if you *alter your original decision because of her simple disagreement* – she will lose respect for you.

Really understand that. Because that's really fucking important. One of the major things that will cause a woman to lose respect for you is if she is able to overpower and/or change your decisions.

And don't confuse my words here. I'm not saying you can't make mutual decisions and come to agreements on various events/matters in your life. But I am firm when I communicate the advice that, as a man, if you make a decision and a woman disagrees with you, don't let her get her way or she'll lose respect for you. And when she loses respect for you, it's hard, if not impossible, to get it back.

Take-home points:

Be forward and approach those you're interested in. Don't be afraid. If someone's not interested, calmly just leave.

Never be afraid of approaching someone who's in the direct line of sight of someone who just rejected you (e.g., at a coffee shop, etc.). In other words, if a girl rejects you, it's her issue. Let her watch you approach a second girl and regret forgoing the opportunity she had.

Have approach integrity. If someone you're talking to isn't very receptive toward you or seems boring, don't hesitate to leave. Be non-needy. And don't over-think it either. Just go with your gut.

Always speak your truth. Don't censor what you're thinking out of fear that you might offend a woman. Not only will she be *glad* you're speaking the truth, but *not* saying what's on your mind means you're changing your behavior *because of her*. And if you change your behavior because of her, you'll emit tiny nuances of neediness that she will pick up on. In other words, you create huge positive momentum for your own behavior when you just conduct yourself naturally.

In order to truly be able to not change your behavior for a woman you're interested in, you have to genuinely be willing to have her walk away because of it. And the only way to truly not care if she walks is by approaching and getting rejected a lot.

Never let a woman override or change your decisions. This is not synonymous with being an obdurate prick. You can reach mutual decisions and share constructive input, but if you *really want something and feel strongly about it, or if you make a simple decision on behalf of both of you, it should stand.* If you allow her to override or alter your decisions against your will, she'll lose attraction for you.

So yeah, that's basically all I have to say for this essay. I could continue on, but I'm content with this flow of thoughts for the time being.

WHY GUYS FEAR SAYING HI TO GIRLS

What I find interesting is that 99% of guys want to avoid rejection as much as possible, yet that in and of itself is the mindset that is inadvertently causing them to change their behavior and, by definition, not achieve optimal attractiveness.

Rejection is a necessary part of meeting women. There's no way around it.

Now this is going to sound a bit fucked up (because in a way it is), but you have to actually *want to encounter* rejection, and then *want to embrace it when it occurs.*

In other words, you can't avoid it. Ever. So your options are: either embrace it, or do everything in your power to get around it.

If you try to get around it, the result is you won't approach at all (vast majority of guys), or if you do approach, you'll change your behavior (i.e., needy facades/tactics [essentially a lot of what the past decade of "game" is premised on, and actually works against you]) or chicken out when you think the scenario carries a high risk of rejection (all in your head anyway, because you never know which girls are truly receptive or not).

So one of the first steps in becoming more confident and being able to approach is knowing that:

You will get rejected a shit-ton no matter who you are, what you look like, what you say, or what you do. Learn to like rejection.

It is merely the case that depending on how you act, the subset of *which* women who are into you changes (see chapter: The most fundamental rule of approach). Realize that every rejection you take makes you more confident and bold, which in turn makes you more forward and fearless with subsequent women you encounter.

There are times I approach women already with the presumption that the percentage-chance of a rejection is very high, but I do it anyway *because I'm very aware of the confidence points I get from the mere approach* **regardless** *as to the outcome.*

For instance, I was walking in a mall area the other day and passed an attractive Japanese girl with light blue hair. I blew my natural approach window and was aware of it. I had probably a 2-3-second span in which I could have naturally said hi to her as we were crossing paths somewhat perpendicularly, but I didn't say anything for whatever reason.

I looked back at her as she passed me and had a "damnit…" moment.

The next thought that went through my mind was that there's never a zero-sum situation with meeting new women. You either go up or down in confidence based on having approached or chickened out. It's one or the other. It's that simple.

Sure, I don't have to approach absolutely every girl I see. Of course not. But in this particular case, I actually *wanted to*, so I knew not flipping open an emergency valve and saying hi would actually decrease the probability of me having a positive interaction on the *next* approach.

So I just turned around, walked somewhat briskly back to where she was walking and introduced myself. She looked at me for about a second, then looked down at the ground and ignored me.

Cool. End of interaction. Her issue not mine.

I saw the whole thing coming actually. It was predictable. I had a good feeling it would be an instant deflection based on the crowded area I was in, but you really never know the outcome of any approach, and I've had many seemingly low-probability approaches convert, so sometimes these "guaranteed rejections" can be some of the more rewarding approaches if they do turn into conversions.

The net result of my rejection in this case:

I walked away feeling more confident. It was instant. I didn't get all butt-hurt about it. This is fairly routine for me at this point. Let's just say I embraced the rejection from before it even occurred.

As I talked about in the chapter 'The more experienced you are, the lower your percentages,' I would say **if you're being aggressive enough,** roughly 80% of the women you say hi to should reject you instantly or ultimately decline a number exchange. Some days you might go 0/10. Others might be 4/6. But either way, with respect to a long-term average, I'd say roughly 20% of women will give you their contact if you ask for it.

(As I mentioned in that chapter, here in Japan, as of April 2019, I would guess I average 20-40 approaches per day, with a typical range of 4-11 contact acquisitions. I never count my approaches, so that range is subjective, but my # of contacts is objective since I can clearly look at them afterward.)

So yes, I'm more than fine getting rejected a lot because I expect it, and that's where my confidence stems from the most I'd say. I handle my rejections really fucking well.

You might think that getting rejected incessantly makes you less confident, but **the exact opposite is true.**

Getting rejected in the **short-term** can sometimes feel like a drag, but that's normal. Some days it won't feel that way. For whatever reason, it just depends on the random mental state you occupy on a given day. It is the potential short-term drag that blockades a lot of guys from ever unraveling their approach potential.

For instance, if you are just starting off (i.e., you've never made any approaches before) and got rejected five times in a row, understandably one might think that would work against, not for, your confidence. But trust me, the rejections help you.

You have to just trust it. It's slow-building. In the very, very beginning, your adrenaline and prior insecurities will cloud your head a lot. But just know that every approach you make – *and all rejections you incur* – make you more confident. Always.

There's a large activation energy, or "hump," you have to push yourself over in the beginning, but once you start getting a few receptive responses, you'll be like, "Wow, I didn't realize it was that... uncomplicated." And you'll eventually view many of the hostile rejections you get as funny because they're almost never about you and more just a reflection of the "state" of the girl you've said hi to in that exact moment.

Some people are just fucking downers in life. Don't let that rub off onto you. The vast majority of the rejections you receive have nothing to do with you. The guy she's rejecting in a given moment is almost always completely interchangeable.

When all is said and done, at the most simplified level, any apprehension a man has with regard to meeting women comes down to fear of others' opinions and judgments, whether that be the girl he's saying hi to or the surrounding audience.

By accepting that rejection will occur no matter who you are, what you say, or what you do, that reduces (and eventually eliminates) this fear.

I'm serious. You have to actually want to get rejected. If you can own that mentality, you win, because then there's no reason *not to* approach.

I'd say audiences are the biggest imaginary barrier to approach as you gain experience. In the beginning, the biggest "fear" is the response you'll get from the actual girl you're approaching. But as time goes on, any tension you feel will be linked to the surroundings (e.g., there's people sitting around her in silence at a cafe), rather than her in isolation.

As your approach count grows, your developing confidence translates into the act of not changing your behavior for her and a realization that rejection is GOOD, not bad (see chapter, "The five stages of approach").

PLAYING THE FIELD FOREVER?

When you're a young guy, you have huge sexual potential. You have zero reason to commit early, and you shouldn't. You're only young once. What's the rush to tie yourself down? But to what extent is approaching girls potentially a "forever thing?"

I have an awareness that I'll very likely never commit sexually to one woman (see chapter: The five stages of approach). However if there were a gun to my head and I were forced to make a wild, shot-in-the-dark hypothetical, any commitment on my end would certainly never occur before 40. And probably not even before 50 either.

As a man, my belief is that you should date lots and lots of people in order to figure out what kinds of qualities you're interested in and what you're willing to tolerate in a relationship.

The luxury we have (which women don't have) is *time*. Women peak in their late-teens/early-20s; we guys peak in our mid-late-30s. That doesn't mean I take time completely for granted, but I'm aware I'm still on the way up in terms of my sexual market value (SMV).

If there's any propensity to think that I'm anti-relationship, that's only because I'm using my peak years to enjoy my sexuality and meet new personalities. What incentive do I have to commit right this second? As I said, you're only young once.

I don't think a confident male who is aware of his sexual market value should commit early. "Early" can mean whatever you want it to, but I generally think of that as sub-30. Some would even say sub-35. Once again, as men, we peak in sexual value in the mid-late-30s, so right now, at the age of 32, I'm not quite ready to cash in.

And by cashing in, that doesn't necessarily mean for the prettiest or smartest girl, or for any single characteristic in a woman – I mean settling down in general.

Most of the women I've ultimately let down have believed that *they* were the problem somehow. Truthfully, I've met amazing women who I might have entertained the idea of committing to (although still not likely) had I been decades older. It's your own timing that's often the deciding factor in things, not the actual woman.

Likewise, many women who won't commit to you when they're 23 might do so when they're 38. It's an SMV thing whether people want to accept the inconvenient truth or not.

Once again, any guy who is aware of his sexual potential has zero reason to commit early. Because what happens is, you enter into a commitment, and then you're like "Wait, what incentive do I have to miss out on tons of sexual opportunities during my peak years?"

It's guys who aren't aware of their sexual potential, or who think it's strictly tied to their physical appearances, who are the ones who strive to find the prettiest girl possible at an early age and then commit hastily.

Young guys tend to feel insecure because they've spent their whole lives until 30 having an SMV less than that of women's. Girls who tie guys down in their 20s, prior to the male peak potential, have won the sexual game. Most men lose the sexual game because they cash in far before they've hit peak potential, completely unaware of it.

In short, I'd say my confidence level pushes my sexual market value to be standard deviations higher than normal. So even if I'm past my physical prime (i.e., in my 40s), I'm confident I could still match with plenty of women in their early-20s. How do I know? Because I'm really confident. That's how I know. That's why I'm not interested in settling right now. A woman who'd be able to tie me down now would be exceptionally lucky.

A male's status is determined by his confidence level, which grows steadily with time. When you're young, you're scared of everything. Older guys have a way of cashing in for a reason. In addition, social proof and income are found to be sexually valuable in men.

Doesn't matter if a woman wins a Nobel Prize at age 44. A man would never date her because of it. Women peak early because their SMV is determined almost exclusively by their looks/fertility. However, a *guy* who wins a Nobel Prize at age 44? Yeah, that would win him plenty of young women.

How I see a relationship is a very general question, and a good one too, but for starters, I believe as guys we can establish plenty of different types of relationship patterns that don't necessarily involve commitment.

Some women are OK with lack of commitment. If you don't believe me, approach enough and you'll meet some who would rather date a man who is promiscuous, but extra-confident, over a guy she can forge monogamy with, but who's a lame beta.

What I can tell you is I'll probably – if eventually – choose a woman who is not by objective standards any particular superlative, but with whom I feel a strong emotional connection. I do not believe in any "one true love."

All of that nonsense is a societal plot to feminize men into monogamy. We grow up thinking that we're searching for "the one." In actuality, there are lots of "ones" in every fucking country around the world, waiting for you, and you'll never meet them.

There are magical "ones" for you all over the world. It all comes down to where you choose to be at a given point in your life, and whether you're forward and confident enough to actualize on your potential.

I could go to, e.g., Argentina or Iceland for the next year and meet plenty of marriageable people. I'm in Japan now, and I've met plenty here as well.

So my point is: Do not carry the mindset that there is a "one and only" waiting out there for you. It's also a needy mindset too because it inadvertently causes you to place a lot of supra-relationship or moral emphasis on an interaction, when in reality, there is a surfeit of similar interactions you could enter into around the world at any given time.

The most important thing in a relationship to me is respect.

Honesty and trust are also vital, but I'd put respect as the highest. I would imagine any relationship I'd enter into as ebbing and flowing such that there are times when I'm not interested at all in my partner, but that I *respect her too much* to cut things off. Then when we come out of whatever ebb we were in (or whichever transient one was in my head), I'd be glad I kept the relationship going.

I also would not be with a woman who is overly dominant or about herself. I like submissive women who defer most decision-making and guidance to me. Essentially, I just want to live my life and whomever I'm with is on for the ride. She's in my frame 100% or there's no relationship at all, and she'd be very aware of that.

Now I know lots of people would vehemently disagree with me here and push the whole notion of 50/50, but what I can say is we all screen for different types of people, and there's no right or wrong with respect to the types of relationships you want to create for yourself. A woman who enjoys my confidence and solidly dominant frame is the type who might not be interested in a guy who's softer. Likewise, there are tons of women out there who come across my content or meet me in person and think, "Wow, fuck that guy." So we all screen for different types of people.

In short, I'd say: A submissive woman whom I feel innate emotional connection with, whom I grow to respect highly over time, who's aware I see other people in the present but who still stands by me unconditionally, is one whom I'd keep around for the longer term.

Notice I don't say super-pretty or smart. Once again, those things aren't vital to me. I would say "pretty enough" and "smart enough" are sufficient. But I'm not chasing the superlatives.

WHEN MEETING WOMEN, THERE'S NO SUCH THING AS GETTING LUCKY

At the cafes I frequent here in Japan, I see plenty of cute baristas, many of whom I have opened and closed.

There's one attractive barista I had seen somewhat frequently during my first six months or so of living here, but for whatever reason, I had never talked to her. For one, I never felt any urgency to open/close her because I saw her working all of the time, and two, she was always working behind a wide counter with a big, hectic team, and the opportunity to isolate or get close to her never presented itself.

Either way, the point being: I inadvertently let her slip through the cracks.

And I say "slip through the cracks" because I eventually stopped seeing her at that cafe. She was gone. The incredibly long approach window that I had, and didn't act on, came to an end.

I didn't overanalyze it, but I assumed she had likely just changed part-time jobs or was a busy university student.

Maybe a month or two after I stopped seeing her at the cafe, I was walking through a busy train station and saw her pass me going the opposite direction. I could have opened her had I been aggressive but didn't. I won't make excuses. The bottom line is that I blew the approach window, and I knew it.

I realized shortly after that moment that the chance of seeing her again in a big city was extraordinarily low, so not opening her was a big mistake.

No matter how experienced you become, you will always occasionally blow approach windows.

Now not to sound like a complete and utter creeper, or needy, or just really fucking weird, but over the course of the year that followed that blown approach, she probably crossed my mind three or four times. Not because I gave a fuck about that one opportunity in particular, but because:

The opportunities you blow will stay with you as negative energy. Approaching and getting rejected is superior 100% of the time compared to a non-approach and subsequent rumination.

"I should have just said hi to her."

It's the opportunities we blow/pass up that are the only regrets we have. Sometimes you might hesitate making an approach, but after you actually do it, you **never** regret it. However we do regret – always – not saying hi to a girl when we could – and should – have.

So as I said, over a year went by since passing her in the train station, and one day I randomly skipped my Japanese class because I didn't feel like going. My tentative plan was to just skate to a random cafe to write.

As I was skating through my neighborhood and toward the city, a feeling came over me that I just wanted to approach a little before settling down into a quiet headspace.

I was essentially like, "I wanna meet some new girls today. I'm not quite ready to write just yet."

In other words, I consciously made a decision that I was going to spend a little time going out of my way to approach. I could have gone straight to the cafe to write, but I chose to create opportunities instead.

I did a little approach on street level, then ventured down into a crowded, underground passageway connecting two of the big subway stations here in Osaka.

One of the girls I approached in this passageway I chatted with for about five minutes. She ultimately declined the LINE (Japanese messaging app) exchange, and the conversation came to an abrupt end. Because of this, I can surmise that the interaction terminated probably 20-30 seconds earlier than otherwise expected.

At this exact moment, I turned around to continue approaching and immediately saw the barista from a year earlier. Wow was I glad that first chick rejected the LINE exchange.

This was literally a replay of the situation from a year ago when I blew the approach in the crowded station. Both then and now, my window to act was 2-3 seconds tops.

As soon as I saw her, I'm fairly sure my pupils dilated.

No way was I blowin' the approach this time son.

However, something to consider is: *the barista undoubtedly saw me talking to the first girl.*

When I say I immediately saw her post-rejection, I mean it, with no exaggeration. We're talking a smooth pivot as though I was ice skating, where the amount of time I took between the rejection and opening the barista was under three seconds.

I didn't care. I wasn't passing up the opportunity this time.

In other words, it was unmistakable that I was clearly hitting on a different girl just seconds earlier, but ignored any "negative impression" that may have potentially made on the barista.

In these types of situations, there's no time to over-think. If you over-think, you lose.

My options were: not open her *again* (and probably never see her again), or just open her knowing she clearly just saw me attempting to pick up a different girl.

When I started talking to her, she recognized me immediately, smiled, and was very receptive. We chatted a bit about how she used to work at that cafe I frequented. We talked for about five minutes. Then I got her LINE.

So why am I writing about this encounter? In other words, what's the point of this little story about the barista?

There's actually quite a few "mini-lessons" I could offer up here, such as the importance of acting quickly and not blowing approach windows, etc., but the main point I want to make for this essay is:

You create your own opportunities to meet women. It's up to you. You need to not fucking waste your time waiting for something magical to happen.

99% of the time, you meeting an amazing girl is not a matter of "luck." It's because *you chose to* put yourself in the right place at the right time.

Let me repeat that:

99% of the time, you meeting a great girl is a matter of *you choosing to* put yourself in the right place at the right time.

Your choice. Your active decision. Not a passive miracle.

The supposedly serendipitous encounter of me bumping into that barista in the underground passageway would never have fucking happened had I not consciously chosen to go out of my way to approach that day.

Rather than having bumped into her, I would have been drinking my coffee completely unaware that that opportunity had even been on the table as a potential outcome.

Pretty lucky how that chick I'm banging who's really hot and fun I met in a busy pedestrian terminal under a train station. Pretty lucky how the two of us crossed paths at that exact moment in time, at that exact place, in that exact way. Pretty lucky. Because while other guys were at home jerking off, I chose to go out of my way to approach, which allowed me to have that "lucky" interaction in the first place, which is how I got "lucky" bumping into her. Pretty fucking lucky wasn't I.

There's no such thing as "luck" when you meet women – 99% of the time. You create the opportunities for yourself, and you have to take responsibility for that. You have to take ownership of that.

That hot chick who just happen to be on the bus that day – pretty lucky you were to have slept with her, considering you went out of your way to talk to her in the first place. Weren't you so lucky, considering most guys would never have said hi to her, but you did.

If meeting an amazing girl means being in the right place at the right time:

You're always in the right place at the right time, as long as you put yourself there.

MAKING "IMPOSSIBLE APPROACHES"

I'm going to talk briefly about two "impossible" approaches I made today.

And just for the record, what constitutes an "impossible" approach is completely subjective and arbitrary.

You might disagree entirely and say, "Bro, those approaches you just talked about ain't hard at all. What you on about."

Yeah, I know. Trust me, I agree it ain't hard. So what I'll do is tie more of an objective guesstimate/definition to it:

By "impossible" approaches, what I mean is probably >99.9% of guys wouldn't have come close to making them because they'd be too scared.

And how do I know they'd be too scared?

Because even I felt tension making these approaches, and my daytime approach count probably comfortably clears the 15,000-level. I've done every type of approach you can (and cannot) imagine.

No matter how experienced you become, the feeling of tension when making certain approaches never fully goes away. Therefore your "skill" moving forward is about being able to use the tension to fuel you in a positive way.

Approach #1:

I left my place probably around 2:30pm (Sunday) to go get some Nepalese food.

Now the area I live in is the hood of Osaka, Japan, and probably >90% of the people are over the age of 60, so seeing an occasional young person around, let alone an attractive girl I'd consider approaching, is actually a big deal.

The Nepalese place has a lunch special that ends at 3pm, so I didn't want to waste any time getting there. However, as I was waiting to cross an intersection, I saw an extremely attractive Japanese girl, probably early-20s, about 30 feet away, standing in front of an うどん屋 (Udonya; pronounced Oo-dohn-yah; which means a place where you can get Udon noodles).

As soon as I saw her, I thought, "Wow, she's really attractive. I definitely have to approach."

So far so good. There's nothing "difficult" about that at all. So what's the big deal?"

She didn't see me approaching, but as I got to about 15 feet away, *she entered the Udonya* to have lunch.

At this point, I was immediately like, "Are you fucking serious?"

That Udonya sucks. Nor does it look appealing from the outside whatsoever. Why in the world did she want to have lunch there? Who the fuck knows. But either way, her shitty ass lunch decision killed the super-easy approach I could have made.

My second thought was: "Great, I can't approach now. Fuck that."

Essentially, I felt annoyed that I had blown the approach window by waiting perhaps five seconds too long at the intersection before skating over to her.

I could have easily said hi to her in a natural way in front of the shop, without any audience whatsoever, but now, if I wanted to approach, I had to essentially enter the shop after her and make it an obvious "Yes, I just followed you in here to hit on you"-type of play.

My options were: creeper-style approach, or no approach at all. Fabulous.

Within five seconds of her entering the shop, I paused, as though I was going to abort the approach and just skate off to the Nepalese place.

But then I decided: "Look, you never see attractive girls around here, and you definitely won't see her again. Since you've moved here, you've never seen her. If you choose not to approach right now, you'll regret it. Just fucking do it."

I entered the udonya.

She hadn't sat down yet and was still using the ticket dispensing machine to select her meal.

In Japan, many small food shops you enter will have a little machine in the front where you pay for your meal upfront by pushing a button. It then prints a ticket that you give to the clerk before you sit down.

This shop was quiet and small. There were probably five or six older men sitting down in silence, as well as the clerk, who observed me walk in the store just to hit on her.

I didn't act weird about it. I opened her in Japanese and said, "Hi, I'm Michael. I just wanted to say hi."

After I said this, she didn't come off overtly unreceptive per se. I interpreted her to be neutral but stiff.

*In these types of higher tension scenarios, if you act weird because you're paranoid of your surroundings, that will feed off onto her and make her weirded out too. You literally have to put up an electromagnetic shield to your surroundings and **not change your behavior** merely because you have an audience there.*

If you maintain your strength in high-tension encounters, the girl will sometimes mold to your frame and be MORE receptive versus if she were talking to a guy who she can tell is nervous making his own approach.

I told her I'm a Japanese language student, am from America, and have been living in Japan since summer 2016.

She said she was from Okinawa (southern part of Japan) and only in Osaka for a month. Her demeanor was still quite stiff.

Cool, I've now established that she's leaving town soon, and considering she's not very receptive toward me, I don't really care because there's limited trajectory anyway. Had I not approached though, I never would have known this. Always better to know than not.

Her responses were extremely flat and along the lines of, "Ohh, okay...okay... [nodding her head with a fake smile]"

Japanese girls who aren't interested will sometimes do this really annoying fake smile and head nod in response to what you say, rather than actually saying anything back. Sort of like:

"Hi, I'm Michael. I just wanted to say hi."

[head nod, head nod]

"I'm a Japanese language student."

[head nod, head nod]

"I came to Japan in 2016. I grew up in America."

[head nod, head nod]

It's like, "Do you have words? Are you capable of speaking?"

Some of the girls will reject foreigners by pretending they can't understand your Japanese, which is effective against you when you're first learning the language because you'll be like, "Wait, maybe she really can't understand me."

But now that I can communicate a lot better, I'll cut through their shyness by following up with clear and direct statements, using street slang. If they *still* do the head nod, I'll just leave.

With this particular approach, after about 15 seconds of talking to her, I could read she was unreceptive, so I said 頑張ってください (ganbatte kudasai; which means "good luck"), and I left.

Now I know you might be like, "Why is that approach a big deal? I could easily do that." And maybe you could. I'm not debating how incredible you might be at approach.

But either way, I'd still pin that at probably above the one in one-thousand level for "difficulty" based on the requirement for aggressiveness and audacity to enter the store in the first place, and then holding it together while calmly ignoring the surrounding audience.

*The only difficulty associated with that kind of approach is only ever in your head. Correct, there wasn't anything **actually** hard about it at all.*

But you know what? 99.9% of guys would probably have come up with an excuse or self-policed:

"Oh but that's just too weird. I can't walk in there after her. That's just not okay."

Why is that not okay?

Are there laws against you walking up and **just introducing yourself** calmly to someone: "Hi, I'm George. I just wanted to say hi."

Nope.

*I am **not** talking about making unwanted sexual advances. That is not what I'm talking about.* I'm talking about **just saying hi. That's it.** Big difference.

If after you say hi, she's not receptive, then correct, you 100% calmly and politely leave.

But even if you think your approach might come off too aggressive, the act of merely introducing yourself to someone is confident and a good thing.

Don't "self-police" against saying hi to someone as a veiled excuse for being scared. Do you have any idea how pervasive this defense mechanism is? Merely introducing yourself is perfectly acceptable. And if she's unreceptive, you just leave. It's pretty simple.

After this approach, I stepped out of the udonya and had my Nepalese food. No regrets.

Approach #2:

I arrived at a cafe to write this essay and saw another attractive Japanese girl, about 20 years old, waiting in line for the bathroom about ten feet away from me.

She was first in line and there was one other woman behind her. At first I didn't feel an overwhelming need to approach, but when the woman behind her stepped out of the way, I saw this first girl had an amazing body.

I was like, "Shit, I definitely have to say hi now."

Now this particular girl had walked up the stairs to the second floor to use the bathroom, which is where I was, so if I didn't approach her now, I'd have to go down to the first floor to approach her, probably in front of a friend or two she was with. And it's not that that would have necessarily been a problem, but I literally just wanted to write and not deal with packing up my laptop and going downstairs, etc. So this was my best chance to have a quick chat with her in isolation.

A few seconds later she stepped into the bathroom.

Then something really interesting happened:

I looked to my right and there were two Japanese guys, probably in their mid-30s, looking at her as she stepped into the bathroom. Then they looked at me. Then one guy's face got red. *Then so did mine.*

You're like, "Huh? What do you mean?"

Yeah, I know. It was a little weird. But basically the situation was:

It was obvious that all three of us guys were looking at her but half-pretending we weren't, so when this guy and I caught each other looking, we blushed. Why? I don't know. I wasn't shy about anything. But that's just what happened.

At this moment I thought, "This guy and I aren't competing for this girl right now because I can read 100% that he's chicken, so he's going to get a free mini-tutorial from me on how to do a direct and confident approach."

(Had I interpreted through his demeanor that he had been intent on approaching, I would have made sure to beat him to it by standing up immediately next to the bathroom, essentially to mark territory, but fortunately I didn't have to do that in this scenario.)

In general, the chance of *actually having to compete* with an unknown guy for a day-game cold approach is fantastically/astronomically low, but that was something, based on the two of us blushing here and now, that I had to tangibly consider.

I thought, "Okay, well I've definitely got an audience now. And these two guys will invariably observe my approach, so I'll make it good."

When she came out of the bathroom, I got up from my seat and walked over to her confidently and without hesitation. The entire floor of the cafe, based on its open layout, could easily observe my approach, and everyone was dead-fucking silent.

I would say 15-20 people observed the approach in silence, in addition to the two guys who were clearly analyzing my every move.

I stopped her in her tracks quickly and said (in Japanese):

"Hi I'm Michael." That's it.

I didn't lower the volume of my voice just because I knew people could observe. In other words, I could handle the tension of my own approach.

She was receptive and smiled. In the back of my mind I was like, "Wow, I'll be totally fucking honest: I did not think she'd be this receptive."

I've done approaches like these innumerable times. And whether the girl is receptive or not is 100% of the time a total crapshoot.

You never fucking know whether a girl will be receptive or not.

Even at my level of experience, I can't predict these things. That's why every approach matters. It's the ones that you sometimes think will be outright rejections that can turn out to be rewarding conversions.

As long as you're direct and confident, a rejection has little/nothing to do with you and is mostly related to her mental state in that moment.

I chatted with her for about two minutes – no more – as she said her friend was waiting for her downstairs. I was actually the one who cut off the conversation, telling her she should return to her friend. I then got her LINE (Japanese messaging app) in front of everyone on the floor observing in silence, and returned to my seat. I made quick eye contact with the guy I had exchanged glances with moments before, but didn't make an arrogant production out of it, and just quietly and quickly resumed writing.

Take-home message:

As you gain experience, tension never goes away; it just takes on new forms. When you're first starting out saying hi to girls, the tension you feel is usually related to approaching the *actual girl*. That's stage zero: merely saying to *the girl*.

As time goes on, no woman in isolation will "scare" you. Any tension you feel will be linked somehow to the surrounding audience.

The majority of the time, the approaches you chicken out on and consider difficult are the ones where you're afraid of being bold in front of other people.

Approaches with very narrow windows (e.g., 2-3 seconds when walking past someone in a train station, where if you don't act fast, you miss the opportunity) *I would say are less a function of actual difficulty and tension* as much as they are related to your instinctual ability to calibrate quickly depending on your circumstances.

The "difficulty" of an approach is defined mostly by the degree to which you need to shield out a surrounding audience.

It's only your fear of what other people are going to think that is holding you back.

I've said it before and I'll say it again:

I've never actually had a single surrounding person react negatively to any of my approaches, and I've approached thousands of women. Any potentially negative response you think you'll get is all in your head.

Surrounding people won't react negatively to your approaches. It's all in your head.

If you can learn to get over your fears of the supposed judgments and opinions of surrounding people, any difficulty associated with an approach is drastically reduced. There's nothing impossible about "impossible approaches." Any hesitation is self-created.

Yeah, I know, these two approaches I just talked about might not seem like a big deal to some guys reading this. But believe it when I say 999 guys in 1,000 would chicken out in similar situations. You don't have to agree on my exact numbers. The bottom line is:

Most guys play chicken when they have nothing to worry about. That's my point. Interesting how one of the girls was actually receptive and gave me her contact. You never know when a girl will be receptive and when she won't be.

I didn't write about these two approaches in order to promulgate how incredible I think I am. I wrote about them to demonstrate that making supposedly difficult approaches is sometimes what you have to do if you want to meet new women.

HOW TO BECOME AN APPROACH MACHINE

I've been asked recently how the stuff I write about applies to you based on your specific age (i.e., if you're 18 vs 28, etc., does that change anything?).

This essay is about reframing your mindset as *early* as possible, regardless of your age, in order to save you a lot of fucking time and annoyance later on.

The process of going from zero to full-on in terms of your approaches simply requires getting over an initial "hump." First and foremost, the most important piece of info I can impart to you is:

Do not take rejection personally.

You're probably like, "Okay…well that I understand. What next?"

No, but I'm actually really serious. I'll say it again:

Do not take rejection personally. Don't.

This is a theme I reiterate quite a bit in my writing.

I'm saying this firmly to start because it lays the groundwork for any thought process you apply toward the women you meet.

Realize that rejection is NORMAL and will happen no matter who you are, what you look like, what you say, or what you do – let that hit you like a lightning rod. I am deadly serious.

**Rejection will never go away. It is the *norm*. It is not the
exception. Learn to *like* getting rejected a lot.**

"So Michael, what you're saying is, I should *want* to get rejected a
lot?"

"Yeah."

This understanding is the primer/key to unleashing your directness
and forwardness with women, because if you go into your
interactions expecting that rejection *shouldn't* occur, you're setting
yourself up for constantly being let down.

I get rejected more than any guy I know. I'm also more confident
than any guy I know. The two go hand in hand. If that sounds
counterintuitive, it's because you don't approach enough.

*The probability of rejection **fucking far exceeds** the probability
she'll be interested. Doesn't matter who you are, what you say, or
what you do. If you understand that, you win.*

That alleviates the vast bulk of your approach anxiety because you
can be more realistic going into your approaches.

And don't confuse my words here. I'm not being pessimistic. I'm
telling you the truth surrounding what you need to expect.

**In other words, what I'm doing is suffocating your current
beliefs around rejection, whether that's inconvenient to you or
not.**

Because:

If no one hammers this truth into you – that rejection is normal, will happen all of the time, and will never go away – you're stuck thinking the rejections you get are somehow a problem with you, when they're really not.

Don't over-think the rejections you receive. They will happen all of the time. For the rest of your life. Forever and ever. They ain't goin' away.

Guys tend to get rejections *and then after the fact think about **why** they received them.* And my point is that there's zero room for post-rejection contemplation. You can be your most attractive and you'll still get rejected all of the time.

Your rejections are NOT a reflection of you doing something "wrong." As I said, they will never go away. Stop fucking thinking you're doing something wrong in your interactions. As long as you're forward and not needy as fuck, that's all that really matters.

I say this because I hear a lot from guys incessantly about "what they did wrong" during their approaches, etc. And whilst on some level genuine reflection is OK (i.e., about not blowing approach windows; being more direct and forward; approaching more to decrease one's neediness, etc.), the vast majority of the reflections guys tend to make are more micro-detail oriented (e.g., "Should I have been talking about things that interest her more?" [answer is No btw]).

In reality, the micro-details don't matter. I preach deregulation and 100% winging your conversations because *it's the mere act of you being comfortable in your own skin and being yourself that is in and of itself what is most attractive.* It's not about what you talk about that matters. And if you get rejected, good, because that's normal.

And I can guarantee it wasn't because you talked about sports over her shopping.

Your focus needs to **not be** how to avoid rejection; it needs to be *how to handle/stomach your rejections.*

When I go say hi to a new girl and she rejects me, I'm not all butt-hurt about it because I understand that female non-receptiveness is the default setting. It's the norm. It keeps me hyper-realistic. I'm not expecting to get her number. I'm not expecting that she'll want to talk to me. I anticipate the most likely outcome is I'll be turning right back around within a matter of seconds.

The reason I'm confident is because I can handle rejection, both on an absolute and relative scale, really fucking well. I'm not confident because I don't get rejected. I'm confident *because* I get rejected a lot.

Let that really sink in.

That is probably one of the most epic pieces of advice anyone will ever give you in life.

The more you get rejected, the more confident you become. Not the other way around.

The vast majority of the terrible advice out there is centered around avoiding rejection. That's the number-one worst thing ever because you can't advocate for something that's not possible. If your focus is to avoid rejection, the result is you'll change your behavior in an attempt to circumvent it.

My philosophy is: go chips all-in on the most raw, direct, and uncensored version of yourself. It's the act of you not changing your behavior that will make you your most attractive to the girls you meet.

The most attractive version of you is the one that doesn't change his behavior for the girls he meets.

The only reason I can handle rejection *really well* is because I've internalized *really well* how normal and expected it is. And I've internalized that only because I've taken an obscene number of rejections.

I've taken thousands of rejections. I don't change my behavior for anyone anymore.

The reason guys fear rejection so much is because they don't understand it's actually the default setting for women.

*The only way you'll truly understand that rejection **actually increases** your confidence is to approach a lot and get rejected a ton yourself. You have to learn the real way – the hard way. There's no way around that. My writing is more just the "buffer" to help you get over that initial hump of approach anxiety.*

Every single approach you make – rejection or not – increases your confidence baseline. When you first start out approaching, if you take rejections right off the bat, you might think you're worse off, even though in truth you're actually more confident. This could be thought of as a "false diffidence" phase, where you might have a tendency to abort making future approaches out of fear, even though this is the most crucial period to fight through.

Taking rejections as your first several approaches might make you feel a bit dejected, but **this is transient and represents a really important hump you need to get over.**

You're going to get rejected way fucking more than you'll get any positive responses from the women you meet. If you've never made any real approaches before and take ten hostile rejections right off the bat, well no shit you're going to feel like ass.

This is where most guys give up.

You have my promise: if you fight through your initial rejections, you WILL encounter girls who are receptive toward you. It's not a matter of if; it's a matter of when. I'm not fucking with you. If you can make it through this phase, your life will be changed.

Why the fuck do you think I'm so passionate about writing this stuff. It's because I was once there – really shy and scared – and I came out of it. I rose out of it, all the way to the top. I want the same for you. And those changes in *you* mean more to me than anything.

And just for the record, I'm not talking about night-time bar/club/party-style approaches. I'm talking about straight-up daytime approaches – streets, cafes, public transportation, in the campus courtyard, etc.

Your initial approach phase (probably the first 20-50) is when you'll experience the greatest apprehension at any stage in your life. But it's make-or-break. You've got to fight through it.

After the first 1-3 receptive responses you get, your increased confidence will be noticeable to you. **It will be the memory of that feeling you get from your first few positive approaches** that will give you the momentum to get through your subsequent rejections. After a while, you'll see that rejections are commonplace and not a big deal.

It will take you thousands of rejections before you start to see that they're GOOD for your confidence, not the other way around. Once you see rejections are beneficial, you become more and more process-oriented because you're not trying to avoid them anymore. In the beginning, approach is all about outcome-orientation (i.e., getting her number, interest, sex, etc.) while attempting to avoid rejection. So the best I can do for you if you're in an early stage / just starting out is to be an annoying asshole who inculcates that rejections are NORMAL.

My role is to essentially step up and be the guy who will tell you, with conviction, that if you cannot learn to accept rejection as a normal and integral part of approach, you will never be as successful with women as you're capable of.

None of us are entitled to being successful with women. The same way 98% of people who start a business fail, most guys who put themselves out on a limb and begin introducing themselves to girls fail because they are overly outcome-oriented. They're fixated on not getting rejected. They see rejection as a repudiation of them. They worry too much about people's judgments and opinions of them.

If you want to be in the smaller percentage that breaks through and generates significant efficacy with women, you need to stop your fucking whining and understand that **rejection will never go away.**

Before you even make your first real approach, it's completely normal to have a certain apprehension level. If you get rejected right away, this feeling might increase, making it *even more* difficult to approach. However, if you get lucky by encountering a few girls who are immediately receptive toward you, you might quite possibly "escape" the hump you need to get over. **However this escape is exceedingly rare.**

I won't act like I'm special. As I said, I used to be really shy and scared of approaching girls. I talked about how for my first approach ever I got really, really lucky to have literally had the most positive outcome possible. This made things so much easier for me going forward. But I'm **very fucking aware** that had I gotten rejected harshly that first time, the trajectory of my life may have been very different.

Then, as though that wasn't enough, *the second* approach I made I *also* got lucky and the girl was very receptive. Trust me, this was just pure chance. I've made thousands of approaches and have taken some unimaginably harsh rejections, so the fact that for my first two real approaches ever I encountered very receptive girls, was a complete toss-up. Had those girls not been receptive, you might not be reading this today.

In the chapter, 'When meeting women, there's no such thing as getting fucking lucky,' I talk about how **you merely meeting a great girl** *is not a matter of luck; that's just a matter of you choosing to put yourself in the right place at the right time.* **However the receptive vs unreceptive state** *of any one girl you say hi to you cannot control. I just want to be clear here in terms of when I use the word "luck."*

There's lots of guys out there who will never actualize on their approach potential because they'll retreat after getting rejected a few times in the beginning. Once again, it is paramount you persevere through this initial shitty period of heightened apprehension.

My first real approach was when I was 25 and a half. Any self-confidence I had up until then was significantly dampened because I truthfully just didn't know any better. I didn't have any guidance. I took absolutely everything personally.

"Oh it must be because I'm not good-looking enough, or tall enough, or incredible enough, or talented enough, etc."

I used to analyze all of my rejections in such a way that *I would actually search for what the problem was.*

I'd say, "There *has* to be a reason."

I used to probe for "the reasons" I got rejected and would synthesize what I felt to be plausible explanations. I would attempt to intellectualize and draw a conclusion from absolutely everything.

I think until I was 25, I believed most of my rejections were probably related to not being good-looking enough.

What I didn't understand was that it was the lack of confidence I had in myself **because this was my belief** that in turn probably resulted in needy behavior and *even more* rejections.

Yes, rejections are normal and never go away. But needy behavior will cause even more of them. The way you eliminate any needy behavior you have is by increasing your approach count, plain and simple. Once again, there's no way around it and you can't fake it.

I only know this now because I've done thousands of approaches in order to figure out that confidence is what actually matters. I've also observed the gradual eradication of my prior needy behaviors. It's only when you've started to change that you can look back and see how you once were.

If you don't believe me or understand what I mean, it's because you haven't approached enough. I would say it requires getting above 2-3,000 approaches before the insecurities you have about yourself will be shattered in the face of internalizing that women care most about raw confidence. It's not your "looks," or "lack of looks," that matter as much as you think.

It takes a minimum of 2-3,000 approaches to see that confidence can compensate for "lack of looks."

(And 2-3,000 isn't high to be honest. It's all relative.)

Your confidence isn't ever *dependent* on approaching, but meeting lots of women will help you see that the shit you think is the most important (i.e., looks, wealth, etc.) isn't, and then *that in turn* will spawn *even more* confidence because slowly you realize you've already got what it takes to attract women.

It was the realization that things I supposedly "lacked" weren't actually part of the equation that was the real game-changer for me.

So what you need to do is:

- Understand rejection is normal no matter what. Regardless of who you are, what you look like, what you say, or what you do, you will get rejected a ton.

- The success is making the mere approach, not the outcome (that gives you a 100% success rate insofar as you say hi, irrespective of whether she rejects you).

- Take tons of initial rejections and handle them. Stomach them. Stop your whining. Don't fixate on outcome.

- Get in a routine of approaching new girls every day. Just say hi if you want. If you're feeling like shit, **literally just ask them for the time if you have to.** The mere process of introducing yourself to new girls will be extremely powerful for your confidence level.

- As your approach count builds, you'll notice the difference in your confidence. You'll slowly realize that things you thought were so important (i.e., your looks, what you wear, etc.) don't matter *as much as* you think they do. You'll start to say, "Wow, I'm slowly becoming a more confident person…It feels really weird to fucking say that."

– You'll start to see the ramifications of your increased confidence level on all other areas of your life. Learning to be more forward with women will also give you the confidence to make bold moves doing other things (e.g., jettisoning your career in medicine to move to Japan because the latter interests you more).

Rejection will never go away no matter who you are, what you look like, what you say, or what you do. Don't attempt to draw causation from your rejections. They will occur no matter what, and often. Your quality of life going forward will be largely dictated by your ability to understand that rejection is normal.

THE FIVE STAGES OF APPROACH

One's ability to introduce himself to women ascends sharply as approach count builds, but the concomitant mental changes (i.e., elements of "approach wisdom") are slow-rising.

Here I discuss the evolution of a male's thought process as his approach count ascends. This could be considered a mix of major realizations, or "breakthroughs," and general reflections + observations relating to one's environment / surroundings.

Stage 1 (0-1000 daytime approaches)

- The approach itself is the success.

Merely saying hi - not whether you get her contact - is in and of itself the success. If you get rejected, great, because that's not the metric for success. It was the act of simply introducing yourself that was. With this mindset, you always have a 100% success rate. In order to go from zero to something, I believe the main unlock is the male being able to convincingly say to himself, "The approach itself is the success. Saying hi alone - that IS the success." Once again, as long as he says hi, it's a 100% success rate.

- The manner in which you approach women naturally filters/selects for those with whom you'll pair.

You carry a lot less hesitation saying hi to girls because you recognize that no matter how you present yourself to the world, you naturally select for corresponding people. How you act/present yourself doesn't change the number of girls who will be interested in you; it merely changes *which* girls will be interested in you.

Even if you're needy as fuck and carry a lot of emotional baggage, you'll still select for a certain subset of girls.

If you're a geek who wears Pokemon shirts, is an avid gamer, likes to go bowling 4 days a week, and studies computer science, you'll naturally select for girls who find that sort of thing quirky and appealing.

If you're a gym-junky, have lots of piercings + tattoos, and own a yellow sports car with vertical-opening doors, you'll naturally filter for women who are attracted to that.

Likes select for likes. People filter for those similar to themselves. That's why you never have to force anything.

The combination of understanding that the approach itself is the success + likes select for likes (and hence you never have to force/change anything about you because you'll select for *somebody*), I believe is the "potent duo-unlock" for getting a male from zero to something in terms of his approaches. In turn, his conviction in these two points is his major breakthrough during Stage 1.

- Crippling approach anxiety falls.

By the end of Stage 1, saying hi to girls isn't a big deal anymore. The girl next to you in the library cubicle; the girl in the courtyard on campus; the girl on the bus – by ~1000 approaches, the male has opened himself up to introducing himself in a more diverse array of environments and in front of surrounding audiences.

He knows he is capable of putting himself out on a limb. He's starting to be able to palpate, in an unfamiliar way, that his confidence is growing. He senses that taking risks won't kill him. A girl declining his advances isn't such a scary thing the way it used to be.

Stage 2 (1000-2000 daytime approaches)

- Confidence can compensate for "lack of looks."

This isn't to say that looks can't assist in his approaches, but he's now aware that forwardness and directness are *actually sufficient* to make breakthroughs with women he once thought were unreachable. It's not that he's putting female looks on a pedestal; it's more of just a passive reflection that he's now sleeping with attractive women *because* his confidence is what propelled those interactions forward in the first place. He's developing an increasing conviction that forwardness, directness, and confidence - combined - are the number-one thing women are looking for. The same way female looks could be thought of as an asset, he now unequivocally sees his confidence as an asset *that can be swapped for looks.*

By the end of Stage 2, he's aware he can out-compete guys more physically attractive than he for the same girl. He'll encounter scenarios, e.g., at the gym, where despite not being the biggest, tallest, and/or most attractive, *he is still the one* getting the contact of the girl who just got off the treadmill while the other guys look on.

- Promiscuity is attainable via playing the sheer numbers game.

The notion of promiscuity isn't a foreign mindset anymore. He sees that his high approach numbers are translating into sexual outcomes based on mere probability and frequency of "collisions" / interactions. He knows that earning the privilege to sleep with large numbers of women requires a corresponding ability to stomach rejection and continue approaching anyway.

He does not yet view rejection as a good thing and wants to minimize it. He carries a sense of entitlement for women's interest, even if subconsciously, because he believes his newly found asset of confidence merits him results. Although he is slowly becoming more resilient to rejection, he is still overall very much outcome-oriented. The terminal Stage 2 male is characterized as highly confident yet resentful of rejection.

Stage 3 (2000-7000 daytime approaches)

- The more bold/audacious you are, the LOWER your percentages.

High conversion rates aren't something one should be proud of. They either mean the guy is embellishing or that he avoids approaching in high-tension/-risk scenarios. If you say hi to a girl shopping with her mom, or on a crowded, silent subway, or walking through an alleyway at 9pm, you're more likely to get rejected versus only saying hi to girls at cafes, book stores, or on the street on a sunny day. During this stage, the male's approach prowess undergoes significant ripening and he becomes much more fearless to engage the highest risk situations.

A girl in a silent study area at the library surrounded by her friends? A bank teller who's standing next to her group of coworkers in silence? Singling out a girl in a trio walking briskly through the subway station? No issues whatsoever. He sees that his high level of audacity/boldness *is the reason* he takes fractionally more rejections than most other guys just starting out with approach.

- The big man on campus.

He's not afraid of being known by others as "the approach guy," nor does the word "creepy" scare him. He sees his confidence level is beginning to push him off the right end of the spectrum. He's certain he has now become a guy who is simply "good with women." Not in a self-aggrandizing or -inflating way, but secondary to the knowledge and experience he's acquiring by having absorbed a few thousand rejections. He may or may not start to have casual conversations with other guys, e.g., at the gym, where he incidentally finds himself to be an informal mentor.

He sees that most other guys who are "good with women" are actually afraid of rejection and do their best to minimize it. In contrast, he's slowly starting to see that he really doesn't care about taking on rejections. He's beginning to truly own them and doesn't change his behavior or implement needy tactics to try to avoid what he sees as inevitable. This comes from genuine non-neediness.

Other guys or girls may occasionally challenge his views on approach and dating, and he can hold his ground. He's okay having these conversations because he's developed a confident core and is aware that others might have difficulty understanding his perspectives. He *literally is* confident that he is confident.

- Frustration breeds fire.

He also enters windows of reflection where he can now look back at his previous, non-approach life and see many of his missed opportunities with an unusual clarity. He being witness to some of his "riskiest" approaches converting over now brings into laser focus for him the inconvenient, undeniable, and irreversible awareness that many of the girls he never hooked up with years ago were in fact at his fingertips and he repeatedly blew it. This is not an absolute negative, however, as frustration breeds fire. This awareness for overwhelming missed opportunity from the past heralds a positive "chip on the shoulder" that fuels him going forward.

Stage 4 (7000-15000 daytime approaches)

- The majority of the world sacrifices happiness out of fear of others' opinions and judgments.

The male palpates that he's shifted further off the right end of the spectrum in terms of confidence. It becomes increasingly difficult for him to relate to other guys as far as dating and meeting women are concerned. He doesn't feel the need to convince others who are skeptical or contemptuous of his intentions and promiscuity that his approach to dating is correct because he knows it works for him and that's all that matters.

He has core confidence in place and is developing ever increasing resilience to others' judgments and opinions. He's able to reflect upon the profound disparity between his current mindset and that from his pre-approach life and can see that the main crux of his confidence converges back on not caring about others' opinions and judgments above his own. Near the end of Stage 4, he can "see" the level of fear in those around him.

- Confidence comes from rejection, not sexual outcomes.

He doesn't view other males' lesser degree of confidence in a condescending light because he knows full well that he was there not too long ago. He starts asking questions as far as *how* his current level of confidence has come about and arrives at the understanding that it has been all of the No's, not the sexual conversions, that have cultivated his fearlessness and resilience.

This is a major, high-level breakthrough for him, as he then begins to view rejection *as a good thing.* This further incentivizes him to not change his behavior for women because he's not trying to avoid negative outcome in any way; rejection *is literally sought after* because he views it as the win. This propels him upward to an even higher level of pure non-behavioral change for those he meets.

Whereas guys in earlier stages would view going, e.g., 1 for 20 on a given afternoon as a waste of time, he sees this as a very successful day because of the ramifications on confidence augmentation.

- Confidence acquired through rejection can be redistributed to *non*-dating life.

He finds that his courage to make bold or contentious life decisions (e.g., jettisoning a lucrative hospital career to bum around in East Asia) was actually acquired through - and arbitraged from - the dating process. He can trace this back to, at the most fundamental level, no longer caring about others' opinions and judgments above his own.

Material wealth becomes less important because he understands that he doesn't need it to achieve dating and relationship efficacy.

He also doesn't need to prove himself to anyone because he's developed an internal locus of confidence that supersedes any degree of extrinsic validation he may still be seeking, subconsciously or not.

- Rejection in dating and adversity in life are the same thing.

Rejection in dating is unavoidable the same way setbacks, frustrations, and annoyances in everyday life are. Confidence comes from overcoming repeated rejection the same way it comes from overcoming adversities and setbacks in general life.

The male's unwavering conviction in the positivity of incurring rejection through dating becomes translatable to an embrace of setbacks in *non*-dating life. This results in less complaining and greater happiness.

He also starts to see how the degree to which people complain is therefore a direct reflection of the extent to which they do not embrace adversity. And if they don't embrace adversity, they must view life through an outcome-, rather than process-, oriented lens. Happiness comes from embracing adversity and process, so unhappiness in the world is largely linked to outcome-orientation.

He begins to wonder if he can help others achieve greater happiness by encouraging them to become process-oriented. If he can "coach" others into embracing adversity through dating (i.e., rejection), then he knows their embrace will translate over into *non*-dating life and make them happier overall.

In short, Stage 4 is predominantly characterized by slow-growing realizations and reflections that transcend the dating process itself.

Stage 5 (>15000 daytime approaches)

- You're on your own.

The male takes on a sense of responsibility in searching for ways to telegraph his mindset to others across the expanses. Rejection and "positive outcome" essentially collapse together as a uniform, liquid process. One doesn't exist without the other, and they alternate in constant equilibrium, like a boat swaying side to side on a still lake beneath crepuscular skies. He pellucidly sees rejection as the core/paramount factor contributory to growth in confidence. Contact acquisition and sexual conversions are incidental and secondary. He will always enjoy outcome but is strangely still "in it" at this stage strictly for the rejection process.

The hallmark of Stage 5 is a complete embrace of rejection as the absolute focus of approach. It is quite possibly this latter point that most distinguishes his mindset from males in the other stages.

Other "experienced guys" out there will have their convictions that differ from his, but he's happy not forcing any of his viewpoints onto anyone else because he knows that he, himself, would never have been convincible during the earlier stages of his process. He has a level of humility commensurate to his sometimes obnoxious level of confidence and is able to empathize that others' varying degrees of contempt for his lifestyle and mindset originate from a place of non-understanding and self-preservation.

The Stage 5 male identifies that the "primer" for seeing through to other males' confidence and experience levels is the degree to which rejection is embraced over outcome. The Stage 5 male can see that others don't come close to his degree of rejection-/process-orientation. Pretty much any/all dating advice out there involves some degree of outcome-orientation, which he's already shifted away from. He sees he's on his own.

- A return to monogamy won't happen.

He sees that society romanticizes monogamous marriage as "the peak," or something we should all strive for. In fact, he viewed it the same exact way when he was younger. He used to imagine he'd be married by his early-30s – a typical linearity of sorts – meet a great woman, get married, have kids, live happily ever after. He now views this social construct as conducive to the masses because the overwhelming majority of males will never come close to actualizing on any latent ability to foster promiscuity. Monogamous marriage is essentially a species-wide self-preservation mechanism that benefits both genders – females retain male provision; males receive sex and can reproduce despite not approaching.

He will always have sexual options, and even if he encounters novel situations (e.g., changing countries, dramatic changes in income level, etc.), he knows he can still easily create new opportunities. He's approached enough women to know that some *don't actually care* about his non-committal sexual patterns.

- Marriage isn't necessary to have children

This is the viewpoint that the Stage 5 male finds hardest, if not nearly impossible, to telegraph to others. He's aware that the overwhelming majority of the population would judge him as disconnected, insensitive, and/or unemotional. This also reinforces just how far displaced he's become mindset-wise from others. He knows he will never be able to return to true monogamy, so having children outside of wedlock is the only pragmatic way to reproduce. His view on rearing children is a complex and lengthy discussion. (I discuss this latter topic in extensive detail in my YouTube videos and podcast).

HOW TO WIN BACK YOUR EX

"I love you, but had you chased me when I broke up with you, we wouldn't be here right now."

This is a fully loaded topic actually. Firstly I'll just say straight-up (because I'm an advocate of no bullshit):

There is no one-size-fits-all answer to this question because it goes without saying that the nature of every single relationship is different.

How you win your ex back versus how your friend could theoretically win his back might be entirely different depending on your unique scenarios.

Maybe she dumped you because you hooked up with someone else.

Maybe she hooked up with someone else first, then dumped you.

Maybe her mom is a devout Christian who opposed your relationship, and that's why she dumped you.

Either way, there's a million reasons why you guys may have broken up, and I can't possibly analyze them all to the depth/profundity you're probably hoping for. However what I can do is essentially "attack/probe" the most foundational mindset of a girl who doesn't want to date you anymore.

In other words, I can tell you how to maximize your probability of getting her back if you really want it to happen, regardless of the specific reasons you guys broke up.

It's actually not the specific reasons you broke up that are as important as you think; it's channeling her mindset, in general, that is how you'll get her back.

The two main scenarios for breakups are:

1) Your ex cut things off with you. You want to get her back straight-up. Emotionally, the ball is in her court and you both know it.

2) You actually cut things off with your ex, but after weeks or months have passed, you decide for whatever reason, sexually or emotionally, that you want to rekindle things with her. Maybe she was extra good in bed and you miss it; maybe you've had a change of mind about her emotionally. Although she's still very attracted to you and you know it, she's hesitant to get back with you and is resisting your re-engagement. Emotionally, you're aware the ball is in your court, but the question is: how do you poke through her apprehension smoothly and effectively without inadvertently driving her away.

First I'll address scenario #1 (the more common of the two).

How to get your ex back after she broke up with you –

If your ex has cut things off with you and you want her back, the first step in making this happen is demonstrating that *you are able to move on and don't need her back.*

In other words, the first step in getting your ex back is ***actually not trying to get her back.***

Now right away you're probably like, "Okay…well how the fuck does that actually do me any good cuz then what? What am I supposed to do then?" Yeah, I know. Good question.

*The correct answer is: **you have to let her come to you.***

If she cut things off with you and you're unhappy about it, the emotional leverage is in her court. The only way you can regain that leverage is by genuinely not giving a fuck about whether you get her back or not. This will create one of two trajectories:

1) The relationship fizzles/disintegrates further and you guys both move on. There's nothing you can do about it and this is your best chance to walk away holding onto your dignity (also, the more you fight against her decision, the harder the breakup will be for you).

2) She will pick up on your fleeting interest in her and slowly come back to you.

The true equilibrium point of your interaction with her will win out.

In other words, if it's meant to end, it's meant to end, but fighting / pushing to get her back will only make you *more* likely to lose her versus if you just keep your cool and let her "equilibrate" back to you.

If she's actually still into you on some level, distancing yourself when she cuts things off with you is the best thing you can do because it will incite trajectory #2.

If she really isn't into you anymore and it's meant to end, trajectory #1 will occur, and that's good, because had you fought against her decision instead, you'd just be creating undue misery for yourself and even more tormenting "heartbreak."

When a girl breaks up with you, if you fight against her decision, you will push her away even more. The best shot you've got is to be non-needy and respond to her act of pulling away by just keeping your cool. If she genuinely still has a desire to be with you, she'll come back. If she doesn't come back, she wouldn't come back regardless of what you do.

And don't misconstrue my words either. I'm not insinuating that you should play games and pretend like you don't care. That's not what I'm saying. I am saying you have to genuinely be non-needy and willing to move on.

The person who cares the least is the one who has the leverage in the relationship.

The number-one thing that will absolutely drive an ex away *even further* is your neediness to get her back.

If you want her back, you have to genuinely – with all of your fucking bullshit aside – be willing to walk away and not care about whether you actually get her back.

There's no way around it and you can't fake it. If you fake it you'll lose, or you'll create distrust and unhealthy games in your relationship. Take me for my word here because this is paramount:

If you want her back, you have to *genuinely be willing to lose her.*

If you can accept losing her, you might just get her back.

As soon as she cuts things off with you, you have to literally flip on a switch and say, "Okay, her issue not mine. I'm just going to go approach 10-20 new girls starting today/tomorrow and build back up again."

This is **not** synonymous with, "Okay, I'm just going to act cold and distant for the next two weeks no matter what in order to create the illusion that I don't care." Because what that will do is create unnatural / artificial behavior that she will be able to read as *you actually caring too much, which is **truly the case.***

Neediness always permeates to the surface.

You can't fake that you don't care. So the only way to *actually not care* is by creating new opportunities for yourself.

The only reason you "care" is because you've got all of your emotions tied up in one person – her. She's your only focus at the moment. So you have to **not make her your focus.** And rather than doing that by pretending she's not, create an environment for yourself where **she literally is not.**

How do you do that? Approach.

If she cuts things off with you, the main way to create true non-neediness as fast as possible is by approaching new women as soon as possible. Even if they reject you, this will shoot up your confidence in terms of *you knowing you could at least meet more women if you choose to.*

Even if you get rejected a lot – and that will happen way more than you'll get any positive responses from the girls you meet – approaching new girls is the #1 way to shift your focus away from your ex.

If you want your ex back, start approaching new people.

If you're too nervous to do that, **just ask girls for the time.** I know it's not 1990 and everyone carries a smartphone, but literally take off your watch and say, "Hi, I'm Jared. Do you know what time it is?" Then walk away. Do that five times as a starter. Then as the sixth approach, say, "Hi I'm Jared. I just wanted to say hi." Or, "Hi I'm Jared. I thought you were attractive and wanted to say hi."

(I'm not going to turn this essay into a focus on approaching, as I have other ones about that stuff, but I'm just making a point that if you are reading this right now and are thinking, "Yeah, easy for you to say. But I'm just not good at approaching girls." Then asking girls for **just the time** can be a benign / easy way to break the ice on making yourself less needy toward your ex.)

You can't just pretend like you all of a sudden don't care about your ex. If you really want to genuinely not give a fuck, you have to approach other girls, starting right away. There's no way around it. Because unless you meet other people, you're stuck in your own headspace where she carries way more importance than she actually should.

The more options you create for yourself = you become less and less needy = you care less and less about your ex = she senses your non-neediness = she becomes more and more attracted to you = you can get her back.

Having no options (because you don't approach) = you carry needy behavior = you care a lot about your ex = she senses your neediness for her = she distances herself even more from *your neediness.*

Your ex is only as important to you as she relates to your lack of other options.

If I were in a hypothetical relationship where the girl I was seeing cut things off with me, I personally wouldn't even want her back because I'd view the situation as she's blown her chance and it's not my issue. But for the sake of this essay, if I *actually* wanted her back, the primary way I'd go about it is by just approaching from day-zero and starting to see other people right away. No questions asked. Her loss not mine.

A girl who'd have the "audacity" to give up a confident, high-status guy (status as in confidence) would pay the price by watching you immediately not care because you'd already be off creating other options. **You can't fake your lack of care.**

I wouldn't even focus on my ex whatsoever. I would literally just skate around and direct approach the entire next week, just as *a starter.* Based on the numbers game alone, I'd pick up a new sexual partner fairly quickly.

I would actually say this is what makes me non-needy in all of my interactions/relationships – knowing that I never *need* any one person because *I know I could* match with many others just as easily. If you carry a "she's my one-and-only and we're supposed to live happily ever after" mentality, you'll lose.

So even if I were to emerge freshly out of a committed relationship and not currently be seeing anyone else, *it would be my awareness that I could find other people easily* that would keep me from being needy.

Essentially, if I could sense any girl becoming lukewarm toward me, my focus on her would evaporate because I'm already off approaching other women.

I'm never needy toward any one girl I'm seeing because I'm always approaching / am aware I could easily approach. You can't fake an abundance mentality.

The result of my behavior is that it would *literally be impossible that she'd care less than I.*

When I preach to you that you need to start approaching immediately, the purpose of that is to force you into a situation where you unequivocally care less than she. Only if that situation manifests will she become more attracted to you.

One could argue that the process of approaching a lot *as a compensatory response* to a breakup is in and of itself needy behavior, but I would actually counter that by saying: Nah, not even close. It's actually the best thing you can do.

There's no such thing as "needy approaching."

Why?

Because your only other option in life is: "Okay, don't meet other girls. Have fun jerking off at home alone while guys like me capitalize."

If you want your ex back, approaching other girls will stir natural, non-needy behaviors on your end that will increase the probability she'll be interested in you again.

If you think my emphasis is a little overkill when it comes to approaching in order to get your ex back, then I don't know what to fucking tell you. It's like, have fun not getting her back. Not my issue now is it. I'm just being straight with you. And it's honestly the best advice you could get.

Essentially, if you got broken up with and we went out approaching together, you'd have several girls you're texting by the end of the week, and probably at least a couple dates by the end of the second week.

In under one month's time, you *would be* sleeping with new girls again if 10-20/day is your approach rate. If you don't believe me, it's only because you're not approaching enough. Even if you can only muster 2-5 approaches per day (which actually just means you're making bullshit excuses about "not having time," etc.), that's still better than zero. Anything is better than nothing.

When it comes to getting your ex back, something you should think about is:

You should never have to qualify to anyone, nor should you ever need to fight for someone who's tepid/lukewarm about you.

If your ex cuts things off with you, what does that say about your own integrity if you don't just move on right away.

The same holds true for *new* girls you meet as well. If a girl you're texting isn't eager to hang out with you, why waste your time with her? Her issue not yours. Find someone else instead.

Never fight back against someone's lack of interest.

The notion that you should be persistent in order to get women should not be overgeneralized. Persistence has a time and place, such as with always approaching new girls and fighting through your approach anxiety.

But when it comes to girls whom you've already established a conversational pattern or relationship with, if you sense they're not interested, just find other girls instead.

Why waste your time with people who aren't fully interested in you?

You should **always** be non-needy and forward-looking. You don't *need* your ex anymore. There are literally tons of girls out there whom you could meet today, tomorrow, etc., so to be fixated on her reflects a mindset that a guy *doesn't think he can get/meet other girls.*

There are lots of girls out there for you to meet. You just have to...say hi to them. You can't wait for magic to happen. You have to create the opportunities yourself.

If you were to meet some "amazing" girl tomorrow, you'd all of a sudden find you're no longer so fixated on getting your ex back. Pretty fucking convenient isn't it.

It's not your ex whom you truly give a shit about. It's the **mere idea** of being with someone – any girl – period. You just want **a**

girl there. You want the sex, or the emotions, or the connection, or a cute face – that's it.

If you think you and your ex had some magical connection that was super-rare, the person is actually interchangeable whether you want to believe that or not.

The way you feel about any one girl is easily transferrable to another. It really is not a magical/unique feeling as much as you might think it is.

Your fantasy of a "one true love" across the universe will only hold you back in life. There are *lots* of "true loves" out there for you. No matter where you are in the world – by all means you could move to Paraguay or Iceland next week – you will find girls whom you have strong connection with.

You might *really want* your ex back, but what I'm saying is, guaranteed that if a random hot chick popped into your life tomorrow, after she starts being all cuddly and affectionate with you, you'd be like, "Wow, I've got a really great connection with this new girl I just met." Then you'd go off to tell all of your friends about this amazing chick you met.

Suddenly your ex means jack shit to you.

So however you feel/felt about your ex is easily transferrable to another girl. The only question is: are you
looking **forward** or **backward**? Are you willing to approach other girls and make the above scenario a reality, or are you going to dwell forever about some lukewarm girl who isn't worth your time.

The other thing to bear in mind is: your feelings toward your ex are *falsely heightened* simply because of the perceived difficulty of getting back with her.

This is called **barrier bias** (slightly different from "hard to get" because you've already had a relationship with her), where a perceived barrier makes you think she's more amazing than she really is (this is also the case with travel; e.g., you meet a great girl on a cruise ship, then after you go back to your respective homes across the world, you fantasize about her being more amazing than she really was).

In other words, if you *actually did* get back with your ex, after a week or so, you'd probably find there's nothing so out-of-this-world amazing about her anyway. It was the mere idea of her being "at a distance" that falsely accentuated any emotions you felt for her.

*After you get back with her, you might be surprised to find that **you** are the one who isn't that interested after all.*

I actually talk about in the chapter, 'End of the beta male,' how I got my ex back through genuine non-neediness. I felt on top of the world for a few weeks. But reality slowly crept in again and *I* was the one who cut things off a second time.

However significant you think your connection was with your ex, a lot of it is a false byproduct of barrier bias. You're creating a fantasy about her because she seems distant from you now.

The same as with infatuation, sometimes when we carry emotions for a girl, things can spiral out of control if we build up a fantasy around her.

Now I'll quickly address the other common scenario.

How to get your ex back after *you* broke up with her –

If you broke up with your ex for whatever reason, firstly just ask yourself whether you *really want* to go back there again.

If she was awesome in bed but turned out to be a psycho, ask yourself whether banging her once more is *really worth* all of the bullshit you'll have to experience as a result of her emotional blowback once you cut things off with her again.

*I know it might be tempting. But ask yourself whether you **really** want to venture back there again.*

You're like, "Fuck yeah. I actually do. She was great in bed."

Okay, well remember when she flipped out those few times and you were like, "What the actual fuck?"

*Yeah, that's what I thought. Do you **really** want to go back there? I mean **really**.*

Even though you broke up with her, if you find yourself wanting to rekindle, truly and honestly look at your situation and ask yourself if the reason is because you don't have other options right now.

If you are currently sleeping with other people and options aren't an issue, it really just comes down to whether you want to deal with the breakup again when it occurs.

You can even ask yourself whether putting **her** through emotional turmoil again, if you have no true intention of a relationship with her, is something you want to pursue. I'm not going to tell you how or whom you should date. That obviously is your call. But if she's *already moved on* and you're aware fucking her again will incite her turmoil, just ask yourself whether that's an avenue you're looking to go down.

Some girls are just better off left alone. Be glad you got out earlier rather than later.

If you have other options, my advice is to just do your best to move forward. If you cut things off at one stage, it was probably for good reason.

However, if you *really* want her back and she seems resistant, approach the situation similar to how you would had she broken up with you:

Just be non-needy by making sure you're approaching other girls. And if you decide, even after you've opened up other opportunities for yourself, that you *still* want her back, your behavior will be in its most attractive state by just keeping your focus not exclusively on her.

You honestly might not even want to date your ex once you've started to pick up other girls.

But either way, you can tell her you guys should hang out. See how she responds. If she's resistant, you've got to allow her to take that space. Just move forward. Maybe she will come back to you. But if you fight it, suddenly you'll find *she's* the one "ending" things with you after all.

So in summary:

If you want to get back with your ex, regardless of who broke up with whom, be non-needy and you'll maximize the probability she'll come back to you. The best way to create genuine non-neediness is by approaching/meeting new women.

You can't fake your non-neediness, and approaching will create natural and attractive behavior on your end. If you don't approach, you'll stay needy, and that will be reflected in your behavior.

Your emotional neediness, or lack of neediness, will always shine through. Being non-needy and not protesting her decision to cut things off is the best thing you can do. If this doesn't work, she wouldn't have come back to you no matter what you did. Pushing back against her resistance will only drive her away further.

Have some integrity and realize that you should never have to be with someone who isn't fully interested in you. Whether it's your ex or a new girl you meet, if she's lukewarm/tepid toward you, why would you waste your time with her. There are lots of other girls out there you could easily meet. You just have to approach to find them.

The way you feel about your ex can easily be transferred to another girl whether you realize it or not. Any feelings you have right now toward her about how amazing she supposedly is are falsely elevated secondary to barrier bias.

If you were to have your "fantasy" fulfilled and get back with her, you'd find after a couple weeks things weren't so great with her anyway.

Once again, there are literally a million scenarios we could dissect in relation to specific breakups, etc., the main idea is that the vast majority of the time, the minute circumstances surrounding your breakup aren't quite as paramount as you might think in relation to being able to recreate lost attraction.

THE SEXUAL GAME DOESN'T GIVE A FUCK

One of the most important pieces of advice I can tell you is that how you feel about meeting new women is 100% irrelevant in terms of actually making positive outcomes happen.

No one gives a fuck about how you romanticize the dating process. The more you romanticize/fantasize about how meeting women *should be* a certain way, the more you can count yourself out of the sexual game.

In life, you never know who will be receptive. Ever. That cute girl who walks past you whom you choose not to say hi to because you don't want to "be creepy" would have gone on to date you had you simply introduced yourself.

I live by that mentality because when the thought that I might not approach a girl sometimes crosses my mind, and then I end up doing it anyway, occasionally that girl really does go on to be a sexual partner, girlfriend, etc., and then I'll reflect and think, "Wow, crazy how that interaction came so close to not existing."

And I've told girls that too, sometimes months/years after the fact. This is very real.

Yet again, no one gives a fuck how close I've come, or haven't come, to having a sexual interaction in life. And no one gives a fuck about how that plays out for you either.

There are sometimes girls you'll cross paths with (e.g., at university, etc.), whom, in a parallel universe, *you've already slept with* had you just opened them a year ago outside that lecture hall, or 18 months ago on that shuttle bus, etc.

That cute girl who sometimes comes in and out of the cafe you frequent **should actually be** your girlfriend, but you'll never unlock that pathway because you've chosen to care too much about others' judgments and opinions of you. You're always too scared to just open her.

Every time you see a girl and choose not to approach her, you're wiping a future girlfriend off the face of the earth without even realizing it.

If there were some magic genie/deity who appeared out of nowhere and showed you misty images/videos of all of the opportunities you've passed up in life, you wouldn't come close to believing it's real. You'd wake up and say, "Ok cool, that shit was just a dream." But it's not.

Yeah, I know. It's fucked.

There was a girl I once approached on a pedestrian foot-bridge crossing over a highway. She and I ended up cruising around the Maldives and going to New Zealand together. No jokes, my friend.

Some guys might wonder why I approach so much. It's not strictly to make up for lost opportunities from my past (although in the beginning, there was perhaps a component of that). I'd say it's more that I've now reached an incontrovertible stage of profound awareness of the true abundance / opportunity out there, and passing it up is nonsensical/basically impossible for me now.

When you consummate your approach/sexual prowess and irreversibly become aware of what's truly possible for you, you begin living life in a very strange place. The degree to which you feel blessed for your awareness is met with a commensurate sensation of visceral insatiability for the approach process.

In other words, guys with no real "appetite" for approach exist in that mental state because it corresponds directly to the magnitude of their lack of awareness for the opportunities they're missing out on.

I'm not saying you have to approach every single girl you see no matter what. What I am referring to is the *general process* of crossing paths with women in every day life, whom you choose not to open, when in reality, that's a big, big mistake on your end, and you have no fucking clue.

I don't mean to be all movie-esque, quixotic, and overly romanticizing, but I have to drill the point into you that some of the girls you've chosen not to approach in life *really did* exist in a parallel universe with you, where you guys dated, went hiking, traveled together, etc.

And if you're not into any of that cloying bullshit and want me to put this into strict sexual terms instead, then that girl you chose not to say hi to on the bus the other day; *you really would have* gone on to sleep with her had you not been so afraid of surrounding people's opinions.

You caring too much about the opinions/judgments of others = you living life not being nearly as bold/forward as you need to be = you missing out on golden opportunities. Plain and fucking simple.

Pretty much every single girl I've had a sexual interaction/relationship with, when I reflect on how I first met her, the initial situation could have been perceived as weird, or awkward, or "creepy."

That girl who will want to marry you in the future is the same one you approached "so creepily" on the bus, on the street, in line at the cafe, etc.

You supposedly "being creepy" is actually what will translate into a success story for both of you.

She'll say she doesn't like creepy guys. But years from now, she'll be glad you put yourself out on a limb and risked "being creepy" to say hi to her.

You: *"I really did come so close to not saying hi to you on the bus that day."*

She: *"Yeah, that's kind of crazy actually."*

I once met a woman at a bus stop. We got on the bus together, had a short chat, and I got her number. Maybe a few days later, I happened to have run into her again while commuting, and as I was getting off the bus, I asked her to come have a quick meal with me. She hesitated and almost said no, but decided to just go for it. We went on to date for a few years. I told her more than once that had she not gotten off the bus and come to dinner with me that day, I would have deleted her number instantly. And I was serious. I would have interpreted the situation as, "Well, the chemistry obviously wasn't sufficient, which is why she said no, and I don't like girls who are lukewarm about me, so fuck that."

People make quick gut decisions in life that sometimes manifest hugely in sexual/relationship terms. My gut instincts told me to "be creepy" and open her at the bus stop the first time we met. Then, her gut instincts told her to just get off the bus with me the next time around. You almost always have no fucking clue how the most seemingly tiny gut decision transforms everything for your future. It might sound obvious that that's just how life works, but I really want you to take that point home.

Once again, pretty much all women I've had sexual patterns with; how have I met them?

In "creepy" ways.

Because I was forward and confident. And because other guys were too scared. That's why *I was the guy* they dated.

At a bus stop; on an actual bus; on a train; in a cafe; on a shopping street; by a lake; on a bridge walking over a fucking highway – wherever.

That cute girl you see on the street today; that girl you see on the bus tomorrow morning; that girl you'll see in line at the cafe next Tuesday; you not saying hi to her is wiping a future girlfriend, or even a wife, off the face of the earth. And guess what, you probably think I'm talking quixotic bullshit. Trust me, I'm not. This is real.

If you want to meet women in life, you sometimes have to risk being a creeper. You have to put yourself out on a limb. It's you caring too much about the opinions of others that is directly related to you not meeting new women. However, the truth is that those thoughts are not part of the equation.

The sexual game doesn't give a fuck about your discomfort opening women on the bus/train just because the morning commute is "too silent."

It doesn't give a fuck about how creepy you think saying hi to women on the street is.

It doesn't give a fuck that you constantly hesitate opening that barista you think is cute because you're afraid her co-workers will smirk.

It doesn't give a fuck that your university campus is small.

It doesn't give a fuck that your town is small.

It doesn't give a fuck that you think you're only average in appearance.

It doesn't give a fuck that you're not tall.

It doesn't give a fuck that you work 8-10 hours a day in an office and are "too tired" to approach when commuting home.

It doesn't give a fuck that you're butt-hurt about the last streak of rejections you took.

It doesn't give a fuck that your ex-girlfriend is dating someone else.

It doesn't give a fuck about you whatsoever. And it doesn't give a fuck about me either.

And it most certainly doesn't give a fuck about your whiny bullshit excuses.

Because when you're old, and your one at-bat in life – let me repeat that: your one at-bat in life – has passed you by and you're regretting it, you'll realize all of the insecurities you clung to so tightly during your peak years didn't mean jack fucking shit.

I get it. You find it difficult to rack up the courage to approach. You find it weird. You find it creepy. You find it hard to get used to. You find that dating apps are better catered to your laziness. I get it.

However you choose to analyze it, don't make fucking excuses. Because the sexual game doesn't fucking care about all of your mental bullshit.

While you're coming up with reasons not to approach, just bear in mind you're passing up life-trajectories with women and are completely oblivious to it.

Trust me, I'm on your side. I want you to win. I'm here for you. I'm passionate about getting my message across to you because it only takes one fucking rant of mine to change you. And maybe it will be this one.

As you move through life, you'll see that no one actually gives a fuck about you or anything you do. No one cares what you do.

If you want to say hi to a girl who sparks your interest, then do it. Because as I said, no one fucking cares.

When you realize no one cares – and that the sexual game doesn't care – about your thoughts, or your hesitations, or your insecurities, **that** is the unlock for you being as effective as you can possibly be. And I want that for you. I want you to create positive outcomes for yourself.

So yeah, cut your bullshit excuses. Start putting yourself out there. Meet new people.

Something *will* come of it.

PERMEATION OF APPROACH INTO YOUR NON-DATING LIFE

Approach starts off as this "thing," or "activity," that we guys experiment with in order to meet new women. It's a mere external locus. It's an idea at best. It's something we might "try after work tomorrow," or "try this weekend when we go to town."

After about 1-2 months of actively integrating approach into our **daily** routine, it's no longer this weird or scary external idea anymore. At this early stage, it hasn't yet permeated our deeper character in such a way that we no longer think about it, but we've now certainly identified it as a **positive integration.** It's becoming more established as a habit and we're aware our confidence is growing.

As the first 1-2 **years** of daily approach ensue, approach grows to be a core component of our lives. During this time, there's an undoubted self-awareness for the ascension in self-confidence. Eventually, it permeates our character forever.

The permeation can be palpated as an irreversible awareness that the insecurities one had supposedly clung to for so long simply don't matter after all; it's the unexpected arrival of this incipient conviction that coincides with the male being able to "see" his confidence as a concrete, tangible attribute he's developed.

The same way a guy might be aware of his height, or skin/eye color, or chubby/muscular physique, etc., self-confidence can now be felt as an unquestionable self-attribute. I'd conjecture that this point of irreversible permeation manifests around the 2-5,000-approach level. At this stage, you say hi to women anytime, anywhere, in any circumstance, and don't even think about it. You also grow to "see" that the vaster population lives in a fear bubble. The quantity of rejections you take in just a single day or two exceeds that of most men's entire adulthood. **But most importantly, the confidence you have now permeates other areas of your life (i.e., decisions with school/work, general life choices, etc.).**

It cannot be stressed enough that as your approach prowess matures and emboldens, one of the most unanticipated and profound realizations is your nascent ability to make audacious life-decisions **that have nothing to do with dating whatsoever.**

*The audacity (or fear) a male carries with respect to introducing himself to new women is a direct reflection of his audacity (or fear) surrounding **all of his other life choices**.*

The only reason most guys avoid approaching is because they're too locked up in giving a fuck about what other people think, whether it's the girls they're saying hi to or the surrounding audience.

Giving a fuck, or not giving a fuck, about other people's judgments/opinions of you isn't ever specific to one area of your life; it's a mental state that is pervasive across all areas.

You being afraid of what a girl thinks of you says you're also afraid of what everyone thinks of you in general. These two seemingly distinct domains *are actually the same thing*.

A guy's ability to approach women is actually a "primer," or gateway, into understanding how he approaches life in general. You either carry fear or you don't. It's that simple.

It's not a coincidence that my content (i.e., blog, podcast, and videos) is a mix of talking about meeting women + living life true to yourself/not giving a fuck about others' judgments/opinions of you.

It's because the two are linked. By overcoming the fear of approach, you actually overcome a lot of fear in life *in general.*

In other words, you might think I just preach a lot about how to approach women, but in reality, if we go much deeper than that, much of my passion is rooted in knowing that if we get you to overcome any fear-mindset associated with meeting women, the rest of your life will improve as well, in ways that, right now, you have no fucking clue.

Approaching a lot + taking incessant daily rejections → slowly no longer giving a fuck about what girls + surrounding audience think of you → slowly no longer giving a fuck about what *anyone* thinks of you → slowly starting to think more for yourself rather than to impress/appease other people → slowly starting to make life-decisions unrelated to meeting women that are *for you and not anyone else* → decreased desire for material wealth + increased desire for life experience + learning + giving back to others.

The only reason you're reading this right now is because I'm not trying to impress anyone. I spent a good chunk of 2018 investing almost all of my money into Facebook ads to help spread what I'm passionate about, with the trade-off being I pay jack-shit for rent and live in a tiny apartment here in Osaka, Japan. Unless you're literally a family member or close friend of mine, we both know the only reason you're reading this book is because you "found" my content through a Facebook, either because you saw a sponsored post, or because a friend encountered one and shared it with you. Yeah, well that wasn't a fucking accident now was it.

It's because I regard *giving you value* above any investment in dumb material shit for myself.

It's also because I have tremendous gratitude for realizing how ultra-low-probability it was having met my Italian housemate that changed my life many years ago. Now I want to do everything I can do be that person for you. I want to transfer all of that to you.

So why am I mentioning all of that? Because the audacity and confidence to not care about the judgments/opinions of others, stemming from my incessant rejections, **is why my content exists in the first place.**

If I cared about what others thought of me, I would have gone on to have some "prestigious and respectable" hospital career after I graduated med school, rather than jettisoning it all to just do what I want in life.

When you absorb incessant rejections day after day and constantly put yourself out there to meet new women, you see that everything else in life follows. Everything that could conceivably be "scary" is really just trivial bullshit. No one cares what you do in life. Life decisions you make that are conceivably such a big deal to you mean close to nothing to practically everyone else.

The confidence you gain from getting rejected incessantly doesn't fundamentally change who you are; it just gives you the courage to bring out who you really are.

WHY YOU SHOULD NEVER FORCE YOUR CONVERSATIONS

When you stop making decisions through the lens of others' judgments and opinions, you can see that you haven't *actually changed* per se; you're now just merely living life as the most unvitiated and raw version of yourself.

For me, when I think about the first real and deliberate approach I ever made, what actually enabled me to do it was knowing that no matter how I chose to approach – no matter what I said or did – that would naturally select and filter for a corresponding female, so there was nothing to worry about.

In other words, the fear a guy might have as far as how to act, what to say, what to do, how to look, etc.; well the most important thing to remember is:

How you act/present yourself to the world doesn't wildly change the number of women who will be interested in you; it merely changes *which* women will be interested in you.

That for me was huge. It meant that I didn't need to act in any particular way, or say any particular thing. It just meant, "Hey, well I can simply be myself and never have to fake/front anything, and that will naturally select for those who are interested in me…just being me."

If there are 100 girls in a room and 7 would potentially go on a date with you, how you act doesn't shift that number wildly up or down; it simply changes **which 7** will be interested.

From the chapter, 'The five stages of approach':

Even if you're needy as fuck and carry a lot of emotional baggage, you'll still select for a certain subset of girls.

If you're a geek who wears Pokemon shirts, is an avid gamer, likes to go bowling 4 days a week, and studies computer science, you'll naturally select for girls who find that sort of think quirky and appealing.

If you're a gym-junky, have lots of piercings + tattoos, and own a yellow sports car with vertical-opening doors, you'll naturally filter for women who are attracted to that.

Likes select for likes. People filter for those similar to themselves. That's why you never have to force anything.

I've had girls reject me for being *too confident,* and I'm okay with that. I naturally pair with girls who are hyper-feminine because my personality style is hyper-male. While one girl might perceive me as over-the-top arrogant and say, "Wow, fuck that guy," there's another who *likes* that I'm very sure of myself.

I'm most attracted to very quiet, very shy, very submissive, small-ish Asian girls, with receded chin/jaw, small ears, a big upper lip, and massive cheeks. And I have no idea where that preference came from. I don't really know what to say.

Likewise, I'm really turned off by girls who are loud and assertive, or those who don't follow my lead even 1%. I have zero interest in

50/50 dating dynamics. It's either my way or no way.

Once again, for every girl who'd say, "Unbelievable. Wow. Fuck that guy." That's exactly my point. I have no interest in those girls and we happily screen each other out. Everyone wins. An ideal relationship / interaction is only what the two people in it want it to be. There's no right or wrong. It's just what you both want out of it.

A girl who's interested in me might not be the same girl who's interested in you, and vice-versa. The way in which you approach women naturally selects for those with whom you'll pair.

I reiterate these points because this means you never need to worry about how to make an approach. You never need to worry about what to say or what to do. Just say hi as your natural self; speak however the fuck you want; conduct yourself as you please; and you'll naturally filter for *somebody*. If a girl you say hi to isn't interested, good, because somebody else *will be*.

It's also really important to reinforce that rejection will always occur no matter who you are, what you look like, what you say, or what you do. It will never go away. And the vast majority of the time, it actually has nothing to do with you.

The only way you can truly understand the above point is to do **a lot** of approaching yourself.

I hear from a lot of guys about how they think their "lack of looks" holds them back. And my response is:

*It's your **belief** that your "lack of looks" is holding you back that is reflective of your lack of confidence, and **that** is what she is turned* *off by. It's your perception of yourself that she reads and is either attracted to or repulsed by; it's not your "lack of looks" in isolation that she truly gives a shit about.*

Even if you think a girl supposedly rejects you for your "lack of looks," you'll find that a girl *much better looking than she* is happily willing to go on a date with you.

Really digest that for a second.

For every girl out there who supposedly rejects you for your "lack of looks," you'll find that if you approach a lot of women, there's an *even better-looking* woman out there who is **more than happy** to go on a date with you.

I get rejected all of the time, and I can tell you unequivocally that the face on a woman doesn't relate in the slightest to whether she'll be interested in you or not.

This is not a debate.

For every "plain" girl who rejects me, there's a "hot" girl who happily goes on a date with me.

And for every "hot" girl who rejects me, there's a more plain-appearing girl who happily goes on a date with me.

Women are all the same.

One of the major ways you can gauge how confident/experienced a male really is is by learning his perspective on how a woman's physical attractiveness relates to her personality or supposed willingness to reject. If he talks as though "9s and 10s" are different in any way, he's secretly a coward and puts them on a pedestal. **It means he changes his behavior for those whom he perceives to be of greater status than he.**

But the thing is, when you're a male of really high status (confidence), you don't change your behavior for anyone. The way I approach a more plain-appearing girl is exactly the same as I approach someone who I'm aware bears more preferable physical attributes.

It's actually not even something I think about.

When I see a girl whom I'm really attracted to and go and say hi, the only variable that sometimes fluctuates is my extra fervor/drive to initiate the approach, but the approach itself is exactly as I'd make any other – i.e., **100% improvisation and just saying whatever the fuck I want.** My behavior never actually changes from person to person.

A female's physical attractiveness only really changes *how likely I am* to make the approach; it doesn't change the approach itself.

Don't ever overanalyze the rejections you receive. I know you want black-and-white answers. But the only thing I can really tell you is that for you to understand that rejection is normal and actually not about you the vast majority of the time, you have to do a ton of approach yourself. There's no way around that.

Lots of factors play a role in why we, as guys, will always receive tons of rejections no matter what. I can say with strong conviction that women are often just in a "state." That is, sometimes they'll reject any guy who approaches them – any guy – it doesn't matter who he actually is.

For instance, if you've seen any of my rejection videos, you'll notice that for many of the rejections I absorb, the girl doesn't even look at me.

I would probably conjecture that where a woman is on her menstrual cycle is the strongest, albeit not the sole, determinant of the "state" she's in.

The more masculine and bold your approach, the more you select for women who are within a few days of ovulation (i.e., days 11-14). That girl who rejects you on a Thursday at the bus stop is the same girl who, last Monday, would have been receptive in the campus courtyard. Approaches are largely a crapshoot.

That doesn't mean women who are premenstrual / menstruating might not be interested in your bold approach, **but all factors cancelled out,** I would probably peg where she is on her cycle as the biggest influencer of her receptiveness.

Guys who are softer and "nicer" attract women around the time of menstruation. Once again, this isn't even a debate. This is just biology.

I naturally select for women who are peak-cycle. I'm short, direct, and confrontational with my approaches. That's just what it is. Want to call me a jackass? Knock yourself out. My fucks given are zero.

As long as you walk up and say hi, irrespective of whether she rejects you or not, *that's a successful approach.*

Rejections will happen way more than you'll ever get positive responses from the women you meet, so if success is framed as the *outcome*, you're always set up to be disappointed. It is this "mal-framing" that is actually the root cause of all of the poor dating advice out there.

I note that pretty much all dating advice out there is structured around – in some way, shape, or form – avoiding or reducing rejection. I believe this is the worst mindset possible.

The best advice is to actually **want to get rejected and accept it as normal.** The idea isn't to learn how to avoid rejection; it's to learn how to stomach your rejections and continue approaching anyway.

I really cannot emphasize this enough:

Pretty much all of the poor dating advice out there is structured around essentially changing your behavior/approach in some way in order to avoid/minimize your rejections. If this is your mindset, you've already lost.

My philosophy is that the more experienced / confident you are, *the more* you get rejected because that means you're more willing to put yourself out on a limb and create audacious encounters.

When I make absolutely outrageous statements such as saying that I'm the best in the world, *it's because I've taken more rejections than anyone else in the world.* I don't think any other guy out there even comes close.

That's not a fucking accident. I'm not here talking about how amazing I think I am because I have "success" with women. My status/confidence level is strictly linked to the **number of rejections I stomach.**

The more rejections you absorb, the less you subsequently change your behavior for the women you meet – or for anyone. Once again, you can't fake this non-behavioral change. You only get there through getting rejected a lot. And there's no way around that.

If there's one key philosophy I want you to take away from my content, it's that your aim should be to **embrace** rejection, not avoid it.

Embracing rejection and continuing to approach anyway will masculinize your behavior and make you high status.

I'll approach anyone, anywhere. I don't really care. However if a girl is actively talking on the phone or is smoking, those are probably the two approaches I don't make.

I hugely advocate winging your approaches and not thinking about what you're going to say whatsoever. Your mind should be a clean-room basically. You might know as a vague idea that you'd be inclined to ask, e.g., her age, what she does for study or work, etc., but as a whole, it doesn't really matter, as long as you approach as your natural self and are 100% deregulated / winging it.

One of the most important take-homes from this essay is that you never need to force your conversations to be any particular way because no matter how you choose to interact with women, that will naturally filter/select for those who mesh well with you.

HYPERGAMY AND THE FEMALE STRATEGY

Hypergamy is the continual / unabated biologic process in which females always seek the best genes possible and will unapologetically swap male partners, i.e., "trade upward," if Male #2 is adequately forward. A woman must debate provision vs genes and will, at times, forgo upward gene acquisitions and/or relationship trades if the decision necessitates a loss of provision. It is this balance of provision vs genes when deciding – subconsciously or consciously – to trade upward that defines hypergamy. Males continually seek out younger, more fertile female counterparts, yet the notion of provisional trade-off isn't inherent to his decision-making. His partner choices therefore fall external to the envelope of hypergamous behavior.

This essay comprises three sections:

1) When's your ovulation day?

2) She's like a lioness

3) The female strategy

When's your ovulation day?

I moved to Osaka at the end of June 2016 after having spent 6.5 years in Australia.

In the half-year or so leading up to the move, I had self-studied the Japanese hiragana and katakana characters and practiced writing them out in mini-flipbooks. At that point, however, I didn't yet know any conversational language.

It was my first week in Osaka, and my immersion school wasn't starting until the following Monday, so I was at a cafe pre-studying vocab and phrases.

A very young family entered the cafe and sat at the table next to me. It was a girl, 21, and her partner, 24. They were mildly hipster. He wore a fedora.

The girl was wheeling a pram with her newborn baby, who was 3 months old. The first word that came into my head was "congratulations."

I had just studied that word on the plane and tried saying it: "oh..mayy..dayy...."

"Shit I forgot."

They were looking at me wondering what I was trying to say.

I scrambled through a little vocab book I had and found it: "omedetou gozaimasu," meaning congratulations (very formal and polite).

They didn't know English. I didn't know Japanese. I relied almost exclusively on my Google translator.

Our "conversation" was basically just them teaching me some basic words. I learned for the first time how to say north, south, east, and west, as well as "from" and "until."

I thought nothing of the conversation apart from that they were a really nice family and I was grateful for having met them. Not everyone is so patient and friendly when you're trying to learn a new language.

They said we should all meet up and talk again the following Saturday. I thought it was an awesome idea. I was already on my way to making new friends. The girl gave me her contact and we all said bye.

When Saturday arrived, it was only she who came to meet me at the cafe. I don't even remember what she told me as far as why her partner and baby weren't there, but nevertheless, it was just the two of us.

When I first saw her, we came face-to-face by the entrance, and I noticed right away that she had big, beautiful eyes. There was a slight moment of confusion and awkwardness because, for some reason, I didn't 100% recognize her, and at the same time, I didn't know how to say anything, so we were just standing there looking at each other.

In the back of my mind, I probably thought she was cute. But she was a new mom and I had *just met her partner and baby.* My headspace wasn't even 0.1% thinking of her in that way. I was literally there expecting it to be all of us again.

I respected that she was a new mom and had just started a family. I was appreciative that she was willing to take time out of her day to talk with me a little so that I could start learning Japanese. We chatted for maybe an hour and then she had to go.

Over the next 1-2 months or so, she texted me a few times, mostly expressing an interest to learn English. She would try writing a few simple sentences and ask me how her grammar was. In turn, I would ask how her family was doing. And that was pretty much it. Once again, I thought nothing of it.

The bottom line was that I respected her situation and family unit. We were simply not part of the equation in each other's lives. Our texting stopped.

At this point, I was in level-one of my immersion course and was starting to meet new people and going on dates. She didn't even cross my mind, but nevertheless she was still in my contacts.

Now the way LINE (the Japanese messaging app) is set up is very much like a micro version of a FB newsfeed, where you have contacts that you text message, but if you happen to update your profile or photo, a notification gets posted to the mini-newsfeed.

I think it was probably around April or May of 2017 (i.e., ~9-10 months after last seeing her) when I saw an update of hers on the LINE feed. I messaged her asking how she was doing.

She said she was pregnant again but that we should meet up at a cafe some time. I once again thought this was a good idea. After all, she was one of the first people I had spoken to after coming to Japan, and it would be great to catch up.

A few weeks passed and the time came for us to meet, but she said she was sick and couldn't. I told her that was perfectly okay and not to worry about it. I mean, she was pregnant with a second kid and clearly (with no sarcasm) had bigger priorities. I understood and just let it be. I didn't try to arrange another time with her.

Then maybe *another* 9-10 months went by (so now we're talking around Feb 2018, ~18-20 months after last seeing her).

I must have seen another update of hers on the LINE feed, and I once again shot her a hello. She asked if I had Instagram, and we exchanged accounts.

We didn't even really start up a conversation. It was more that I now could just see countless photos of her and her **two babies.** There were also some lone photos of her from before she was pregnant, posing and looking kinda cute. I didn't see any of her partner.

At the same time, I wondered whether she had looked at my blog at all because the link has always been on my Instagram.

Even though she didn't know English, the pages can easily be Google translated into Japanese. Either way, it wasn't hard for her to simply click into my blog and gain a sense of my lifestyle if she wished. I imagined she had.

I wasn't trying to hide anything from her. I didn't care if she knew about my blog.

All bullshit aside, any thoughts that had crossed my mind about her didn't extend further than: "This chick is undeniably cute. But she's got two kids and a family. I respect that situation and it's just 100% not anything I have a place getting involved in. End of story."

I noticed, however, that her recent Instagram "highlights" photos were only ever of her alone, and they were cute/sexually flaunting.

I didn't overanalyze anything, but I was able to assess, just via gut feeling, *that she was sexually available.*

My intuition could gauge that, at 22-23 years old, although on the one hand she was probably really happy to have her kids, *she also secretly knew that she had cashed in too early on family life and passed up the chance to experiment sexually during her youth.*

Right or wrong, that was just my intuition. But I believe my assessment was correct.

So a few weeks went by and one night I randomly messaged her. We struck up a convo pretty quickly. I could text in Japanese now without a problem, so we had a more extended back-and-forth.

She said she thought I was cute. I told her she was also pretty cute.

Now before we go any further, I want to bring up an important thought process I was going through regarding her partner.

I'm 100% not okay crossing guy friends and going after their girls. I see that as insurmountably douchey and unforgivable.

So when I thought about this guy, I considered that I had met him only once almost two years earlier, when I couldn't even communicate with him apart from "north, south, east and west." And I hadn't had any contact with him since. He seemed like a "nice" guy at the time, but I truthfully just didn't know him. I wasn't friends with him. I didn't know the circumstances surrounding their relationship, nor was it my business.

Part of me wanted to tenaciously adhere to some arbitrary moral high-ground and conclude that talking to her, with intent of interest, while she was in a relationship, was not okay. *But I truthfully just didn't know the guy whatsoever, so I decided that chatting with her was OK. I didn't feel overly stellar about it, but I reasoned that it was FINE.*

But I didn't act surreptitiously and ignore the topic when messaging her:

I asked how her partner and kids were doing. I was genuine about it.

She said her partner was out of town on business and coming back in two days.

I said we could meet up for coffee tomorrow.

She said only her daughter was enrolled in childcare, so if we met up tomorrow, *it would have to be her, me, and her 6-month-old son together.*

I then made what I consider to be my first statements to her conveying my intent, **but I did so tacitly:**

"Can you get your mom or someone to look after your son tomorrow?"

She said her mom was working tomorrow.

I said, "Are you able to bring your son to childcare for just one day?"

In other words, why should it even matter whether her son comes along tomorrow? What does it convey to her the fact that I'm trying to get Baby out of the picture? I wasn't consciously thinking about it, but I knew that she was aware of my tacit message/intent. It was obvious. And by the way she was responding, I could tell she was "working with me" to see what she could do. But ultimately, there was no getting her alone tomorrow.

So now what? Even if I met up with her tomorrow with intent of interest, she'd be bringing her baby along. I was 100% sure we were mutually attracted, but the situation and its logistics were next to impossible. Why was I even bothering to see her? There was no way it would go anywhere.

I believe the reason I chose to meet up with her was because, despite not having logistics, I was genuinely OK with the idea of simply seeing her to catch up. So even if nothing happened – which I was like >98% sure nothing would – I thought just having a simple convo with her was *fine*. I mean, why not?

The next afternoon we met up by a station near where I live. She had driven about an hour into the city to meet me. It was cloudy and cool, as it was March and still winter.

When I saw her, she was carrying her baby against her stomach/chest, using one of those front-side slings, sort of like a reverse knapsack. She was wearing a white pollen mask covering most of her face and no makeup. Her hair was up in a bun and slightly frizzy.

She 100% didn't come dressed to impress me at all. She clearly put zero effort into trying to look good for me. It was evident that even the 1-2% notion that anything would happen between us was all in my head and I was just being an idiot.

I mean, really though, what the fuck did I think was going to happen?

So here I was, walking around with this girl and her baby. I felt like the dad, but not really. It was weird and out of place.

But nevertheless, who cares, because there was nothing wrong with just grabbing a simple coffee with someone I hadn't seen in a long time. No harm, no foul, right? I didn't have to make it long. But it was nice to catch up with her either way.

We went to a cafe a 5-minute-walk from my place. The ambiance was small and quiet. She placed her handbag full of toys, bottles, and nappies on the chair next to her. While we were talking, her baby slept against her chest.

I could now speak with her in Japanese without a problem. I said that she was one of the first people I met when I came to Japan and that we obviously weren't able to communicate back then.

After talking to her a little bit about hobbies and whether she has siblings, etc., I directed the conversation into more personal topics.

I asked why she entered a serious relationship and family life so young. I told her I recalled that she and her partner had met at a BBQ north of Osaka years back.

She was impressed that I had remembered that detail and said that she settled into the relationship because she had gotten pregnant, so it was convenient.

I asked her how she felt about that.

She gestured, essentially implying, "It is what it is."

She asked me if I was dating anyone while in Japan. She said she imagined I was "popular."

I didn't answer her question directly but told her that sometimes girls who want to practice their English get excited when they meet me.

I then turned the convo back onto her and asked if she still was wanting to learn English, etc. She said yes, but that she didn't have any time.

I then switched into fast English and, for ~30 seconds, rambled about the stuff I had already told her, i.e., about my immersion course, how I liked Japan, that it was good seeing her again, etc. I could gauge that she understood absolutely zero of what I was saying, so I then said to her, in extra-fast English, something along the lines of:

".........Yeah and on top of that you're sitting in front of me right now and I'm really attracted to you. I think you're so hot and sexy baby. And what's really interesting is I can just say whatever the fuck I want right now, such as how I want to bang you and go all out on you, and you have no idea what I'm saying which is great. So yeah, I would totally bang you. I think you're really **sexy."**

And I said the final "sexy" with Japanese pronunciation, and more slowly and strongly, as I was looking her in the eyes.

She was able to retroactively infer exactly what I had said. She blushed.

I then switched back into Japanese and said to her, "Do you like forward guys?"

She immediately nodded her head and said yes.

I said again, "You like forward and direct guys."

She nodded again.

At this point, her baby was starting to wake up and cry a little. She used a toy to calm him down. Probably 30 seconds or so went by where she tended to her baby and I just checked stuff on my smartphone.

Cool, well being a little flirtatious on the surface is always fun and harmless, but yet again, this still ain't goin' anywhere. She's a cutie though.

I then said, well anyway, we can get going. I paid for the coffees and we left the cafe. We were probably there for 45 minutes to an hour.

It was now starting to drizzle, so walking around indefinitely outside wasn't a viable option.

After walking with her for about 50 meters or so, I said to her – completely genuine and with no bullshit:

"So which direction do you need to go. I'll walk you to your car."

We crossed the street. I knew she had parked her car in the opposite direction from where I needed to go, so I was either walking her to her car or parting ways with her here.

So I said to her – once again, with no bullshit:

"Well, thank you for the conversation."

In other words, I was genuinely saying goodbye to her and seeing her on her way.

The convo then went something like this:

Her: I've still got more time if you want to do something else.

Me: This area doesn't really have other places for us to go.

Her: Where do you want to go?

Me: We could go to my place.

Her: That sounds good. Let's go.

Me: It's like a 5-minute walk this way.

Her: Yeah that's good.

Oook.....so I guess we're going to my place... ...

In my mind I was thinking: "My place is tiny – the size of a single room at a college dormitory. I'm just going to go back there with her and her baby? What are we even going to do? This doesn't even make sense. But wonderful Michael. Let's just go shall we."

Now when I say my place is tiny, I really mean it. You basically walk in and there's literally just my bathroom, a sink, my desk, and my bed. That's it.

So we walked in and I just sat on my bed. She stood next to me, rotating her body side to side gently to rock her baby to sleep. He soon fell asleep.

Another 10-15 seconds went by and then I said, "Ok…well…you can take off your baby if you want and lay him next to my pillow."

She immediately unstrapped herself and laid him down on the bed. He was sound asleep.

She made a slight sigh and said sometimes it can strain her lower back to carry that weight.

I said, "Where does it hurt? Here…?" [And I gently touched her lower back with my thumb, index, and middle fingers]

She blushed when I did that.

I told her she could sit down.

She did.

Then we were just sitting next to each other in silence, with her baby sleeping on the far end of my bed.

The silence lasted maybe 5-10 seconds, and then I said to her, "Sitting next to you…there's definitely……a different energy."

She said yeah.

I put my right hand behind her head and just leaned in and kissed her.

I could tell by her response that she was half really into it, half unsure/confused. That is, she was blushing, but also touching her fingertips gently against her lips, essentially with the expression of "Omg…I can't……cheat on my partner….?"

I didn't overanalyze it, but I was surprised for some reason that I could taste cigarettes when I kissed her.

We spent another 10 seconds sitting beside each other in silence.

I then kissed her again. Just a repeat of a few moments ago.

I started touching her leg a little.

And then the turning point came:

As I was touching her leg, she looked excited but unsure. I paused for a moment, then said to her, "daijoubu desu ka?" Meaning, "Are you okay? / Is this okay?" And I used polite conjugation. She replied, "daijoubu." Meaning, "Yes, I'm okay. / This is okay."

I started unbuttoning her shirt. It was an unflattering, loose-fitting, green velvety one with caked-on saliva stains from her baby, who was still fast asleep beside my pillow.

The thought very briefly crossed my mind: "She's probably……..
breastfeeding still? Probably…..? I don't even want to know and it
grosses me out thinking about it. I'm just not going there."

Our shirts never actually came off. It all happened so fast and the
next thing I knew I was in her.

I looked to my left and her baby was starting to wake up.

"How the fuck is this what's happening in my life," I thought.

I was getting closer and closer to coming. The main thought that was
now racing through my mind was, "I just………I just don't want to
destroy her family or create problems for her……..she has it so
stable right now…….I just don't want to fuck that up for her."

I also thought she was cute……..*but not cute enough* for me to just
come.

It's weird, I know. Call me an asshole, but that's the truth.

The implication being, "What, so if she had been 'cute enough,' you
would have just come?"

Correct, probably.

I'd say my thought process was 75% on not wanting to fuck up her
family situation; 25% was I didn't think she was cute enough + the
cigarette taste gave me a bad impression.

All I can really say is that, mid-sex, I wasn't intellectualizing, hyper-analyzing, or compiling an Excel spreadsheet of pros/cons. The interaction was a fast, limbic blur.

I pulled out and put on a condom.

As I was walking her to her car, I didn't even need to ask, but I did anyway:

"When's your ovulation day?"

"Umm………..tomorrow."

I was like, "Yeah, no fucking shit it's tomorrow."

"Do you understand that if I didn't use a condom we would have had a baby?"

"Yes."

We got to the parking lot and I paid the 10ish dollars for her parking. She had driven over an hour to see me and probably would be deep in thought on the way home. It was the least I could do I thought.

I didn't kiss her goodbye.

The next day or two, she created a new Instagram account specifically as a back-channel to contact me, separate from her normal account. She said we should just chat through this new account from here on out.

She's like a lioness

In the mean time, I was due to meet up soon with a friend of a friend who was currently visiting Japan from Australia. He was born/lived in Australia but was 100% Greek heritage.

I say "friend of a friend" because I had only met him once or twice through mutual friends back when I was living in Australia, and we had never actually had a one-on-one conversation before. I knew he was in Japan because I had coincidentally seen a post of his on the Facebook newsfeed.

So the situation was essentially, "Oh cool, you're in Japan? Yeah, let's grab a beer or something if you come through Osaka."

He was traveling with a big group of guy friends, so when I met up with him, he was with another guy. The three of us did street approach together. They were both shy, so I basically played the role of opening trios and groups for us while we walked around the city for a few hours.

At some stage, the second guy returned to the hotel, so now I was just out with the Greek guy.

In Japan, it's legal to drink outside, so we grabbed a couple beers and started drinking on some random street. I chatted with him a bit about my blog and ideas surrounding approach/confidence, etc.

He came from a conservative Greek Orthodox background and had a slight traditionalist air about him. I suspected that although on the surface he may have seemed intrigued/amused by the idea of my approach lifestyle, that secretly, maybe he didn't fully agree with or understand it. It wasn't anything I consciously thought about. It was just what I sensed.

Nevertheless, I told him the unabridged story about the girl I saw the other day. I was waiting for him to give me a somewhat critical and/or disapproving response, but I didn't care. I was ready for it.

I think the reason I told him the story in full detail was because I wanted to hear his criticism.

I wanted him to tell me he didn't agree with my actions/thinking.

I wanted him to tell me that sleeping with a girl who has a partner made me a douchebag, irrespective of the fact that I didn't know the guy at all.

I wanted him to tell me that having sex with her next to her baby, on my bed, was an absolute shocker and outrageous.

I wanted him to get angry at me.

I wanted to absorb his disdain and then rise above it.

With all of the approaching/dating I do, which isn't looked highly upon by mainstream, feminized culture as it is, I've learned to shield out others' opinions without a problem. But perhaps I secretly felt deep down that this particular situation was crossing a line somehow.

Perhaps I felt my actions were worth condemnation. Perhaps he could be that person, here and now, to give me the explication I needed to hear so that I could grow and be a better person.

His response was:

"That's a pretty crazy story. So yeah, now I'll be honest with you...................

..................I'm kinda jealous actually."

"Wait.... what? Really? Why do you say that."

"I mean, that's just crazy. Like, who the fuck has life experiences like that. Basically she's like a lioness who entered your den with her cub. You chose not to take her in, essentially, but you could have. What happened was, she went to you for your genes, and then went back to her provider. That's just how the animal kingdom works."

"Well then I have a bit of a fucked up question for you...."

"Yeah that's fine."

"No but I mean, I really do have a bit of a fucked up question for you...."

"Go for it."

"I almost didn't put the condom on. Part of me wonders whether.......I should have just came? In that moment, I genuinely didn't want to fuck up her situation – her stable family unit / support system – and, I know I come off like an absolute asshole saying this, but I just... didn't think she was cute enough either."

"Look man, that's not fucked up. There will probably always be a percentage of you that would have wanted to, but I think what you did is actually really admirable. What separates us from other animals is that we have intelligence and self-control. As guys, I mean yeah, we always want to spread our seed. It's in our nature. But I think your ability to exert self-control was really good, especially in a situation like that."

"So you think it was good that I put the condom on?"

"Yes, I think it was a good idea. If I were her partner and found out she was pregnant with your kid, I would absolutely leave her. And I'd probably try to track you down and kill you. It was definitely a good idea."

Call it fucked up all you want. But that's what I thought/felt about the situation, and I was glad to just be able to chat with him about it. A small percentage of me – my animalistic side – reflected and felt like I should have just had a kid with her. But when I actually had that chance, I knew I never would have become a support figure for her. I never would have looked after her. So I saw it as being *in her best interest* to not go that route.

The female strategy

A week later she came to see me on her own at night.

This time she was fully done-up for me. Her hair was long and curly, with brown highlights. She wore hipster style jeans and a blouse.

We made our way back to my place through the small, meandering, dark alleyways of the slums I live in.

As we were walking together, our conversation was quiet and boring. I looked at her and specifically thought to myself that, at 23 years old and as done-up as she was, I "had her" tonight as the most physically attractive she'd be for the rest of her life. I was aware she was at peak-SMV and this was the pinnacle for her. This was it.

Tonight was literally her pinnacle. And she was there with me.

It was nothing I was wanting to be a superficial asshole about, but it's just what was going through my mind. That's the truth.

I believe the reason I was having those thoughts then and there was because had our circumstances been much simpler, i.e., had she been single and without children, I don't think that would have changed anything for me. I could just sense, through gut feeling, that she very likely would not have been more than just a casual sex partner for me. For whatever reason, I had that awareness in the moment.

When we got back to my place, the vibe was very different from the week before. Maybe it was just the charged tension of the interaction the first time that had given it such a limbic flame, but this time our pheromonal/sexual chemistry was average at best. And it was nothing that could have been controlled.

While we were having sex and she was looking me in the eyes, her expression was that of enjoyment – but also that of a deep yearning that had nothing to do with me at all. As she stared into my eyes, she wasn't gazing into me; she was gazing *through me.*

She didn't come to see *me* that night. That's not why she came. It was just getting fucked, by someone she perceived as an alpha, in this exact fashion – here and now – tonight – that she longed for. I was giving her what she hadn't ever had in life. Something she knew she would never have as she grew older if she didn't make it happen here and now.

And then afterwards, reality sorta just hits ya.

We both knew there was no flame between us. We both knew our circumstances didn't align. Nor would they ever. We both knew she was going back to her partner and that's what she saw as best.

She had two children. It was impossible that I'd ever be any type of provider for her. She knew that.

In retrospect, I can see clearly that the non-perpetuation of our interaction beyond that night was strictly linked to her need for continued provision.

Here she was in my tiny apartment in the slums. I knew she lived with her partner in a much nicer and bigger place based on her Instagram photos. I felt like the plumber that the rich housewife secretly chose to fuck on the bathroom floor, but after all was said and done, why would she risk losing everything she had from her stable provider to continue the interaction with me?

After that night, I decided to lend space to the interaction. There was no analysis. It was just what seemed reasonable. I noted of course that I hadn't heard from her at any point either.

I shot her a message a few weeks later telling her that the following weekend would be good. She said she didn't have much time. So I told her to create the time.

She replied by saying that had we met years earlier she would have wanted to date me, but that right now she was really busy. I could easily infer from her use of the past-tense that she had no intention of ditching her family or seeing me again.

I asked if she loved her partner. She said yes.

I asked if they have sex a lot. She said yes, a lot.

So I just blocked both of her accounts on Instagram. I saw that as best.

A day later she created a Snapchat account and added me there. So I blocked her there too.

This is of course bearing in mind that I hadn't blocked her on the main LINE app. I was fully aware she found my Snapchat through LINE because I had posted the QR code to it just days earlier.

I believe the reason I didn't block her on LINE, yet had done so on Instagram and Snapchat, was because I wanted her to know that whilst I wouldn't tolerate her rejecting my proposition to meet, I nevertheless respected her as a person and didn't view the situation as negative between us whatsoever. I was conveying that I was moving forward instantly, but was essentially leaving the door open for her to message me months from now if she changed her mind.

And that's exactly what she did. Four months later.

I was in Korea and she messaged me one night while I was out getting chicken and beer.

She said something along the lines of how she had a Japanese friend who needed a medication for something, and she wanted my opinion on what was best for her.

I replied saying that's clearly not the real reason she was messaging me.

She said it was. She just wanted my opinion on medication.

I was already a few MODERN CHICKEN beers in and told her something along the lines of, "Or are you bored with your partner and are messaging me bc you want real excitement."

She didn't respond to that.

Then maybe 5ish weeks after she messaged me in Korea, I returned her gesture with a hello of my own. She replied that she was pregnant a third time. She asked how I was. I didn't even respond and blocked her instantly.

I imagine she never told her partner about me and that, if anything, her experience with me only brought them closer together.

It's not really my job to speculate on that situation. And it doesn't even matter.

I wrote this essay to reinforce the point that women are never unconditionally loyal to men. And I say that with zero cynicism. This is actually a positive statement. It brings awareness to the fact that it is in female biology to weigh provision vs genes, and those decisions are unrelated to how much we think a woman loves us. Hypergamy doesn't care about your feelings. It doesn't care how much you romanticize relationships. It's agnostic. It's unemotional. It doesn't give a fuck how "nice" you are. Hypergamy isn't always convenient. In fact, it's not. At all.

THE MOST IMPORTANT THING TO KNOW ABOUT NIGHT GAME (Bonus Chapter)

*What you choose to do in the **first 60 seconds** you walk into a bar/club determines how potent and efficacious you are for the rest of the night.*

The results you experience when you're out are often a total crapshoot, and lots of factors come into play that are not in your control (i.e., you could do everything "right" but still not get an outcome you're looking for), so I can't go so far as to say that what you do in the first 60 seconds necessarily determines the *final outcome* for the night, but what I can unequivocally tell you is:

There is no other time for the rest of the night that more greatly impacts the trajectory of your momentum apart from those first 60 seconds after you walk through the door of that bar/club.

The earlier you approach → the earlier you get one or more rejections out of the way → the earlier and more greatly you're "immunized" against further rejections → the earlier and more greatly you reduce all fucks you have about any additional rejections → the more bold and fearless you become → the less likely you are to change your behavior for the girls you meet AND the more approaches you make overall → greater overall potency (how likely it is a girl will be attracted to your confidence + how quickly you'll get results that night) and efficacy (the outcome you're looking for).

The absolute worst thing you can do when first entering a bar/club is what 99% of guys do: walk through the door and immediately get a drink.

Whether you walk right up to the bar and get a beer, or find a table first and order some gin-tonics, it doesn't matter.

The worst thing you can do upon first entering a bar/club is to "take a few moments to just grab a drink, chill, and settle into things."

You don't have to agree with me. But I'm telling you that if you choose to chill and settle into things, you're fucking up the rest of your night. In contrast, if you approach within 60 seconds of entering a bar/club, you will be on fire from that point onward. It's that simple.

And when I say it's that simple, I mean it's that fucking simple.

If it's a harsh rejection you receive right off the bat, you'll be **even more** on fire. In truth, the best outcome you could have is to actually take a harsh rejection instantly because that effectively "immunizes" you against giving a fuck about all subsequent ones for the rest of the night. Then, you'll be more likely to open the 2nd, 3rd, and 4th girls AND be more likely to have a "preferred outcome" with them. You'll be more direct, forward, and confident as compared to having protracted making your initial approach.

One could raise the argument that a rapid-fire, shotgun style approach instantly upon entering a bar/club may be overkill/needy in some way. In other words, one might ask, "But what's wrong with just spending a little time getting settled in? You're really going to tell me I should approach, literally, within the first minute of entering a bar?"

"Yeah."

Even if you don't "like" my advice, it's the best you could possibly get. In fact, it's world-class.

Sometimes when something sounds weird, it's just because you have to get used to the idea of it.

Remember, 99% of guys don't approach within the first minute of entering a bar/club, so of course that idea is going to feel weird initially.

If you and I were out together, that's what you'd see me do. And pretty much right away you'd be like, "Holy shit, Mike Mehlman really is straight to the point and direct as fuck. Wow."

I think if you were to see a genuinely non-needy and confident guy do it (like me), you'd be able to see how powerful those first 60 seconds really are.

You would more than likely watch me take an instant, harsh rejection (or two) within 60 seconds of entering a bar/club. You'd laugh. Then I'd be like, "Ok, who's on fire now, you or I? Who's still approached zero girls, you or I?"

(If I'm ever out with guy friends, that tends to happen by the way. They may or may not poke fun at how I get rejected a lot. But when all is said and done, they've approached zero and I've gone 2/20. **And those small numbers add up and I'm the only one getting dates. Real fucking convenient isn't it.**)

So why are most guys subconsciously in the default state of getting settled in with a drink for the first 10-15 minutes or so? Because 1) they secretly have approach anxiety, and 2) they want to get a small buzz in order to overcome it.

For the overwhelming majority of guys, it's an immutable, fundamental prerequisite to have a drink before even contemplating any kind of approach. This all comes down to approach anxiety.

You can say you want to "chill and spend time with your friends" all you want, but my advice is to "chill and spend time with your friends" any other time of your life apart from the first 60 seconds you enter a bar/club.

Make it a priority to say hi to at least 1-2 girls before getting any alcohol. That momentum is huge.

If you choose to "settle into things," it will be harder to reverse the lack of momentum you've set for yourself.

If it's a small bar you're in where you feel compelled to sit and order right away, ask yourself why you've chosen to go there in the first place. If you're literally just catching up with some old guy friends from high school to have a drink or something, that's fine, but if you're genuinely looking to do some form of night game, choose a place where you have a little bit of breathing room and aren't mandated to order the instant you enter. I've walked in and out of venues instantly before. If I see there's nothing there for me, why would I waste even one additional second of my time.

If you're waiting to get into the bar/club, that doesn't count toward your first minute by the way. If you want to open the people in front of or behind you, then do it, but it's not mandatory. You can just chat with your friends.

When you enter, first "scope out your surroundings" and quickly make note of who's around you. I'd say a good 10 seconds of stationary observation from the front of the venue is good. Don't worry about who may or may not be looking at you. That bears absolutely zero importance. You don't need to feel compelled to walk immediately to the bar (or anywhere for that matter).

Take 10 seconds or so to observe your surroundings from the front of the venue when you first enter. It's alright to be stationary and just look around. If a girl happens to look at you, good, then you can take 3 seconds to decide whether you're going to approach her.

Scan to see where there are cute girls you want to say hi to, and quickly improvise how you are going to approach.

Are there 5 girls at a table in the back of the venue? Is there a duo at the bar that's caught your attention? Is there a girl by herself sitting on a high-stool?

These are quick observations you can make in the first 5-10 seconds upon entering the venue.

After you've identified a girl you want to say hi to, just walk right up to her and introduce yourself, without hesitation, and without a drink in your hand. Once again, this should occur within the first minute you're in the venue. Likewise, if you're with a guy friend and there's a duo, then by all means open them right away. After your first one or two approaches, sure, grab a drink, but your positive momentum is now set.

You should essentially go into a bar/club with the mindset that you "don't have permission" to have a drink until you do at least two approaches.

If you're with a wingman and see a single girl to approach, one of you should break away from the other and approach her solo. The other should disappear into thin air. Your friend should be off approaching someone else without hovering around you.

If you're with a wingman who's shy or lame for whatever reason, you have to step up on behalf of both of you and tell him that the first minute matters the most. If he's a whiner/downer (lots of guys reveal their true colors in these settings), then approach a single girl on your own so he can observe how it's done. Don't let him hold you back. If you had eyeballed a duo instead, then simply walk up and approach them without your wingman.

Never let shitty wingmen drag you down. Be confident in your own ability to generate momentum quickly, and if guys you're with can't handle approaching and are like, "Nah man, let's get a drink first." Just calmly break away from them for a little bit. Have empathy for the fact that most guys (even your close friends) have approach anxiety.

What a male chooses to do in the first minute he enters a bar/club is a big indicator of his status / confidence level.

If you're normally more of a silent-wolf type but need to transition into taking on the overt leadership role, then do it. Situations like these can be important times to effectively teach your guy friends how approach is done.

Once again, after that first minute, by all means grab a drink and take a moment to "chill and spend time with your friends." Just bear in mind I'm giving you the best advice you could possibly get regarding how to spend a mere 60 seconds of your life any time you go out. So yeah, that's my two cents on this point. Everything else in relation to night game is secondary.

WHY GETTING REJECTED IS SO IMPORTANT

I have an awareness that my confidence stems from the process of overcoming repeated adversity. I've come to identify rejection through dating as just a form/type of adversity. This is why repeated rejection via dating is the core pillar of confidence augmentation.

The reason I'm passionate about getting my message across to people is because I can see that the process of overcoming repeated rejection via the dating process creates confidence that transfers over into other, non-dating aspects of life.

I call this "the arbitrage of confidence."

In other words, confidence accrued from overcoming adversities in one area of life can be packaged, stored, and then **arbitraged and redirected** to overcome adversities in completely unrelated areas of life.

Every time you take a rejection **and continue to introduce yourself to new people anyway,** the more fearless you become to go after **everything else in life as well.** That is, you'll start to observe your behavior unrelated to dating (i.e., career, lifestyle, living abroad, etc.) and see that the confidence and audacity to go after what you want can actually be derived from repeated rejection via the dating process.

It's not an accident that I abdicated a medical career in order to move to Japan and live a life true to myself. I was able to package and store the confidence from one realm of my life (i.e., dating) and apply/redirect it toward non-dating aspects of my life.

That doesn't mean confidence *must be* derived from dating/rejections. It just happens to be the case that rejections have been *the mere type of* adversity I've repeatedly overcome that has led to my present-day confidence.

I'm sure there are many ways to grow one's confidence, but at least for me, putting myself out on a limb and constantly getting rejected by people has been my way of making it happen.

I believe confidence comes from repeatedly overcoming adversity, not from a lack of it. Repeated rejection is essentially just a form of repeated adversity. Therefore, it represents a mechanism via which one can achieve confidence.

Outcomes associated with the dating process (i.e., "sexual conversions"; "whether she's into you"; "getting her contact"; "creating a relationship with her," etc.) can create positive emotions, but it's actually the ongoing process of getting rejected that builds one's core confidence.

I don't really care about getting a contact exchange the same way I don't care if a girl rejects me on the spot.

I don't care so much about getting a "sexual conversion" the same way I don't care so much about a girl ghosting or flaking on me for whatever reason.

This isn't about suppressing emotion. This is about perspective. My focus just isn't on the outcome. It's on the process. I acknowledge the positivity of occasional preferred dating/approach outcomes, but I don't fixate on them, nor do I dwell about the negatives.

Detaching oneself from the outcome of approaches doesn't just happen automatically; it happens abreast a growth in awareness that the process of getting rejected is by far and away the most paramount.

I believe rejection and confidence are embedded in a positive reinforcement loop. In other words, the more you get rejected (i.e., arguably the "non-outcome" component of meeting new people), the more you begin to see your behavior becoming more audacious and confident. Over time, it becomes undeniable that one's change in mindset is derived from overcoming continual adversity, not from "positive outcomes."

This might seem counterintuitive, and in turn, often isn't conspicuous early on. That's why my content is really important for keeping you on track early.

As time progresses and you begin to notice your growth in confidence, there's an increasing awareness that it comes from rejection, not from "positive outcome."

The result is a change in one's perspective to begin viewing *rejections* as the win.

This embrace of rejection in dating then translates over into ***non-dating*** aspects of life.

I believe happiness is tied to our embrace of adversities in everyday life. Adversities, setbacks, frustrations, and annoyances will never go away. So it's a matter of embracing them as positive – because you see how they're tied to confidence and happiness – that is a big determinant of quality of life.

Once again, the confidence accrued *via the process of incurring repeated, daily "mini-adversities"* (i.e, rejections) can be arbitraged and redirected to **other areas of life completely unrelated to dating.**

This wasn't ever something I psychoanalyzed for the first 5+ years I was approaching, nor did I even care.

It's more that I can observe the trajectory of my life – i.e., living a life true to myself – and when I reflect, I can see that what makes my path possible is not caring about what anyone thinks about me above what I think of myself.

And when I consider where that mindset has come from, it's the resiliency attained from having been rejected at least 10-15-thousand times.

When you get rejected over and over again by women, that's *already* checking off the "hardest box" to begin with, so every other criticism or judgment you could receive in life seems trivial by comparison.

I view meeting women day in and day out, and getting rejected incessantly, as a huge win because I'm very aware of how those adversities/setbacks are the major contributor to not just my confidence but my embrace of setbacks in everyday life.

I empathize with anyone who views me disdainfully as a pick-up-artist douchebag. Yet again, I'm not entitled to anyone spending the time to acquire a deep, thorough understanding of my mindset and philosophies.

I'm okay with the socially contentious nature of my content because I don't need everyone to like me, the same way I don't need all of the women I say hi to to like me.

Do you see how being able to handle rejection in dating actually makes it really easy for me to handle "rejection" when it comes to lots of people not liking me for my content?

I've received many emails where some of you guys have said *you're so glad I'm writing about the shit I do because most guys wouldn't have the guts to do that.*

Yeah, I guess you're right. But hopefully that serves as evidence in some form that you can just do/go after what you want in life when you learn to not care about others' opinions and judgments of you so much.

The only reason I was able to begin producing content is because I don't care about others' negative judgments and criticisms of me. That's not an accident.

My content exists as an anomaly in the dating world (because it's the best out there) the same way my mindset about rejection is an anomaly.

There's a parallel between my <0.00001% life trajectory and my >99.99999%tile embrace of rejection. This isn't magic.

(Nor are those numbers. I'd peg the frequency of someone graduating med school with top board scores, yet jettisoning that sure-fire lucrative/prestigious route in order to move to east Asia, live in a tiny apartment, and become a socially contentious dating

blogger, as probably eclipsing the 1 in 10 million threshold in the population for rarity.)

I want to see people embrace rejection in dating because I know, *if they can get to that point,* the effects will translate over into areas of life that transcend dating itself.

Rejection through dating has been my way of becoming a much happier person. That's been my journey so far. I don't fret over setbacks in life the same way anymore because I know they're a win. I see them as the driving force for a positive mindset.

I suppose my core passion is about getting you into a mindset where you can just go after what you want in life so that you can be much happier.

I don't *need* you to become successful with women. Why should I care? How does your ability to approach directly affect me per se?

It's more just that I want you to be happy with respect to whatever your natural equilibrium point is. And I know that if I can help get you into a headspace of not being afraid to simply introduce yourself to new people, then that confidence will translate over into you living life true to yourself, completely unrelated to dating, whatever that may entail.

So go out there. Start getting rejected. Maybe in six months' time you'll finally have the courage to quit that job you hate and move to Thailand or Japan like you've been thinking about.

Feel free to reach out to me through my blog (mikemehlman.net). You'll also find links to my videos, podcasts, other articles, and more. Thanks so much for giving this a read. ~Mike

www.ingramcontent.com/pod-product-compliance
Lightning Source LLC
Chambersburg PA
CBHW050225270326
41914CB00003BA/575